2,001 Innovative Ways to Save Your Company Thousands and Reduce Costs:

A Complete Guide to Creative Cost Cutting and Profit Boosting

By Cheryl L. Russell

2,001 Innovative Ways to Save Your Company Thousands and Reduce Costs
A Complete Guide to Cost Cutting and Profit Boosting

Copyright © 2007 by Atlantic Publishing Group, Inc.

1210 SW 23rd Place • Ocala, Florida 34474 • 800-814-1132 • 352-622-5836–Fax

Web site: www.atlantic-pub.com • E-mail: sales@atlantic-pub.com

SAN Number: 268-1250

ISBN-13: 978-0-910627-77-1 • ISBN-10: 0-910627-77-0

Library of Congress Cataloging-in-Publication Data

Russell, Cheryl L. (Cheryl Lynn), 1967-
  2,001 innovative ways to save your company thousands by reducing costs : a complete guide to creative cost cutting and boosting profits / Cheryl L. Russell.
    p. cm.
  Includes bibliographical references and index.
  ISBN 0-910627-77-0 (978-0-910627-77-1 : alk. paper)
  1. Cost control. 2. Corporate profits. I. Title. II. Title: Two thousand one innovative ways to save your company thousands by reducing costs.
  HD47.3.R835 2006
  658.15'52--dc22

                                    2006021597

EDITOR: Marie Lujanac • mlujanac817@yahoo.com

PROOFREADER: Angela C. Adams • angela.c.adams@hotmail.com

ART DIRECTION & INTERIOR DESIGN: Meg Buchner • megadesn@mchsi.com

BOOK PRODUCTION DESIGN: Laura Siitari of Siitari by Design • www.siitari-design.com

Printed in the United States

TABLE OF CONTENTS

Introduction

"**A** *penny saved is a penny earned,*" said Founding Father Benjamin Franklin. That pretty much sums it all up. To earn money for your company, simply save it. Don't spend it to begin with — at least not on things that aren't really needed. Sounds easy enough, but in practice it takes a very specific vision to cut costs to the max effectively.

If you're a business owner, manager, or even a cost-conscious employee, you can be the catalyst for saving money by cutting costs, or making money by boosting profits at your company. In many cases, all it takes to start a cost-conscious initiative is the inspiration of just one person. If you're reading this book, odds are you are willing to be that person.

Some of the ideas you'll find in the coming chapters require only one person to implement, rather than the approval of committees or a board of directors. Small ideas do add up.

Other ideas are more complex and will require a carefully considered, planned, and implemented cost-cutting strategy. Failing to plan makes your efforts counter-productive from the onset.

When planning the larger cost-cutting initiatives, one of the first things you should do is determine what your objective is: are you in such a pinch that your immediate need is to keep the company from folding? Or is your company in relatively good shape but not really competitive in your market? Or are you in no immediate danger of shutting down but want to find an extra competitive edge by being leaner or more innovative than your competitors?

Look at your company's mission statement, its objectives. Keep these in mind as you prepare to embark on this journey. Build your cost-cutting strategy around your mission-critical activities. Make them stronger, not weaker, with your efforts.

Another top-priority is to decide on an approach. There are two ways to think about cost cutting, what I call the *itch* and the *rash*.

In the *itch* approach, you see a single activity that takes time but doesn't add anything to your product or profit. Or you realize that you've been purchasing one item over and over and even though it's used, you could do without it. When it dawns on you that these things are truly unnecessary, they become like an annoying little itch; you *have to* scratch it, and you won't be satisfied until you do.

Neglecting these little itch-items only increases your annoyance. Itch-items are fairly easy to take care of, simply by eliminating the small thing or process that's costing time or money and not earning anything in return. If you prefer, think of the itch-items as a mosquito circling you just looking for a chance to drain you of a bit of blood. That's what itch-items do, drain bits and pieces of profit away, and often you don't even realize that it's happened until it's long done.

Yet once these itch-items are spotted, you can treat that one spot and see results from that one effort on your part. Treating an itch item often involves cutting away money-sucking practices, processes, methods, or other specific targets of good health for your company. Train your eye and the eyes of every employee at your company to spot needless purchases, processes or profit-suckers.

The rash items, then, should be easy for you to imagine. These are not just single things that can improve your health and well-being when treated. Rather, they are like a muddy river running through every corner of your company and requiring serious measures. The effects of rash-items will not simply run their course and stop draining your company of profits and productivity on their own. Their problems tend to multiply and continue their money-grabbing until they're stopped.

Some examples of rash items are an unpleasant company morale, or corporate culture, as it's often called or a workforce whose numbers far exceed the available work. These items shouldn't be treated like itches: they cannot be cured with a single memo announcing that this or that is no longer going to be purchased or implemented.

Rash items require careful evaluation and implementation to be successful. Like a surgeon who very carefully searches for every last remnant of a tumor, those who are attempting to eliminate the rashes have to treat not only affected areas but the entire company. Treating a rash requires full-body attention. The entire company, department by department, is subject to scrutiny and disinfection.

The full-body treatment also takes more time, more planning, and the involvement of every employee from the top down. In essence, cost cutting is infused into the work ethics, the corporate culture, and in every step of the day-to-day running of the business. Every employee contributes, even without knowing it, by being cost-conscious every day.

Even if urgent need suggests you take an itch-approach right away, set the wheels in motion for the longer-term effects of the rash-approach as well. Getting each worker to take ownership of their own cost-cutting measures builds more than strong balance sheets.

Knowing where you're going with your efforts to cut costs will help you plan properly along the way. And when you've built your plan, use this book as an idea-generator, a quick-list of ways to implement your plans.

Before delving into the myriad of tips to come, here are just a few thoughts about this book, what it is, and what it isn't, and how to get the most out of it.

First, be aware that creative cost cutting can mean a variety of things to different people. It may depend on your own personality. Some business owners, managers, and employees are more able to think outside the box than others. However you define creative cost cutting, be prepared to be introduced here to more ideas on how to cut costs for your company and boost profits than you have ever seen in one place before.

Not every tip will work for you. Many of them may seem like variants on the same theme, and indeed, they are, because while one variant may not be applicable to your situation, another might. Some basic ideas can be used in many departments and in a different ways throughout your company.

Some tips are size-specific. There are techniques that simply work better in larger companies than smaller ones and vice versa.

Another thought is the miniscule nature of some of the tips you'll be given. Even if implementing these *tiny tips* saves you only pennies after implementation costs, it's a start that will lead to other savings. No matter how small the tip, I've included every single thing that I found in my research and especially those that were shared by the business owners, managers, and employees whom I interviewed.

Some tips are industry-specific. Tips about how to be thrifty with your napkin supply might be useful for a family diner, but may not be for a Fortune 500 company, but then again, the larger your company, the greater the opportunity for savings.

This book was written using many research and interview sources, and it covers items applicable to both small businesses and large corporations. However, very little time is spent educating the reader about topics that naturally come up in the discussion of tips. If these very specific tips are applicable to you or your company, you'll likely be familiar with the accompanying concepts already and will know how to use the tip. If, on the other hand, your company just "doesn't go there," you can probably skip those tips altogether.

In addition to the boxed tips and stories, you'll find numerous true stories of companies all across the country and the innovative ways they are cutting costs and boosting their profits. Learn from the story of Qwest's Idaho Falls call center, where the manager is not afraid to dress like an insect to elicit a few yucks from his employees. And don't miss out on the good advice from Doctors Foster and Smith who have found that cost cutting doesn't really enter their corporate conversations so much as something they call "balanced efficiency."

You can also use the book by perusing the Table of Contents and choosing a target area that you want to consider first, such as The Human Element—cutting costs related to your workforce—or The Intangibles, cutting costs that are hidden or often overlooked. If you've got a pretty good handle on one area, you can start your focus on a different area.

While this book is a source of cost-cutting tips, don't neglect the information in the final chapters. Like the old adage, *a chain is only as strong as its weakest link*, a business is only as strong as those who show up every day to turn the wheels of commerce and industry. It is possible to go overboard in a moment of zealous cost cutting and do damage to the very company you sought to strengthen. Read about the common ways that cost cutting gone awry can deal a blow to your company's health and well-being.

Finally, take a "health check" to assure you that your company is on the road to recovery after your cost cutting. Make the cuts that you identify in the book as being applicable and worth trying. Let your imagination take over and you will find that you can be even more creative than the companies that provided these tips. Then come back and review the health checklist again.

I'm sure you'll be pleased with the results!

Biz Wiz Says . . . Throughout the chapters you'll find boxes such as this one highlighting a particularly important tip or thought from Patrick Walden, a 13-year veteran of corporate accounting and small business consulting. Patrick holds a Bachelor of Science degree in Accounting from Minnesota State University. His extensive work as a contract consultant for the Small Business Development Center and years in corporate accounting have given him a good look at what companies sometimes do wrong— without even realizing it. Patrick's tips and stories serve as extra reminders to do the obvious, even when it isn't.

Foreword

One of the most challenging aspects of reducing costs in your organization is to think through every item in your business including workforce planning, production costs, office supplies, vendors, and suppliers. Yet, you must first begin with determining what you want to accomplish before you absently cut costs in your organization.

Before you embark on the journey, review your organization's mission statement and its long-term goals. Locating the information you will need to make the journey a success is often quite difficult and time-consuming. This book provides the reader with the information necessary to make successful decisions about reducing costs and ensuring your organization reaches its goals.

In my position as Vice President of Human Resources, I am often consulted regarding the people aspects of business and how we can save money by reducing the workforce. I recommend considering other aspects of the organization that can be reduced before letting go of an organization's greatest asset — its people:

1. Decrease the number of office hours,

2. View your health insurance provider as a supplier,

3. Adjust inventory flow to be more effective,

4. Streamline productivity processes,

5. Be creative in advertising and marketing,

6. Increase time frames for Accounts Payable,

7. Decrease time frames for Accounts Receivable, and

8. Consider reducing the overlooked costs of building/ equipment leases, utilities, and office supplies.

These areas are part of a larger cost-cutting initiative that will require careful planning and involvement of every employee within the organization. This publication provides a larger scope for reducing your organization's costs and will enable you to develop a savings strategy that will keep your mission-critical activities intact.

> *Denise Starcher, MBA, SPHR, is currently the Vice President, Human Resources for a Web services and consulting company headquartered in Atlanta, GA. She is an innovative HR professional with expertise in change management, organizational effectiveness, talent management, employee relations, compensation and benefits, and training and development. For the past 18 years, she has focused on enabling organizations to achieve sustained business growth while embracing change in technology, hospitality, healthcare, and energy industries. She holds an MBA in General Management from Georgia State University, and a Bachelor of Science degree in Psychology from Centre College in Danville, Kentucky.*

PART 1:

Cutting Costs
Related to Your Workforce

"The most powerful force on earth is that spontaneous cooperation of a free people."

—Woodrow Wilson,
28ᵀᴴ President of the United States

daho Falls, Idaho, is a medium-sized town of just over 50,000 where unemployment is reasonably low and the scenic beauty ranks high on the list of reasons to live there. But in 2003, there was nothing scenic about empty workstations and the negative environment at the Idaho Falls Qwest call center. In fact, it was downright ugly.

The Idaho Falls location was consistently ranked at the bottom-of-the-barrel for performance in most areas: sales were way down, employee grievances were way up, customer service was almost nil and morale was less than zero. Rumors of impending doom kept the employees in a constant state of crushing fear. In the midst of this situation came the person that Qwest hoped would heal the ailing location: Larry Walters.

Walters was anxious to save the Idaho Falls location from closure, and he swooped in with such grace and gusto that the resulting improvements were inevitable. You see, Larry Walters manages in a rather unique manner. He doesn't just hold meetings and make rules; he molds people at all levels and motivates them to higher ambitions.

Since Larry Walters came on board, Qwest's Idaho Falls location has become the most profitable and largest of their call centers. The transformation was so amazing that in January 2005, the Gallup Management Journal took an in-depth look at the blunders of the management before Larry Walters and specific steps he took to turn the location around.[1] Read the entire article online at **http://gmj.gallup.com/content/default.aspx?ci=14593&pg=1**.

One of the items that Walters is best known for is his assortment of zany costumes. Here he is, the highest-ranking Qwest official at this location, and he comes prancing into work dressed like a milkshake bearing a tray of burgers for the employees. Then there's the SpongeBob SquarePants outfit that was given to him by an employee. Walter's thin, lanky frame gets him the perfect

---

1 Rodd Wagner, "Becoming the Best at Qwest: How a self-deprecating manager turned a call center around—and built it into the largest and best in this telecommunications company," January 13, 2005, Gallup Management Journal, http://gmj.gallup.com/content/default.aspx?ci=14593&pg=1, accessed on May 1, 2006.

comedic reaction: the employees love it.

Whether it was making them laugh to lighten their mood, or truly listening to their needs and giving them hope that they'd have a job the next week, putting the employees first was a large part of the plan, because Larry Walters instinctively knows something that has never occurred to many managers: happy employees are productive employees. While turning around the Idaho Falls location wasn't accomplished overnight and it wasn't done through simply making employees happy, the focus on employee issues likely can be credited for a large chunk of the improvements that were made.

Keep this management model in mind as you read about costs and profit-finding associated with what's often the biggest outlay for a business: your workforce.

If your business is booming, why consider cutting costs? Because in today's global economy your business might not be booming in a year or even in a decade. And every bit you can put back into your business or into investments now will be a buffer in the lean times which are almost certain to come at some point. Being aware of a potential for a downturn in business in the future isn't being pessimistic — it's being realistic. The point is, be wise with the savings you reap from your efforts to trim.

There is one common-sense axiom about cost cutting that just can't be ignored. As you'll be directed to do in many of the tips, you'll have to *spend money to save money*. One example is to spend money on the proper marketing studies before planning a new product line. While the cost may seem high up front, weigh it against the cost of a fully-developed but failed product line. Don't think of the losses surrounding the marketing studies — focus on the savings you just reaped by not jumping into that product line! And if the marketing analysis shows the product line will soar? Now compare that small amount spent to the profits of a highly-profitable product line. Spending the money up-front will either save you from a big loss later or help boost your profits later.

In this section, we'll examine all the costs related to having employees: the size of your workforce, the benefits you provide them, the training they receive, your human resources department, and people-issues surrounding the thing all employers strive to achieve most: productivity.

CHAPTER

1

Workforce Size Issues

L ayoffs are, unfortunately, one of the quickest ways to cut costs in a crisis or impending shortfall in the budget. And it's often one of the first suggestions that comes up when owners, managers, or a board of directors tackles issues related to costs. Consider these alternatives to layoffs next time your workforce's wages become a target of cost cutting.

Layoffs have short-term and long-term repercussions on your company. In the immediate sense, you no longer have to pay wages, but you may have to pay severance packages and unemployment costs. Consider these costs as well, as they may add up and make the layoff less attractive.

AVOIDING LAYOFFS

Consider the future before deciding on a layoff. Is the downturn going to be short-lived? If the current changes in business aren't permanent, what are you going to do when you need these employees back? The cost of hiring new workers and training them to take the place of your skilled and trained employees may be too high. Avoid excessive hiring and training costs in the near future by avoiding a layoff in the present.

One oft-used method of avoiding layoffs is to ask employees to consider retiring early. With a small additional incentive (which will be quickly made up by not paying the retiring employees' wages) you may be able to entice some near-retirement employees to rev up their RVs and go fishing a few years early. When employees retire early, you don't have any unemployment costs.

On the flip side, be careful not to make the incentives too generous or there might be too much of a drain on your pension plan and you may lose a good supply of highly skilled and productive workers who will be expensive to replace.

In addition to having employees retire early, you can avoid layoffs by simply putting a halt to all hiring. If you're creative — and employees are aware that this step can save their jobs — you can probably reassign employees to different jobs within the company. There may be some training needed and salaries might have to be renegotiated up or down a bit, but considering the alternative — a layoff — many employees will be willing to comply with changes. To make these changes more appealing, offer a guarantee to employees that when business picks up again or a vacancy becomes available they can return to their old jobs and wages on a seniority basis.

Create a new policy requiring unpaid time off. An employee whose finances would be in shambles because of a total layoff might willingly work one day less every week for a while. Others who wouldn't be able to make ends meet on unemployment, especially those who also might not find another job quickly, will compromise on the 40-hour workweek. Rotate those who are having their unpaid days off so that you don't have too many employees on duty at any one time. Or give employees a time frame and a number of days they must take unpaid days off during that time.

Another possibility is reducing the number of hours your business is in operation. You can reduce the number of hours per day, or the number of days per week that you are open to reduce the wages you will pay.

Instead of reducing your employees' working hours, you could institute an across-the-board pay cut for every employee. Be sure that the cuts are fair and that management feels the pain of slow times as well, or you'll be faced with a morale issue. Airlines often negotiate pay cuts with classes of employees, such as the pilot's union or mechanic's union. At every level of business, employees often will give up a little now to avoid losing a lot later.

Shift some workers from full-time status to part-time status. Start by asking for volunteers and negotiate things like continued health insurance and other benefits. If your work load doesn't require a full force right now, try this rather than a layoff so you'll have a ready, trained workforce to call into action at any moment.

Consider rotating workers from full-time to part-time. For example, divide your workforce into four even groups and every week on a four-week cycle, one group works only part-time. Scheduling may take a little planning and coordination, but it can be beneficial to your payroll woes.

If your workforce contains many highly-skilled employees who would be very expensive to locate and replace in the future, consider offering a sabbatical to them. You can negotiate things like benefits (keeping health insurance active) and a retainer for consulting services if they are needed here and there during their sabbatical. An employee who's been toying with finishing his last year of graduate studies or one who is considering starting a family might find this an attractive alternative.

Offer an incentive for workers to take an extended unpaid vacation. If it looks as though it's going to be a slow summer, workers with young children may volunteer to take the summer off to avoid paying daycare for the children in exchange for a small bonus. Many employees would like to have the winter months around the holidays off work. Those who can afford it may be willing to volunteer.

Evaluate the duties of your highly skilled and your higher paid, employees. If their jobs require them to spend considerable time doing menial duties that could be done cheaper by another employee, then rework job descriptions accordingly so that the work done is equivalent in value to the cost being paid to do it.

If the goal is to increase profits, then the means can be justified. Instead of reducing your workforce, consider increasing it in a manner that benefits employees and increases productivity. During a layoff, overstressed employees who already have too much on their plates might be *even less* productive due to their own increased workloads and reduced morale. If increasing productivity will lead to greater profits (which translates the same as reducing your workforce to cut costs) then try hiring more people.

When pay cuts are necessary to avoid a layoff, make sure the lower paid employees know that even the higher salaried ones are taking a pay cut as well.

Bonuses can often be cut without any employee running into the skids financially. However, find alternate ways to show appreciation. Make compensation variable based on performance. For upper managers who have a direct influence on the productivity of those they oversee, this measure can be a strong motivator.

Have a CEO or company executives trade salary for stock options, in effect getting paid in proportion to the productivity of the company. If a company hasn't been profitable of late, you will incite an energy boost from the top down!

Salespeople can trade salaries for a commission-only scheme. A sales member may work harder and earn more then, rather than only doing as much as the next guy because he won't make any more anyway. Paying him more isn't a problem because he brought more business into the company.

Rather than reducing salaries, simply eliminate all increases for the next quarter or year. Most people would have an easier time living on what they are currently earning rather than having a pay cut immediately.

When layoff rumors are on the lips of employees, they begin to get skittish and perhaps even start looking around for another job. Even if you don't end up laying off workers, you may *lose* good employees to other companies that seem more stable. Avoid losing good workers by keeping abreast of rumors and maintaining good communication with your employees about the actual chances a layoff anytime soon.

There are companies that have a policy, either formal or informal, of no-layoffs. One of these companies has been able to make good on that promise for nearly four decades: Hypertherm, Inc., of Hanover, New Hampshire.

This manufacturer of innovative plasma-cutting products has an official policy of no-layoffs. Founder Richard Couch built the company on a solid foundation that values the input of employees in their workplace. Their employee suggestion program, called the Continuous Improvement Activity Program, is successful in part because employees who feel their jobs are secure have a vested interest in being more productive and profitable for their employer.

In addition to being productive, Hypertherm's employees are eager to be cross-trained so they can be useful in another job during a slower production time. The willingness to do whatever it takes to keep the company productive is a trait that's linked directly to the corporate culture. (Learn more about Hypertherm's corporate culture in Chapter 4).

While Hypertherm is not entirely unique in its no-layoff policies, it is a prime example of the benefits that can be had simply by recognizing the core needs of their employees: to have gainful employment, to be recognized for their contributions to the company (through profit-sharing) and to be valued as individuals and team members both. Read more about Hypertherm at their Web site **www.hypertherm.com.**

WHEN LAYOFFS ARE UNAVOIDABLE

If a layoff is truly the best choice for your company, how do you go about it? One excellent resource is the writing of Dr. John Sullivan, Professor of Management and Corporate Advisor, College of Business, at San Francisco State University. Dr. Sullivan is the author of hundreds of articles about business topics, plus a recent book: *Rethinking Strategic HR*. Published in 2003, this 456-page book shows you "new ways to improve the business impact of your HR function by up to 25 percent," according to the book's description.

In one of Dr. Sullivan's hundreds of articles that you can read on his Web site, "Effective Layoffs: Key Steps to Effective Layoffs," this second part of a five-part series on the topic of layoffs shares with readers some of the things needed for planning and implementing a layoff including:

- Layoff planning and strategy: 17 clear-cut steps to guide you through the process.

- Who should be involved? Plan a layoff team.

- When should it be done?

- Before the layoff process begins: seven things to do.

- Setting the layoff criteria: 11 important criteria for ranking employees.

- The layoff process itself: 19 crucial steps to follow.

- Additional factors: 13 items you may not have thought of.

- Don'ts: Seven things to avoid.

To find the entire series of articles about layoffs, go to Dr. Sullivan's Index page at **http://ourworld.compuserve.com/homepages/ gately/pp15js00.htm**.

Layoffs do have their place in a company's strategic shifting of costs. Use a layoff to reposition people within your company or to restructure your employee base. It can be a positive thing for the company's balance sheet if done for the right reasons.

Another reason that a layoff might be necessary is as a result of hasty hiring. Sometimes, an organization has acquired excess workforce simply because it hasn't been acting in a thrifty manner. A department manager asked for an extra secretary and, at the time, it seemed necessary. A small downturn in business now reveals that the secretaries have excess time on their hands. Excess time leads quickly to excess drain on the company's resources.

To avoid mistakes such as excess staff in lean times, don't jump on the hiring wagon during busy times. This is not to say you should work your employees excessively hard when things are busy, but consider using temporary employees who can be cut from the payroll as easily as calling the temporary agency that supplied them.

Obviously, you can expect that your employees' lives will be disrupted by news of a layoff. If this was coming for some time (perhaps due to a gradual decrease in orders over the course of months), don't keep that information from the employees as things slow down. If employees are aware of decreased order status and then a layoff occurs, they will be less likely to take their misfortune and turn it into litigation. Save your company the possibility of your lawyer being involved by being honest with employees about the state of things.

When you do have to lay off employees, keep a positive relationship with them by offering them a re-hire incentive if they come back to work for you in the future thus reducing the cost of hiring and training someone else. Be selective, however, as a layoff can be a good way to weed out unproductive workers that you do not want to hire back in the future.

You can also prune away the unproductive workers by determining who gets laid off based on their job performance and other factors such as absenteeism, history, and attitude.

Be sure that you aren't bound by union regulations or any other legal issues before handing out the pink slips.

10 Factors That Might Affect the Cost-Effectiveness of a Layoff:

1. **Lawsuits.** Claims of discrimination by any class of employees may cost you more than you saved with a layoff. Make sure you don't target any particular ethnic group, gender, age group, or protected class (such as disabled workers).

2. **Recall decisions.** If you do recall workers, make sure you base your decisions on your business needs and call back accordingly. Don't just call everybody back without being sure you need them all right now. Recall decisions can lead to litigation as well, if you obviously avoid recalling anyone in a group above.

3. **WARN Act.** This federal law requires employers with more than 100 employees to give 60 days' notice of a layoff. If your company falls under its rules, make sure you obtain the advice of your attorney and follow it carefully.

4. **Layoff Policy.** If your company has frequent downturns and layoffs, it may be wise to add a specific layoff policy to your employment manual so all employees will understand the potential for this action. Surprised

employees may be more likely to turn angry or litigious.

5. **Severance pay.** Not a necessary benefit when an employee is laid off, severance pay may be beneficial in reducing discrimination claims. Consider having employees who receive severance pay sign a release form created by your attorney stating that they will not file any claims against you.

6. **State laws.** Your state governs whether unused vacation time is required to be paid upon layoff or not. Find out if there is such a law in your state and follow it.

7. **COBRA and health insurance continuation requirements.** If you have more than 20 employees be sure to investigate these requirements and determine whether you must contribute in the case of a layoff, as state laws may vary.

8. **Collective bargaining agreements.** Contracts may require you to recall laid off employees before hiring new ones. Be sure of your obligations before hiring after a layoff.

9. **Recalling employees.** Try to recall employees with multiple skill levels who can be flexible and perform many functions. Take into consideration an employee's past performance, attendance, attitudes, and embodiment of your corporate culture, and then recall those who fit the bill.

10. **For more information** on layoffs, free downloads of sample policies, and articles to read on this and many other subjects, visit Personnel Policy Services, Inc., at **www.ppspublishers.com/about.htm**.

One hallmark of a wise employer is demonstrating that you care about employees — even those you might one day lay off. What can you do to prepare your employees for that possibility? If there's even a remote chance that layoffs might take place, you can bet your employees have already picked up on that vibe. "Career insecurity," according to authors Anne Baber and Lynne Waymon, "saps energy, cramps creativity and lowers morale." But having some career insecurity at your company doesn't have to signal the end of your productive workforce, if you take charge of the situation.

Baber and Waymon, who have been writing and speaking about employment-related issues for more than a decade, have a mantra that they've developed for employees who face the possibility of a layoff: be eager to stay—and prepared to go.

For the employer whose workforce is feeling the effects of career insecurity, Baber and Waymon suggest that you prepare your employees for the possibility of a layoff by helping them distinguish between "job security" and "career security." If you assist your employees to "focus all resources and energy on being ready to make a living in the marketplace no matter what organizational earthquakes erupt," they contend, your employees will be happy to stay and remain productive.

Baber and Waymon have developed a five-point strategy for preparing employees to be proactive in the case of a layoff. Briefly, they suggest you do the following:

- Encourage employees to **become psychologically employed**. Employees who realize that their career opportunities are in their own hands will be less emotionally dependent on you, their current employer.

- Remind employees that **increasing their employability** is up to them. Even if they may be laid off at your company due to economic downturn, they'd be wise to take available seminars and educational opportunities at every turn. Their future employer may be looking for just those skills they will acquire.

- Help employees **manage their money**. When you provide a paycheck, you may not think about what your employees are doing with it. A good employer assists employees to **safeguard their financial futures by planning ahead.** Provide opportunities for training in financial planning and living within one's means, so your employees won't be financially strapped during a transitional employment time.

- Encourage employees to **develop multiple options** for career success by looking for new ways to advance their skills, knowledge, and ways to apply them right now. Doing so will make them more productive and happy at their current job and serve them well in future employment opportunities.

- Finally, make sure employees **take time to build a safety network** in their own specialty. When your employees are knowledgeable about their peers in other companies and have a network of other professional and trade associations, they will begin to see that the wide world of employment is open to them should the need arise for their current employer to lay them off.

These are just brief snippets of the valuable information found at Anne Baber and Lynne Waymon's Web site. The suggestions above came from an article "What to Tell Your Employees About Career Security," that is found on their site at **www.fireproofyourcareer. com/site/576990/page/336992**.

Baber and Waymon also have a complete e-book available on the topic of career insecurity titled "FireProof Your Career: Be Eager to Stay — And Prepared to Go" that is available on their Web site, **www.fireproofyourcareer**. In addition to the e-book, they offer an audio tape made during a live session with Anne Baber, the opportunity to license their site information for use by your company (which also includes copies of the audio tape), and a

"Corporate FireProof Package" of services including a training seminar, workshops to train your staff, and a site license.

In addition to their "FireProof" site and e-book, the second edition of *Make Your Contacts Count: Networking Know-How for Business and Career Success*, will be available in fall 2006. Co-author Anne Baber calls it "the ultimate step-by-step guide to networking the right way."

CHAPTER

2

Employee Benefits Issues

Employees are as protective of their benefits as they are of their job itself. After all, good benefits often are what attracts quality employees in the hiring process, so you don't want to go overboard in taking benefits away when times are tough. There are many creative and thoughtful ways to reduce benefits without leaving your employees feeling like they have been robbed blind.

HEALTHY EMPLOYEES
ARE HAPPY EMPLOYEES

You'd be hard pressed to find a health professional who wouldn't agree: healthy employees are productive employees who save the company money by not wasting the company's time. They also can affect a company's health insurance premiums and may even qualify for discounts if your company and its employees are smoke-free.

Employee wellness programs can be controversial in an era of cost cutting. If you make certain that the elements of your wellness program actually contribute to the health of your employees, then it is likely very much worth it. If you don't have one already, consider starting one. Research effective wellness programs at other companies to find out what works and what does not.

One corporation that traditionally serves college and professional athletes has recognized the need for their special approach to occupational therapy in the corporate wellness market. The Airrosti Center, a Texas-based company that has developed what they call "Rapid Recovery Treatment" methods that take a unique approach to assessing and treating injuries, has paired up with Cardell Cabinetry, another Texas-based company, to provide occupational therapy for their workers with injuries.[2]

Airrosti believes that by using their rapid recovery techniques that have been successful with some of the best-known professional athletes, they will be able to get workers back on the job sooner and in better condition than before they were injured. Rapid recovery can translate into a significant savings of up to 70 percent in workers' compensation costs.

Conversely, if you have a wellness program in place with ongoing associated costs but your employees do not use it or it has shown no improvement in your employees' health, consider discontinuing it or replacing it with a program that is effective.

Even without a formal wellness program in place, you can conduct informal (and voluntary) exercise sessions during coffee breaks and lunch hour. Your local library may be able to assist you in finding a video that features easy to do office exercises.

One popular workplace regimen includes Tai Chi, a noncompetitive self-paced program practiced in China for more than 2000 years. Originally developed as a self-defense program, it helps produce strong balance, more coping power, and increased stamina — all benefits to an employee during the work day.

In every aspect of employee health, make sure that the leaders set a

---

[2] "Cardell Finds Success with Airrosti's Approach to Occupational Injuries," January 13, 2006, <http://www.prweb.com/releases/2006/01/prweb331738.htm> accessed on May 1, 2006.

positive example. Learn a bit of Tai Chi yourself and then introduce it to your employees. They'll be more likely to participate if they see that you value the benefits it will bring them.

Even employees at a work station should be taught to take a few minutes out of every working hour to change positions and do some simple exercises that will help eliminate repetitive stress injuries such as carpal tunnel syndrome. Some exercises are very quick and simple.

Speaking of those employee workstations, have you evaluated them to be sure they are ergonomically acceptable? Ergonomics, a system of matching up the physical needs of a worker with the appropriate tools, could include changing the height of the workstation, chair, or tools being used by the employee. Proper ergonomics can avoid injuries that will raise workers' compensation costs.

Smoking cessation programs are also becoming increasingly common in the workplace. Here is another excellent opportunity for managers and business owners to lead by example. If you value your own health, your employees will value theirs more as well.

Exercising and quitting smoking are great ways to improve employee health. But what about their eating habits? Contribute to healthy eating by providing only heart-healthy and other positive foods in vending machines or at company-sponsored parties or outings.

It is easier said than done, but de-stressing the workplace leads to greater productivity and fewer sick days for employees. Find out what stresses your employees while they are at work. Is it a constantly ringing phone? Worries about a sick child? A crabby co-worker? Some employees are very sensitive to perfumes and colognes. An employee who's sneezing or stuffed up all day due to odors (even pleasant ones) won't be able to work productively. Survey employees, formally or informally, and make as many changes as you can for their comfort.

Reward the participants of your company wellness program or even your informal coffee-break exercise group. Give them every reason to continue in their efforts to improve their health and productivity.

Publicize any positive results of the efforts, such as a reduction in absenteeism or the number of days without a workplace injury. There are countless web sites devoted to the subjects of employee health and wellness programs. Don't miss out on a way to reap a serious return on your investment (i.e., your employees) by keeping them happy and healthy at work!

Beyond Band-Aids: 10 Things You Should Have in Your Corporate First-Aid Kit

Keep your employees safe in an emergency. The proper treatment right away can reduce the severity of an injury, reducing time-off or health care costs and workers' compensation costs:

1. **Aspirin.** Studies show that taking aspirin early on in a heart attack can be helpful. Heart attacks don't strike just middle-aged men, either, so have some on hand.

2. **Defibrillator.** Having this item alone isn't enough; you need to have people on hand who know how to use it.

3. **Employees certified in CPR and advanced first-aid.** Call your local Red Cross office for classes.

4. **Solar blanket or other way of providing warmth.** You want to avoid shock in an injured employee.

5. **Contamination control items.** Examples are CPR masks and latex gloves.

6. **Back-up light source and energy source.** Emergencies may happen if your power goes out suddenly. Have stations with emergency light and power available.

7. **Specially designed clean-up kits for bio-hazards.** Containers of absorbent material and decontaminants for removing bodily fluids or hazardous liquids are inexpensive.

8. **Ice packs and pre-packaged gel dressings.** You will want to be prepared should someone suffer burns.

9. **Sterile eye pads and eye wash.**

10. **A portable stretcher.** An employee may need to be moved out of danger.

INSURANCE BENEFITS

Health insurance is the bane of every company, from the federal government right on down to the individual working from his own home. Everybody needs health care, but how much should employers be responsible for providing it? Companies that do not offer it can save a lot of money, but do they have more health problems among their employees because of lack of preventative care or early intervention? Do they have trouble attracting quality employees because of the absence of this benefit? Does this benefit pay for itself in terms of a healthier workforce?

The answers are as unique as every company you could survey. But since most companies already do offer at least some sort of health insurance coverage, let's focus on ideas for getting the most out of what you do offer.

One way to begin is by viewing your company health insurance provider as a *supplier* rather than an overhead expense. This change in perception gives owners, CFOs, and managers a different view of insurance. It now becomes something that needs to be used efficiently and a cost to be scrutinized rather than just something the company provides. It's too easy for everyone to take their insurance for granted — sometimes just looking at the same thing differently can help raise the level of awareness about its costs and value.

Although it can be annoying for employees when your company changes insurance providers, make a habit of shopping around. Asking for quotes (which may require employees to fill out a brief form) never hurt anybody, and you may find a company with better benefits for your particular workforce. There is no one-size-fits-all insurance policy.

Larger corporations occasionally have turned to a self-insurance system for their healthcare needs. Under the right circumstances, it is less expensive than farming the benefit out to a provider.

All companies, whether they self-insure or use a third-party system, need to know if their employees' medical bills are accurate. Especially when it comes to hospital stays, emergency room visits, and surgical services, there can be all sorts of errors on the bills.

One way to combat billing errors and fraud is to hire someone who is trained to review bills. For the company who self-insures, having your benefit staff know what to look for is crucial. Training is available for this service as well as a network of professionals already trained and waiting to assist you with your billing review processes. Some professionals will work on a commission basis, meaning they earn a percentage of the savings they find for you in billing errors. Be sure to get all the facts before hiring a professional, as you would with any consultant.

To locate a professional who is trained in reviewing medical bills, one source is the Medical Billing Advocates of America. Their Web site is **www.billadvocates.com**. Another resource you might check into is the National Health Care Anti-Fraud Association at **www.nhcaa.org**.

10 Common Medical Billing Errors to Watch Out For:

1. Make sure that the dates of admission and discharge are correct and the total days billed match that number of days.

2. The time you spend in the operating room may generate a charge based on an hourly rate. Find out if you really were in the OR that long.

3. Be on the alert for duplication. Unless you truly received multiple enemas, be sure you got charged for only those you received.

4. What type of room were you in? If you were in a semi-private room, but you did not have a roommate during your stay, be sure you weren't charged for a private room.

5. Another thing to look out for is separate charges for things that should be included in your room charge, such as linens.

6. Keep a log of all medicines you're getting while in the hospital. Ask the nurse what the medicine is and whether it's generic. Compare that information to your bill; make sure if you received generic, that's what you were billed for.

7. Keep track of anything that is provided to you by hospital personnel. Anything can generate a charge. Most hospitals don't provide a box of tissues in a room anymore. If you ask for a tissue for a dripping nose, you'll be given a box and a charge on your bill.

8. Keep track of services. Did you really get all those tests and other procedures on the bill? Double check.

9. Oops! Sometimes simple mistakes happen. Something was mis-coded. A billing clerk input something wrong, but if you don't compare your bills to your records, you'll never know. A simple error or oversight could cost you big bucks.

10. You have the right to a completely itemized statement

and a copy of your medical records for comparison.

Company-paid life insurance policies are a nice benefit appreciated by any employee. Often, the rates are very reasonable and employees who might not otherwise be able to obtain insurance now can. However, make sure you set limits on the policy amount to keep premiums reasonable. If an employee wants a higher limit and the insurance company will allow it, have the employee pay the difference.

Workers' compensation programs can be costly, so do an audit to be sure that your workers are classified properly. You could be paying more than necessary.

If you are considering eliminating your long-term disability insurance policy, check with your employees about their desire for that coverage. Among middle class, blue-collar workers, that coverage might be very valuable. Offer a compromise and have employees pay some or more of the premium.

To keep your insurance rates from rising, institute a very solid employee safety program. Different from a wellness program, it focuses just on eliminating workplace injuries. Your entire workforce could feel the financial pain from just one severe injury.

OFFER OPTIONS TO EMPLOYEES WHO WANT FEWER BENEFITS IN EXCHANGE FOR MORE SALARY

Encourage employees to use a spouse's insurance plan instead of yours. Reward them with a monetary rebate equivalent to a percentage of your savings.

Raise the percentage of the premium that your employees must pay for their insurance rather than losing some insurance benefits or switching to another provider.

EAPs

While not exactly an insurance policy, a company's Employee Assistance Program (EAP) can do some of the same functions as health insurance.

Six Ways an EAP Can Save Money:

1. It can provide an early detection system, not for disease but for things like employee stress and strain.

2. It can provide preventative maintenance by offering things like financial planning assistance for employees who need help learning how to manage their money properly, thereby avoiding such stressful situations as bankruptcy or homelessness.

3. A good EAP will also provide counseling for the employee's family. Marital and other family issues can be dealt with in a healthy manner, preserving families and leaving the employee more able to concentrate on work instead of being preoccupied with family troubles.

4. It provides a confidential place for employees to find resources for things like alcohol abuse.

5. An employee who can tap into an EAP early on in a crisis will eventually miss less work to deal with it later.

6. An EAP can reduce workers' compensation costs due to treating an issue early that could have led to an injury.

For more information about EAPs and how even small businesses can bring them to their employees, visit the Employee Assistance Professional Association's Web site at **www.eapassn.org**.

Dental and vision insurance are often tossed out the door in an effort to cut insurance costs. However, the premiums for these extras are often not expensive. If a majority of your employees want this coverage, have them contribute most or all of the premium. For families with children or employees who have had prior vision or dental needs, this coverage will be valuable enough for them to contribute to it.

Other insurance options you can offer your employees are called supplemental insurance policies. An employer may be able to get these policies offered to employees cheaper than they could purchase them independently, so look into it. By saving employees a few dollars through a volume purchase, you are inadvertently giving them another benefit, even if they pay the entire premium themselves. Some types of supplemental insurance are long-term disability and coverage that would pay the entire cost of treating a terminal illness.

Regardless of the benefits you offer your employees, they can take an active role in managing those benefits, resulting in a reduction of time needed by the human resources staff for those functions. Your company Web site can help facilitate this change. By placing employees' current benefits information on your site and making it password-protected, you can allow employees to update information such as their tax deductions, their dependent status, their 125c plan reimbursements and their choices for options in the coming year's insurance plans.

Paid Time Off

Almost every company in the United States today offers its full-time employees at least some paid holidays and vacation days. Some are more generous, offering up to ten paid holidays a year, which might include things like Dr. Martin Luther King, Jr., Day or President's Day, or even an employee's birthday. Others stick to the standard six, which include New Year's Day, Memorial Day, Fourth of July, Labor Day, Thanksgiving, and Christmas.

In addition to paid time off, sometimes employees need unpaid time off. How you handle this issue is based partly on law. The Family and Medical Leave Act requires certain things of employers for certain reasons. But what about employees who simply want a day off now and then to run errands or because their children have a day off school?

Your company needs to have policies regarding unpaid days off, as well as those regulating the use of sick and vacation days. Giving employees a clear vision of what they are allowed to do and when will save money in the long run. As with all benefits you offer employees, there needs to be built-in cost-effectiveness.

Just as reducing the number of hours your company is open reduces the wages you pay, it may have an effect on the benefits you pay as well. If your employees' sick and vacation days accrue based on the number of hours they work, then they will not accrue them as quickly on a reduced work week.

Limit or do not allow vacation to carry over from year to year. Because employees earn more money every year, their vacations cost you more from year to year. If an employee banks vacation for five years then takes it all at once, you have to pay for all those days off at their current rate, not the rate of the year in which they earned it.

Do you offer the opportunity to "cash in" unused sick days? Employers who allow employees to do so are just asking for sick employees to show up to work. Consider eliminating that policy to ensure employees use their sick days when they are sick. But what about employees who aren't ever ill? Those few people who are blessed with perpetual good health are "robbed" of their sick days if they can't cash them in. Find other ways to reward healthy employees for using their sick time properly, or you'll find that even the healthy ones are getting suspiciously ill just to avoid losing the time.

Instead of offering to cash in sick days, allow employees to roll them over to the next year, giving them some security should a major illness or accident strike them. However, since it will cost you more to pay the sick days in future years than in the current year because the employee will get their current (higher) rate of pay when they take the sick days, not the rate of pay they got when they earned the days, consider reducing the number of days carried over. For example, if an employee earns ten sick days and used none, at the end of the year they can roll over nine of them. To counter future inflation, set a percentage that can be carried over; for example, 90 percent of the days earned and not used, and the rest is simply lost.

Employers who allow carryover may impose a cap on how much sick time can be banked, and they do some long-term planning at the start. You don't want to be changing the rules after-the-fact because you find that you're losing money. Setting caps, or setting a percentage of days allowed to be carried over, should be done at the outset of a new policy.

Take a close look at your corporate culture regarding sick time. If the managers and the boss come to work ill, the employees may follow suit. Set a good example by using sick days at all levels. Talk about the downside of employees coming to work sick, perhaps by inviting your county health department to prepare a presentation demonstrating how easily germs and viruses are spread.

Your corporate culture might make employees fearful of calling in sick if managers treat them as if they're babies or if they insinuate that employees are not really that sick when they call in. Managers and bosses who become hostile or try to make an employee feel guilty for being sick also are going to find employees coming to work sick just to avoid a confrontation.

These attitudes may be more prevalent in very small companies that nearly come to a standstill when an employee is absent. If attendance is crucial to your company's business, perhaps you need to cross-train employees to fill in for each other, or have managers who are capable and willing step in and cover for an ill employee. Small companies with very few employees may be harder hit by germs and could easily be shut down so it's especially important for these employers to avoid having sick employees at work.

Make sure that employees don't abuse their sick leave, however, because when they take paid sick days inappropriately, you've lost their healthy productivity for that day. And then you lose double when they are absent when truly sick even if they don't have any paid days off left. Your company's production will be affected. However, monitoring sick employees' use of their sick time is a gray area.

Some companies require employees to present verification of their illness, such as a note from a doctor. Since most common viruses and illnesses don't require a doctor's visit, requiring a doctor's note may actually raise your health insurance costs because employees will be going to the doctor for common illnesses just to prove that they are ill.

Ill employees who come to work because they don't have any sick time available or because they feel obligated to be productive really aren't doing anyone a favor by showing up sick. It costs more in the long run to have a sick employee around, so save others from exposure and send sick employees home, even if against their will. You are morally obligated to protect the public in workplaces such as restaurants, daycare centers, schools, grocery stores, and banks.

There may not be one strategy that will effectively reduce your employees' misuse of sick time. Educate employees about the appropriate use of all benefits as well as the losses to productivity incurred when those things are misused. Make policies both understandable and user-friendly. If you aren't sure how your employees really feel about their benefits, survey them in a confidential manner. Do they feel satisfied with the number of sick days, vacation days, and other perks? If not, are their feelings justified?

Having an open line of communication with employees regarding their benefits, including an honest desire to make benefits truly usable and worthwhile, will help build a sense of trust and respect between management and employees. Those two items will go a long way in getting the most from the benefits you offer and avoiding their misuse.

Instead of giving employees a set number of vacation days and sick days, move to a system where they earn paid time off (PTO) instead. Not only will you avoid employees' using up their vacation and sick days early in the year and then quitting, you will assist employees in their true needs. If they are out of sick days and need to use vacation to care for a sick child, they don't have to lie about why they need a day off. On the other hand, if they want to save it all up and use it on vacation at the end of the year, they can do so without pretending to be ill.

Incentive and Other Creative Benefits

Sometimes you can give a benefit to your employees that will also benefit your company as well.

River Steel, a steel fabricating plant in La Crosse, Wisconsin, recently created such an opportunity. They began supplying uniforms for their employees at no cost to their workers. This might seem contradictory: a company reaping a benefit by bearing the entire cost of the uniforms, including laundering and maintaining them but Tim Brennan, CEO, believes it is true. While he admits that "the potential return for the company is indeterminable," he believes that offering the uniforms will assist in things like attracting quality employees. He also hopes to provide a safer working environment with the uniforms, chosen for their fiber content, for the majority of their employees who are welders. They also don't discount the fact that employees will be wearing uniforms with the company's logo on them every day as they travel to and from work, stopping at the bank, running company errands, and whatever else is done on a daily basis. Creating a stronger, and positive, image of their company through the use of uniforms is yet another portion of the payoff.

CEO Tim Brennan notes that "we elected to pay the entire cost with the belief that there would be a comparable benefit to the company, even if it can never be measured in dollars and cents."

Legal costs are expensive, and often employees don't know where to turn for a simple consultation. The stress of legal issues can be counter-productive to employees, so consider offering pre-paid legal benefits for things like consultations and simple items while negotiating a discount on other legal services for your employees. Simply having someone already lined up to consult with is an important benefit, even if they are contributing to the cost through payroll deductions.

Allow employees to trade paid benefits for things that they may value more. Employees whose spouses provide health insurance may forgo using your company's plan in exchange for more vacation time, more sick days, or even *unpaid time off.*

Employees may also want unpaid time off on a one-time basis for personal reasons, such as the opportunity to take classes in something nonwork related, or to prepare for family events such as a wedding, birth of a child or grandchild, or for a long-awaited dream vacation. Having a policy that is friendly to employees taking unpaid time off is an important way to provide a benefit without paying for it.

Instead of blanket bonuses for executives and upper management, give stock options that are tied to overall company performance — rather than division performance — to foster a desire to increase the productivity (profit margin) of the entire company.

Another way to foster positive outlooks and hard work in managers is to link bonuses or stock options to how well they embody the corporate culture. In other words, a manager who makes no efforts other than those mandated by upper management to implement cost-cutting techniques in his department will get a smaller bonus than a manager whose innovations have inspired his division to become involved at every level.

Benefits for top performers in the company can be flexible enough to allow these employees to participate in an *ala carte* system. They can choose more personal days, more sick time, or choose to have more of their insurance premiums paid by the company. Four-day workweeks, ten-hour days, work-from-home and telecommuting are becoming popular options.

Create income for local businesses while scoring a benefit for your employees by negotiating a discount for your employees. Movie theaters, restaurants, and local retailers may be willing to give out a discount temporarily or permanently.

Some companies might even be willing to partner with your employees. Any company that normally charges a fee for their services might be willing to waive the fee if they can do business with a number of your employees at one time. Examples are restaurants or dry cleaners who charge a fee for deliveries; they may wish to offer free delivery, their own way of providing a discount.

Everybody enjoys learning something that's useful to them. Find out if a group of your employees is interested in learning about heart health or organic gardening, just two examples. If you get several employees interested in a common topic, arrange a speaker to give a lunch-hour talk for them.

While most American households have a personal computer, the very rapid changes in technology make the average PC outdated within a couple of years. Would your employees like a chance to purchase a brand new, state of the art system? Negotiate a quantity discount with a major supplier and resell them to your employees. For those who can't purchase them outright, offer a no-interest payroll deduction for a set number of weeks or months.

Host a company-wide garage sale and swap meet day. Invite all employees to bring things from home for a large garage sale. Provide tables, change, and price stickers. Employees can trade with each other or only sell items.

In conjunction with such an event, you can sell off excess inventory to employees during the garage sale day. Be sure to sell items at a reasonable discount.

Creativity with benefits is going to become increasingly important over time. Employees don't stay with companies for an entire career as they have done in the past. Now, they go where the money and benefits are. Creativity will help you offer quality benefits without cutting too deeply into your pockets.

10 Things You Might Not Think of as "Benefits"

1. Optimum work conditions

2. The best equipment available for doing the job

3. Talented co-workers and competent managers

4. Flexibility

5. Tuition assistance/reimbursement

6. Profit sharing

7. Section 125 Plans (cafeteria plans)

8. Floating holidays or the ability to take holidays specific to an employee's own religion

9. Recognition for excellence and milestones

10. The financial stability of the company

RETIREMENT AND PENSIONS

Today's college student works hard for four years, many for much longer, and then graduates hoping to get a job. The student who has job offers before the graduation ceremony is jubilant; obviously far ahead of the majority of graduates in the country. And what can today's college graduate be assured of by his or her new employer?

More importantly, what can the new college graduate be assured *not* to receive: a defined-benefits pension plan. Defined benefit pension plans are going the way of VCRs and cassette tapes. They are considered outdated financial technology, and for many reasons, they no longer do what they were conceived to do: pay retirement benefits for life if the employee met certain criteria. Oh, and the employees didn't have to contribute their own money to this plan, either.

The concept of a defined benefit pension plan is really an amazing one that hasn't even been around for very many decades. It wasn't until World War II that large corporations began to offer such pension plans. There were a few cases prior to the 1940s, but they were extremely rare. However, by the mid 1970s nearly 50 percent of American workers were covered by pension plans.[3]

In the late 1970s the concept of the defined contribution plan, the 401(k) being the most common example, started to push aside the defined benefit plans which were costly to employers. Today, the vast majority of workers who have a pension plan are covered under a 401(k) plan.

Many of our largest corporations are discontinuing their pension plans altogether in favor of defined-contribution plans, to which an employer may or may not contribute. Employers who match employee contributions to 401(k) plans are fast becoming thought of as generous, when 20 years ago they would likely have been

---

[3] Jennifer Klein, "Ducking Out on Retiree Benefits," November 27, 2005, www.h-net.org/~hns/articles/2005/112705a.html, accessed on May 1, 2006.

defined as being cheapskates! In the wake of the changing times for retirement benefits, how does your company help its employees prepare for their futures?

Six Ways for Your Employees to Get the Most Out of Your Pension Plans

1. **Start early.** The youngest set of workers, those under age 25, have the lowest rate of contributions to a company's 401(k) plans. Legislation has been suggested to auto-enroll all new hires if your company has a pension plan, hoping for better enrollments among younger workers.

2. **Participate.** Employer's contributions to a 401(k) are also not used by employees who don't participate. That's like throwing away free money!

3. **Roll it over.** When employees leave your company, be sure to educate them about rolling their funds over into an IRA rather than withdrawing them, which will incur penalties.

4. **Use before-tax dollars.** Employee contributions reduce their taxable income now. That makes using your company's plan cheaper than if they take their after-tax dollars and save them on their own.

5. **Save taxes on interest.** Employee investments grow tax-free until they are withdrawn, ideally only at retirement. No tax is paid on interest earned.

6. **Stay informed.** Many employees simply don't have a concept of what they'll need when they retire. They're too busy working and raising families today. Educate employees about future needs and how investing now is the way to alleviate future shortages.

INFORMAL BENEFITS

Reevaluate your company's annual holiday party or summer picnic. Find a cheaper way to have fun without totally eliminating these morale-building events.

Upper management's perks may have to be trimmed back as well as the employee perks. Those season tickets to the local NBA team may be costing a tidy amount that could be reduced by getting tickets to a local university team's basketball games instead. Minor league baseball can often be as thrilling as the major leagues and at a fraction of the cost.

Do you have a pot of coffee brewing for employees in the break room? You might want to eliminate it or set up a secured place for employees to chip in. Twenty-five cents for a cup of the finest in office coffee, anyone? And while they're drinking that coffee, are they using a Styrofoam cup supplied by the company? Ask every employee to bring in a coffee cup from home. It's likely that a little dish soap and a few towels supplied by the company will cost less than all those foam cups. It's also better for the environment!

Offering things that don't cost you anything, such as credit union membership for your employees, will give them benefits and lower banking costs than they might otherwise obtain. Find out which credit unions will offer membership to your employees, if your company is not large enough to start its own.

CHAPTER 3

Training and Meetings Issues

Whether you're training a new hire or certifying machine operators, your employees need training to stay ahead of technology and keep you on the cutting edge. And meetings need to take place, both within your workplace and with clients, customers, suppliers, and investors who may be anywhere on the planet. Eliminating these categories from the budget completely isn't an option, so how can you get the most for your money in this area?

THE NEW HIRE

There's more to training a new hire than just showing him where he will work and what functions he will perform. If you want your new employees to invest themselves into the company in the same way you are going to invest in them, then introduce them immediately to your corporate culture.

Every year, *FORTUNE* magazine scours the country to find the 100 best companies to work for. Part of the data that they take into consideration is the rating of these companies' own employees. [4]

---

[4] Robert Levering, "Warmer Welcomes, Fatter Profits: Making New Hires Feel at Home Helps Fortune's 100 Best Companies to Work For Boost Bottom Line," January 10, 2006, http://money.cnn.com/2006/01/09/news/companies/bestcos_welcomerituals/index.htm, accessed on May 1, 2006.

The 2006 list included companies such as Starbucks, which ranked 29th on the list overall. Starbucks is one of several companies cited that goes to great lengths to introduce new hires to their corporate culture, starting with day one, or more specifically, their first hour. The "Starbucks Experience," as the company calls their new hire orientation, includes an hour of taste-testing the company's products. Obviously, it's difficult for a new hire to recommend products to customers if they've never tasted them, so the company wants to make sure those recommendations are fervent right from the start!

Twenty-fourth on the list in 2006 was David Weekly Homes, a Dallas, Texas, home builder. Their two-day new-hire session gets right down to the nitty-gritty: home building. If new employees think they're going to swing a hammer while building this home, however, they've got another think coming. The team-building exercise uses Legos®, not 2' x 4's.

FORTUNE magazine also noted that the companies on their Top 100 list often have an ongoing view of training their new hires. Some companies invest 90 days to a full year in training employees to emulate the company's values and culture concepts.

Another practice noted was that assigning a mentor to a new hire was a common experience. Some companies hand out welcoming gifts, others gather all employees to a free lunch with the new hire. Company heads were often on hand for the welcoming party as well. All these add up to one obvious conclusion: the new employee will feel welcomed and needed.

Employees who stay with a company are cost-cutters because they do not have to be replaced. The Best 100 companies often comprehend the savings and do what they can to keep good employees, starting from day one.

If your company has a strong focus on a zero-defects program, instill that desire for quality in new employees from the start.

Demonstrate, and demand, attention to detail and the utmost of professionalism from new employees. Of course, all current employees must embody these same qualities.

While the new hire is in the process of training, ask for their overall observations of your manufacturing or working processes. Make sure you open the lines of communication early, because someone who is new to your process may be able to identify cost-cutting measures more readily than the employee who merely does things because "That's the way we've always done it."

New hires are sometimes criticized by their co-workers for their "at my last job, we did it *this* way" mentality. Such comments don't mean that they don't want to be a part of your team. Rather, by sharing ideas that could save money if you changed your process a little bit, your new hire might actually already be embodying your corporate belief in sharing information for the improvement of all. Mine your new hire, so to speak, for ideas that could bring savings to your company.

Seven Ways to Retain Your New Hire:

1. Let your new employees in on the big picture. Demonstrate to them how their job contributes to their department, their branch or plant, and the entire corporation.

2. Help them to feel like an integral part of your company right away. They may stay longer.

3. Set up a schedule of meetings with new employees, individually or as a group of new hires, to discuss any observations, suggestions, and gauge their overall experience to date.

4. Get your new hires involved right away in any volunteer charities. They'll do so initially to please you, but their involvement may evolve into a sense of pride and accomplishment at your company.

5. Make sure your employees have a positive working environment. Being "new" is hard enough without having to deal with social negativity or unhealthy competition among employees.

6. Foster cooperation among employees by organizing outside-of-work social events where the employees can mingle without the pressures of work. If employees become even casual friends, their working environment will be healthier.

7. Let your new employees know what they can do to endear themselves to you, their new employer. While they may seem like common sense ideas to an employer, employees who know these traits are valuable may be more likely to exhibit them.

Some work habits and traits you may wish to emphasize to new hires as valuable are:

- **Attitude.** Positive attitudes about their duties, their managers, and co-workers are always important. When issues arise, a valuable employee will deal with them in a mature and fair manner.

- **Safety.** Encourage employees to follow safety rules and keep themselves safe off the job by using seat belts and not driving while under the influence of alcohol.

- **Clean and free.** Drug-free workplaces are common, and yet statistics about drug use show that some employees take illicit drugs. Let your employees know your policies and the repercussions of not following them.

- Also let them also know the **resources you have available to them** (such as an Employee Assistance Program) to help them deal with any substance abuse problems.

- **Preparation.** Employees who arrive with their minds already on the work ahead of them are more productive that those whose first cup of coffee is still in their hands. Encourage employees to come to work prepared to work from the moment they arrive.

- **Timeliness.** Showing up to work, returning from lunch, coffee breaks, and meetings on time is crucial.

- **Availability.** Attendance is another crucial matter. Make sure you instill the importance of good attendance in your new hires right away.

- **Communication.** Everybody has a blip on their radar every once in a while such as having a car that won't start or being stuck in traffic. Make sure employees practice proper protocol and call to let you know when they will be tardy.

- **Proper dress.** Let employees know what constitutes appropriate work wear and what does not. Sometimes people are innocently clueless about the inappropriateness of their garb.

- **Open door.** Have an open-door policy for new employees to come ask a question any time they don't understand something.

- **Worth.** Let new hires know that you value team work, but you also respect their individual talents as well.

- **Initiative.** Praise new employees for taking the responsibility to do something they see needs to be done without being told or asked to.

- **Honesty.** The most valued trait is honesty. If your employees are honest, you'll find that most of the troubles employers have simply will not exist.

Employees who embody all these qualities are the ones you'll want to retain. Not all employees will come to you with all of these qualities fully developed, but each one of these traits can be nurtured through praise, fair enforcement of policies, and appropriate rewards, such as job security, promotions, or wage increases.

WHEN ALL EMPLOYEES NEED TRAINING

If you purchase new equipment, negotiate some training costs in the price of the equipment. The manufacturer may not be willing to train all the users but it may have its staff train your supervisors who can then pass the information along. Some manufacturers will even provide extra users' manuals or other training materials for free.

Share the costs of a training session with other local companies whose employees need the same training.

10 Good Reasons to Train Your Employees Better

1. **Competency.** More competent employees free up management to concentrate on other duties.

2. **Growth.** You can be more confident expanding your company's product line or reach if your employees have top-notch skills.

3. **Morale.** Employees feel valued when you invest in their training and ultimately have higher morale.

4. **Loyalty.** Higher morale increases loyalty and reduces grievances.

5. **Turnover.** Recruitment costs plummet when your employees are happy and stay on.

6. **Competitiveness.** Employees who are at the top of their game can help put your company at the top of its game as well.

7. **Safety.** Employees who are highly trained will perform

their jobs with a greater level of safety awareness. They will care more about everyone's safety as well.

8. **Productivity.** Any time you can enhance your abilities of your employees, you will reap rewards of increased productivity.

9. **Happy campers.** Your customers will ultimately be more satisfied with your products and services, thus boosting sales.

10. **Profits.** All the previous trickle-down effects above translate to your bottom line: it will be more profitable.

Simply training your employees may not always be sufficient to maintain long-term happiness. Long range employee training must take on more of an employee-development approach.

Eight Ingredients of an Effective Employee Development Program:

- **Learning.** Different from merely receiving training, learning focuses on things that an employee may not necessarily need to do his particular job, but things that she might value knowing to broaden her knowledge of your company and its operations. See more about learning below.

- **Self-Direction.** Employees who feel they have a say in their career path will be more engaged with their tasks. They see their job as one step of their career, not a dead-end they'll never overcome.

- **Ownership.** Employees should be encouraged to explore and understand their own styles of learning and growing professionally and find unique opportunities to satisfy their need for professional growth and education.

- **Mentoring.** Giving an employee the opportunity to mentor another can demonstrate your confidence in the employee's knowledge and skills. Have the mentor draw up a timeline and set of learning goals to gauge the effectiveness of the transfer of knowledge and skills to the new employee.

- **Promotion.** When a promotion is available, carefully consider all employees who have demonstrated self-direction, learning, and ownership. Note that once promoted an employee may need to do more learning to be competent in their new position.

- **Enrichment.** Even if a promotion is not currently available, enrich the life of employees by offering increased responsibilities and opportunities in their current job.

- **Diversify.** Cross-training an employee in other jobs of similar skill level and prestige can give them a sense of being more valuable to their employer. Short or long-term assignments can also be a positive step in their career path.

- **Moving sideways.** Even if an employee is not able to move up on the corporate ladder at the moment, allow lateral moves to keep the employee from becoming bored and seeking out opportunities elsewhere.

Learning is important both on and off the job. Sometimes, however, the things your employees should be learning, whether formally or informally, just aren't sinking in. Rather than give up on the employee, or feel that you're wasting your money with training opportunities that don't seem to be helping, consider these possible reasons that your employee isn't learning.

- The employee isn't connecting with the trainer. When someone who's receiving training is annoyed or put-off by "just something about" the trainer, the distraction can keep important information from making its way into the employee's store of knowledge. Even simple things, such as the trainer's bad breath, an annoying habit (such as twiddling thumbs) or a sense of arrogance on the trainer's part can cause these issues.

- More seriously, the employee may not be tuning in due to the age, gender, religion, culture, or nationality of the trainer. These issues can have other ramifications that may affect the employee's overall ability to work with and accept other people who are different from him or her.

- While it's often true that the trainer is a person who's higher in the organization or better educated than the trainees, sometimes someone lower in the organization or with less education may be the trainer; however, his or her corporate position, poor speaking habits, or bad grammar may cause trainees to put up a mental barrier to the subject being presented.

- Employees may resist training when they sense it is changing the way they've always done their jobs. Many people who were well into adulthood before the advent of computers have found it difficult to adjust to the training and proficiency needed to do their jobs a new way. Fear or resistance to change can cause a defensive attitude that blocks learning.

- A learning match is the best way to have the training sink in. That is, when the training offered matches the best way an employee learns, the results will be optimal. However, because there are so many different ways to achieve learning, it's nearly impossible for every employer to offer the same information in several training formats. This hurdle can be overcome by a good trainer who will use a variety of methods for instructing, such as visual aids, hands-on examples, and audience input.

REGULARLY SCHEDULED MEETINGS

Do you really need to have monthly departmental meetings? Productivity can be hurt by a meeting that interrupts the flow of work during a shift. If all your employees have an in-house e-mail account, replace the monthly meeting with an e-mail asking for suggestions on the issue of the month. Require each department member to reply and compile the responses for a follow-up e-mail or a meeting if the responses indicate one is needed.

When meetings are necessary, how do you keep them from being a time-waster? Too often meetings get bogged down by getting off track and running over the scheduled time frame.

Save your company time and money by using these 18 suggestions to make your next meeting successful:

- Plan the meeting before announcing it. Having no plan will get you nowhere. Define a specific purpose or purposes and stick to them.

- Don't try to cover too many topics in one meeting or it will become an information overload. Make an agenda to determine what order you'll cover which topics.

- State in the agenda how much time will be spent on each topic and what information will be presented, be it report, demonstration, or previous meeting minutes. You should always strive to stick to the agenda and the time limits.

- Gather any information that could be reviewed by attendees in advance and distribute it along with the agenda. People who are prepared need to spend less time being briefed at the actual meeting.

- Set up your meeting space so that everybody can see the demonstration or the speakers and also interact with each other. Select a space large enough to avoid discomfort. A small room will rapidly become too warm if it's overcrowded.

- Maintain the group's interest in a meeting. When they arrive, give them something to nibble on along with coffee or cold drinks and visual aids to follow along with. PowerPoint presentations, overhead projectors, and handouts help.

- Start on time and end on time. Late members will have to be brought up to speed by someone else, thus encouraging late-comers to be on time for the next meeting.

- Have the meeting's moderator or leader introduce each item of the agenda so that participants know when the topic is changing.

- Encourage attendees to contribute to the discussions, but don't allow differences of opinions to turn into a battle.

- Try to generate new ideas, solutions, or proposals for each item on the agenda.

- Interrupt to end discussions that are getting hostile, unproductive, or redundant.

- Take action. If your group votes on ideas and suggestions, call for a vote when enough discussion has taken place so that all sides have been reviewed, but don't wait so long that you're beating a dead horse.

- Summarize at the end of the meeting what was discussed, decided upon, and what tasks each participant is expected to do before the next meeting.

- Keep minutes or notes so that next time you meet to discuss the same topics, you can avoid repetition. These will also serve to demonstrate your progress over time.

- Set a date and time for your next meeting. You won't

have to try to contact every person at a later time. Besides, people's schedules are more open at this point than if you try to get back to them in a couple of weeks.

- Send a follow-up report within a few days to all meeting participants, which may include meeting minutes if taken, to help people keep the topics fresh in their minds and achieve the tasks they were assigned to do.

- Do additional follow-up midway between the meetings to ensure that participants are accomplishing their tasks and will come prepared to the next meeting.

- Plan for the next meeting. Include anything that wasn't decided upon on at the last meeting on the agenda for the next one.

If you structure each meeting in a similar fashion, eventually participants will come to expect this structure. Your meetings will be shorter, more productive, and useful. A complete guide to successful meetings, including planning checklist and templates for an agenda, can be found at **www.businessballs.com/ meetings.htm**.

Another reason to have meetings is to build teamwork among a particular group of employees. Those who are on the same shift, on the same production line, or working on a common project may need a little training session to put them in sync with each other.

Teamwork doesn't just happen, and it doesn't happen overnight. But if you can facilitate this process, you'll find your teams are more productive earlier on, leading to a faster completion of a project, increased productivity, or better working relationships. All of these improvements lead to the same conclusion: more work being done faster and easier to achieve a better bottom line for your company.

Any method you take to build an effective team should encompass as many of these aspects as possible:

- All persons on the team must be able to think and work independently. Although this seems the opposite of teamwork, it really is an important aspect of it. People who can work independently can contribute more to a team than those who are always waiting around for direction and instruction.

- All team members also must be able to trust the other team members. If there isn't trust, members will undermine each other and be constantly checking up on each other, which is counter-productive.

- The team and their project must have the support of management. If the manager doesn't have faith in their project or work, then the results will likely never be satisfactory to management.

- The team must have a leader, preferably appointed by the team as a whole.

- There must be guidelines defining their purpose, project, and things such as timelines and goals to meet in those timelines.

- All members of the team should share the same basic values. If everybody values the work that they will do together, they will be more productive than they would if a few members feel their work is pointless and a waste of time.

- A team should not, however, be void of diversity. Teams should represent a cross-section of your company.

- One last thought: persons who do not want to be part of a team, such as one that works on a special project, should not be forced to participate. The result would be pandemonium.

LONG-DISTANCE TRAINING AND MEETINGS

Training sessions that have traditionally been held off-site may be able to be held on-site for a reduced cost. Have all secretaries treat it as an off-site meeting (meaning don't let them interrupt it) and have a local deli bring in some sandwiches.

Or better yet, ask employees to bring in a pot luck lunch to an in-house training! Share some of the savings with employees by offering a door prize and even small prizes for employee input and participation in the session.

Scour your local region for less-expensive off-site training options. Many hotels have conferences rooms and in-house restaurants. Their package deals are worth looking into.

Video tape training sessions for use later (with the instructor's permission and knowledge, of course), or see if you can purchase a video with the same information in it for less than you can hire an instructor.

Check with your equipment manufacturers to see if your employees can obtain training over the Internet for their products that are use in your facility.

Video conference is an excellent choice for long-distance trainings and meetings. You can rent a conference room with equipment from many different locations, including some FedEx Kinko's. The downside is that you'll likely pay by-the-hour and you may feel pressured to leave some business unfinished for lack of time.

If you are going to doing a great deal of video conferencing, you may wish to invest in the equipment. The advantage is that you haven't got any mounting fees to force a meeting to close early. The disadvantage is that, like most new technological items, these systems may require frequent upgrades. However, you don't need extremely high-end video conferencing equipment to speak to someone. Webcams and pc microphones can allow you to have meetings with several people in different locations. The scope of what a webcam can do is limited, of course, but for simple matters, it often will suffice.

You can also hold meetings and have your demonstration, such as a PowerPoint presentation, over the Internet. Microsoft Office Live Meeting and other programs by other companies provide software and services for all your web conferencing needs.

If you're interested in web conferencing, check out the Web site **www.thinkofit.com** for a review of all the software and tools that make this a great alternative to live meetings. This independent Web site attempts to be unbiased and up-to-date on all aspects of web conferencing.

Teleconferencing is also an option when you have several people in different locations who need to be given the same information but don't require demonstrations or presentations. Be sure to shop around, as rates can vary widely among companies that offer this service.

You can couple a teleconferencing session with your private Web site where all participants log into the site and view charts and reports at the same time.

THE TRAINERS

Regardless of where you are holding a training session, give employees some reading material in advance to prepare them for the training. Many of the basics could be more quickly learned by reading.

Learn about each employee's learning abilities. Some employees will learn best by reading the manual on their own. Others need to have ideas explained to them by someone who's already trained. Still others may need a formal training session to bring them up to speed. Identify those employees who excel at training, and don't send them to a formal class that costs money (unless, of course, the class is needed for a certification).

You can save some money by having one of your own employees perform a training session, but there may be a downside: lack of respect for the trainer. Some employees will pay closer attention to a stranger than they will a co-worker or manager.

Therefore, consider professional training companies for some of your training needs. They may be able to achieve better results, with better-trained employees and less downtime from errors or fewer calls to a technical assistance department.

Train your trainers. It might be part of a department manager's job duties to provide training to employees, but does the manager know *how to train*? Educating others does not come naturally to everybody, so make sure those whose job it is know how to do it properly. Poorly trained employees can actually be a hazard in the workplace.

Ferret out the trainers in your company. Find the people who, regardless of their level of employment, are natural-born educators. If you can use their talents, you may achiever better results than conducting training by a manager who has no talent in educating.

Thinking outside the box is tough to do when you can't see what's outside the box. Have key employees spend time at your suppliers' and vendors' locations and bring back fresh concepts to your company.

You, too, must think outside the box! Don't automatically send the manager or employee who normally would be assigned to go. Send the employees whose creativity and enthusiasm for your product will motivate them to take the experience seriously and want to provide the best results to you for sending them.

4

Human Resources and Employee Relations Issues

The very nature of work environments requires cooperation among all employees at all levels. Someone needs to make decisions, and someone needs to carry them out. Some companies are more successful at achieving cooperation, yet some companies have friction at every turn. What makes the successful companies run like well-oiled machinery while others are mired in the muck of departmental in-fighting, power trips, and low employee morale?

The key element may be a company's *corporate culture*. A corporate culture is essentially the combined values and ethics of the company's leadership. Think of it as your company's DNA, if you will. Correctly created and implemented, a corporate culture works its way from the top down through management to every level of employment, even if not intentionally.

Therefore, if you don't have a positive message going around in the boardroom or management meetings, you'll soon have a sour workforce. If you fail to create a positive and thoughtful corporate culture, you'll find that one will develop anyway. Often a negative corporate culture develops when management fails to implement a positive one, or none at all exists. Companies where backstabbing and unscrupulous corporate ladder-climbing are the norm are those where no positive corporate culture has ever been established.

Corporate culture is crucial for every size of business. Many businesses have gone so far as to write a definition of their corporate culture which is then presented to new employees so they can understand the company better even before they join it. But putting it in writing and having every employee—from the bottom up—buy into it are two different things. How does a company enforce its corporate culture, especially when it has more than 6000 employees at 45 worldwide locations?

At W.L. Gore & Associates, it's an ongoing job. Just like budgeting or R&D, the corporate culture is given its share of thought, effort, and money in the organization. W.L. Gore & Associates' founders, Bill and Vieve Gore, set up their company in a way that worked for them and is still working nearly 50 years later. What the company calls their "four basic guiding principles" are the building blocks of their positive corporate culture.

These principles specify that employees must deal with everyone at their workplace with fairness. Each employee is also encouraged to see out the knowledge and skills they need to do their jobs at the highest caliber. This freedom comes with the responsibility to assist their peers in doing the same.

Making commitments, whether to a special project or a committee, is also stressed in the guiding principles. Keeping the commitments you make is of utmost importance.

The final principle compels all associates (not employees) to obtain advice and guidance from others with in the company before doing anything that might reflect on the company's reputation.

When Associates come on board and are schooled in Gore's ways, they are sent to work in what the company calls general work areas. Skills are matched up with various projects that are in process or starting and the associates commit themselves to a project, all the while learning new skills and expanding their ability to work within the company.

Those who assist in the skills/project matching and oversee the results are not "bosses" but are "sponsors." Autonomy of the individual associates is the desired working environment; those who lead strive to bring new associates into that mode and assist them to excel once there.

Probably one of the most unique features of the corporate culture at W.L. Gore & Associates is what they term the "flat lattice" nature of their organization. There is no one right way to get to a goal, and communication goes out in all directions, not just up or down to or from the leaders of the organization. To learn more about W.L. Gore & Associates, visit their Web site at **www.gore. com/en_xx/index.html.**

While applicants traditionally have wanted to know the bottom line, hard numbers for benefits and salary, more and more people want to know about a company's corporate culture as well. Merely making a nice salary isn't going to bring job satisfaction for the employee who doesn't fit in the company.

Fitting in is more than what it was in junior high school. If you don't fit in a company, your ethical behavior will be either better or worse than those you work with. Your motivational level will differ, and you will feel out of place. The workplace may be hostile with employees clawing and scratching their way up the ladder and kicking others below them to keep them down. Some people can push aside their discomfort or conform to the environment that they work in. Others cannot and will leave an unhealthy environment sooner than later, leaving you in the lurch for good employees, so the corporate culture can affect the bottom line.

Assessing your corporate culture isn't easy, however, for obvious reasons. The corporate culture is filtered from the top down. If upper management has negative attitudes and hostile methods for dealing with employees, then lower-level managers and supervisors will model their behavior accordingly. Employees at all levels will soon see this is "just the way things are done here," and nobody will even see that it's causing an unhealthy working environment.

If you want to get a real handle on your corporate culture and its strengths and weaknesses, hire an outside consulting firm to perform confidential surveys of your employees, review files, and make observations. Even if it's *the way you've been doing business for decades*, your current schemata might ultimately become counter-productive when it comes to obtaining and retaining quality employees.

There is a tendency among employers to rationalize the loss of quality employees:

- They got a better offer elsewhere.
- They had personal problems that interfered with their career.
- They didn't live up to what they portrayed themselves to be when we hired them.
- They lost interest.

The list is endless. An outside consultant might point the finger elsewhere. Be sure that you are willing to do some hard looking and planning if you're going to change a negative corporate culture.

Fitting in is important for employees, and important for employers to assess as well. Assessing a potential employee for a proper fit is just one of the many duties of human resource managers.

ACQUIRING EMPLOYEES

Hiring is a more complicated process than it may seem. And we're not just talking about finding qualified candidates either.

Today's H.R. professional needs to know more than just a potential employee's social security number and job history. Pre-employment screening companies are doing a brisk business for companies that want to avoid everything from employee theft to violence in their workplace.

I.F.R.S. Group, a California company that provides private investigation services for almost anything imaginable, shares some very compelling statistics regarding the need for pre-employment screenings.[5]

- The Society for Human Resource Management states 45 percent of all resumes contain one major fabrication.

- The *Wall Street Journal* said that 34 percent of all application forms contain outright lies about experience, education, and the ability to perform essential functions of the job.

- College and University registrars report that at least 60 percent of the verifications they receive contain falsified information.

- The Small Business Administration said that employees at all levels falsify their backgrounds.

- The American Management Association and the U.S. Chamber of Commerce said that 30 percent of all small business failure is caused by employee theft.

- According to the Bureau of National Affairs, Inc., from $15-25 billion is lost each year due to employee theft.

Their site, **www.ifrsgroup.com/preemployment_1.html,** also has a downloadable brochure about pre-employment screening services.

Companies like the I.F.R.S. Group use investigative tools to accomplish their mission, while other companies like Robert

---

[5]   www.ifrsgroup.com/preemployment_1.html, accessed May 1, 2006.

A. Cameron & Associates (Web site **www.racameron.com**) use assessment tools: personality tests that assess an applicant's attitudes toward work ethics, employee loyalty, and illicit drug usage. These tests have been designed to screen out those who are attempting to foil the tests by being deceitful.

10 Ways a Pre-Employment Screening Company Can Assist You:

1. Trace a social security number to avoid identity theft.

2. Provide criminal background checks, including any outstanding warrants or restrictions (i.e., parole requiring someone to live/work in a particular location).

3. Verify educational claims, work history given, validate professional licenses.

4. Provide driving records.

5. Check credit history.

6. Check for any ties to terrorist organizations.

7. Perform any necessary checks on current staff persons (even current employees may have issues you need to know about).

8. Guide your company in forming and implementing a policy to safeguard or destroy sensitive information.

9. Help educate applicable human resource professionals in the use and understanding of the national criminal database.

10. Gain access to courthouse records in person, saving your personnel time in tracking down records themselves.

10 Reasons For Considering Pre-Employment Screenings With Potential New Hires:

1. When you inform all potential hires of your pre-screening

intentions, candidates who are honest will think highly of you for wanting to hire only honest people.

2. On the other hand, a candidate with something to hide may back out and save you the trouble of finding information they'd rather you not know.

3. Candidates are less likely to falsify their resume or make claims of experience during an interview that simply aren't true when they know you're checking.

4. Pre-screening will save you money from mis-hiring due to deceit on the candidate's part.

5. All candidates will be less likely to embellish; they'll be themselves during interviews and trial periods because they know you chose them for good reasons.

6. Pre-screening ultimately reduces turnover by helping you make the right choice the first time.

7. They will help reduce violence in the workplace by eliminating those with a history of violence.

8. Employee theft will be reduced by helping to eliminating those who are prone to behaviors indicating the possibility.

9. When your new hires are a good fit and well-received by current employees, your entire workforce is likely to be happier and more productive.

10. Hiring employees who don't engage in high-risk behaviors may ultimately reduce health insurance costs for your company.

To locate potential new hires and reduce recruitment costs, start a referral program for your current employees. Offer an incentive for them to refer potential employees.

Post job notices on community internet bulletin boards and other free sites to gain exposure without the costs of paid advertising. Some of these sites also have places for posting resumes or employment wanted ads.

When managers and company executives travel for work (to trade shows, conventions or meetings, for example), ask them to collect business cards of people they meet who they feel would be a positive addition to your team when the need arises. Keep a database of names and contact information for quick reference.

Stay informed of other local or regional employers who are downsizing and try to snag quality employees from them. Another company's human resource department may be willing to identify employees meeting your needs whom they will be laying off.

When interviewing potential new hires, be sure to inquire about all their abilities and skills. Space limitations in a resume cause job seekers to delete otherwise important information. You could potentially fill a number of needs within the company with just one employee.

Use videoconferencing to interview potential candidates. You will save on airfare, hotel costs, soft-dollar costs (time to travel for candidate). You can also save the conference to video so it can be replayed for other managers to gain their input.

Rather than replacing a retiring or terminated employee, redistribute the tasks to be done among all other employees in the department or among those who do the same tasks as the lost employee.

College interns are often short-term sources of energetic and enthusiastic employment at reasonable wages. Contact your local university or business school to learn how to be accepted into their intern programs.

Hire people on an if-you-do-well-you'll-become-permanent basis. In effect, make new hires into independent contractors until you are certain you wish to hire them.

Many companies hire employees through temporary agencies, so that they can eliminate them easily if they aren't of the caliber desired by the company. The temporary agency will charge more than your cost of wages, however, and may require you to wait an extended period of time before you are allowed to hire the person yourself.

If you do use temp agencies to hire new employees, develop a relationship with just one or two agencies and offer them exclusive access to place their candidates in jobs at your company in exchange for lower fees or other negotiable terms.

Be thrifty with your recruitment dollars. Try online sites where resumes of available candidates appear first before placing an expensive advertisement in a newspaper or other print publication.

If you advertise in a print publication, clearly and specifically state your minimum educational and work experience requirements so that you don't receive hundreds of resumes from poorly qualified people costing you time to process and sort them.

Avoid a mis-hire (hiring someone who ultimately does not work out) by evaluating candidates not only on their qualifications and experience, but also on their personality as it will or will not fit into your company. For instance, if your company is filled with driven and orderly persons, try to avoid hiring a laid-back and philosophical person to manage them.

Additionally, reduce future workers' compensation program costs by making sure applicants are ergonomically fit to perform the jobs they are applying for.

You may be able to reduce future health insurance premiums by raising the health standards of workers you hire. In fact, some companies now have a policy against hiring smokers because of the health issues and future health care costs they may incur.

Match the right person with the right job. A candidate may be eager for a position and will agree to take ANY job but later become unhappy and a poor-performing employee as a result.

Match the employee with the right shift. People have a natural body clock and for some that means being up all night and sleeping during the day. Place an employee on the proper shift based on the person's preferences, when at all possible. You'll have more productive employees if they're not half asleep because they're forcing themselves to work when their bodies prefer to sleep.

Replacing employees can be time consuming, expensive, and stressful. What do you do when you suddenly are without someone in a key position in upper management? Just as people provide documents for their families in case of their sudden death or incapacitation, upper management and leaders should have a plan in place detailing what needs to be done for the company to continue its work in case of their sudden illness or passing.

Understand how hiring someone at a beginner's pay rate will affect productivity. It might seem attractive to let go more experienced employees at a higher rate of pay and replace them with new workers, but the new workers might not be able to do the same job in the same amount of time with the same level of quality. Output is important to measure when considering an employee's true value.

Three Unconventional Interview Suggestions

1. When interviewing candidates, try to focus less on their skills and accomplishments and more on their personality. Would they fit in? Would they give good customer service? Would your grandmother have liked them?

2. Narrow the field down a bit and shake things up at the second interview. Ask the candidate to lunch, but ask them to drive. How do they handle lunch rush traffic?

Do they speak politely to the wait staff? What do they talk about during lunch? Do they spend the whole time reiterating their resume, or do they engage you in conversation about current events and things you may have in common?

3. Narrow the field down a little bit more. Now ask the candidates to attend a nonwork related function with several employees that they'd be working with. See how they interact, especially if they don't realize these are the same employees they'd be working side-by-side with. Are they genuine or do they automatically snub certain people from the get-go? Most importantly, what does the feedback from your employees tell you about whether or not to hire this individual?

"Before you can keep them, you need to get them," notes River Steel's CEO Tim Brennan. He knows all about finding good employees for his family-owned business that recently celebrated its 50th year. This La Crosse, Wisconsin, company has learned the hard way how to choose the right employees for their organization. When the steel industry was in its heyday in the 1970s, River Steel hit its peak employee count of 144 employees. However, having more bodies didn't always equate to getting more work done. A lack of a consistent method of screening and hiring by the management of the day left the shop filled with an abundance of what Brennan calls "breathers," or simply bodies who filled a space and performed a duty. When the steel industry's slowdown began, employment opportunities became "survival of the fittest or sink or swim," recalls Brennan who took over the day-to-day operations of the company in 1987.

By the 1980s the employee count was down to 11. As Brennan remembers, "Old opportunities dried up and new ones were scarce." However, River Steel wasn't about to fade away without a fight. Instead, they viewed their slowdown in a positive light.

"[We] became leaner and prepared for opportunities in a more cautious and thought-out manner," states Brennan.

By early 2006, the shop employees numbered 31, but it is interesting to note that of those, 11 have been with the company for more than 30 years. And of the 42 shop employees hired since 1996, 43 percent have been retained. Not a large number? Remember, it is a huge improvement for River Steel.

What has made the difference? Brennan explains: "I hate to let people go. Whether it's due to lack of work, an employee's misconduct, or my mistake in a candidate's assessment, letting someone go is difficult. It's personal and, without a doubt, the worst thing I deal with in managing a business." So to avoid the problem caused by any of the above circumstances, Tim simply "work[s] harder and smarter to get it right."

Over the years, Tim and his wife, Gloria, who manages the front office, have developed a system of screening applicants. Each applicant starts with Gloria, whose bubbly and caring personality puts people at ease and allows her a chance to assess how someone treats the lowly secretary, as most applicants do not also know she's the CEO's wife.

As a side note, Brennan points out, this technique is also is applicable for meeting potential customers and vendors. He calls it "the waitress guideline." The way people treat those who are, or are perceived to be, beneath them has important ramifications on how they may treat you as a client, customer, or co-worker in the future.

After the initial meeting from Gloria, interviews follow with the manager of operations and with Tim himself. Second interviews are arranged after the pool of candidates has been narrowed to about 10 percent of the initial applicants.

In addition to practical welding tests and written tests, the face-to-face interviews are also a time to assess "whether they are contenders or are pretenders," explains Brennan. "When you consider that about half the waking hours are spent in your work environment, it's important that the employee and the company be a good fit for each other. If the company is going to succeed, the employee needs to succeed," he said. They try to learn about the corporate culture at an applicant's previous employer, looking to make that fit even tighter.

While there's no guarantee that every employee they hire will work out, Tim Brennan's efforts to cull the best of the best for his team are crucial to the lifeblood of River Steel. "I spend so much time on the selection process because it affords us the opportunity to create an organization of individuals that have some commonality in terms of core values and ethics." With their retention rate steadily rising and a CEO and management team that truly cares about the company's culture and those working within it, positive things will surely continue to come their way.

RETAINING EMPLOYEES

Keeping the employees you have is a complex mixture of several issues. Wages, benefits, and corporate culture play key roles, but sometimes excelling in those areas just isn't enough.

One issue that receives a lot of media attention in terms of retention is that of *hiring better* to increase retention. Every company will lose employees every year through the usual attrition avenues: deciding to retire, go back to college, stay home with a new baby, or move away. When you lose employees to these normal occurrences, how do you replace them?

Finding the right fit for the job is important to retention. In fact, some companies believe that it is *the most* important aspect of retention. Consider these cases as reported by CreditUnionMagazine.com[6]:

- One California credit union saw a reduction in their

---

[6] Sarah Fister Gale, "Testing Can Reduce Employee Turnover, Improve Quality," October 2004, http://creditunionmagazine.com/articles/200410_06.html, accessed on May 1, 2006.

turnover rate by adding just 12 minutes to their hiring process. By using a simple 12-minute long aptitude test, along with the interviewing process, to help choose the best people to hire, their turnover rate went down more than 10 percent in one year.

- An Arizona credit union has had good results with using pre-employment testing as well, but one manager learned to trust the results by making a mistake. Despite having low scores on the aptitude tests, two employees were hired because they impressed the manager during the face-to-face interview sessions. Their outgoing personalities and customer service skills were impressive, but just as the testing had predicted, they couldn't make the cut when it came to learning the entire job. After giving extra training time that was more than double the usual amount allotted, the hard decision was made to let them go.

Employees who are proud of the quality of their work are less likely to leave their employer. Make quality work part of your corporate culture and reinforce it in even the smallest ways: company memos, during meetings, and the everyday attitudes of managers and employees.

Even though you want to be heavily invested in your corporate culture, you also want to be appreciative of each employee's differences. Employees who feel they are valued for their individuality will be more loyal than those who feel forced into a mold by the corporate culture.

If you are losing quality employees who won't disclose their reasons for leaving, talk to employees who knew their former co-workers and see if you can get the reason they left. One common source of employee loss is a poor immediate supervisor. Retain good employees by facilitating good relationships with employees and their supervisors.

To build employee loyalty, have a policy of honest and clear communications about the company's financial strength. Employees who are surprised to read about their employer's financial woes on the front page of the local news are less likely to stick around than those who have been briefed ahead of time and been given an honest assessment of where things stand and how they can be improved.

Employees who are dissatisfied often have a jaded view of what the boss earns. If not disclosed, rumors and speculation about the wages and benefits of upper management can turn into urban legends of sorts that can damage morale. Consider disclosing the salaries of upper management and all the way to the top. After all, the wages of the president of the United States, every senator and congressman are a matter of public record.

Reward employees for their loyalty, not just productivity or attendance. Make a point of regularly congratulating employees on their number of years in service to your company. Even if you can't afford big bonuses or expensive gifts, your sincere gratitude will mean a lot.

What parent hasn't been caught by a child's memory that is better than their own? Promising your child a treat at a later date is a sure-fire way to get them to remember something you said. The same holds true for employees. Make it a policy never to promise (or even hint at) some reward that you cannot deliver once they do their part. You won't win many hearts that way, as employees are less forgiving of broken promises than children are.

Managers are often seen as being above the general employee population, in more ways than one. They earn more, they often do less physical labor, and they have more clout. Take away some of the mystification of managers by making sure they *stay real*. To do this, consider these suggestions:

Hire or promote managers who are enthusiastic about their jobs and the company. Managers who take pride in the quality of work that their department or company produces are going to be energetic and able to motivate employees to do their best.

Years ago, I worked in the manufacturing sector of a worldwide computer company. It was a temporary job for me; the company hired a large portion of its production employees with the understanding that you'd work only two years or less and receive no benefits. I spent my nights, often seven days a week, watching two automated machines polish pieces, waiting for the twice-nightly cleaning and hoping it didn't break down, although that could amount to the most excitement of the shift.

Even though I had no real interest in the whys and wherefores of this huge company, I did care about each piece that my assigned machines produced between 10:30 p.m. and 7 a.m. Why? Because I had managers who cared about the machines, the product, and those who watched over them. The department's assistant manager was a young man who knew how to listen to employees, encouraged people to bend his ear and didn't hide in his office.

White shirt and tie notwithstanding, he often was seen donning safety glasses and peering into a broken machine or briskly walking from area to area acting like a corporate cheerleader. "Pound 'em out!" he'd yell, "Pound 'em out!"

As the company-wide softball tournaments began one spring, somebody suggested a name for our department's team: the Pounders. While other departments shrugged their shoulders or laughed, the third shift team and supporters wore their team shirts, sporting a pair of criss-crossed hammers, with pride. I don't recall how well the "Thin Film Pounders" did that year as a softball team, but even though it's ragged from nearly 15 years' washings, I still have my shirt.

Employee loyalty isn't something that goes away when someone leaves your company. Instill pride in your employees for the items they are helping to build, create, or improve, and you'll instill a lifelong loyalty to your company.

Find out what really motivates employees to work hard. For some, it's money; for others, promotions. Be sure to offer a wide variety of rewards for hard work so that everybody has something to work for.

When promoting from within, take into consideration the dynamics that can change when a co-worker suddenly becomes the supervisor. Try to promote but not so that the promoted person directly supervises their former peers.

Have managers perched at the entrances where employees begin every shift, greeting employees by name, thanking them for coming to work and asking for news, such as "How was your weekend?" "How's your new baby/grandchild?" "Has that chiropractor been helpful for your back troubles?".

Not only does this signal to employees that the managers have already been here ahead of them (and already on duty), but it gives managers a chance to show that they do really care about the employees and they do notice when someone doesn't show up to work (other than seeing an empty spot on the production floor). It demystifies the manager, making him or her more real and sincere.

Train managers to have proactive contacts with employees throughout the shift and set a pattern of asking employees what they think (and then listen, of course). A casual query might spark a suggestion that may not otherwise have come to light.

Additionally, have managers repeat their performance as employees leave, thanking them for their hard work that day, wishing them a safe journey home and giving the expectation that they will all be back the next work day.

Another take on the exit procedure is to have the manager be the last one off the production floor at the end of the shift. Let the employees know that the manager comes to work before them and stays after them. Managers can become more to them than "just the guys who get a bigger paycheck" and can seem more "like one of us."

Obviously, these tactics won't work if the managers don't sincerely care about the employees under their supervision. If they don't, seriously consider doing what's known as "assisting them to leave the company" or "freeing them up for other opportunities."

11 Quick Ways to Improve Employee Retention

1. Employees who have clear-cut and realistic-but-challenging duties are happy because they know where they stand when they do their job right.

2. Upper management must provide the same things (see #1) to middle managers so they can provide it to the people they supervise.

3. Ask employees how they feel about their jobs, and listen with an open mind.

4. Find out what your employee believes he/she is talented in and give them an opportunity to display it, especially if you can work it into their current job duties.

5. Do your employees feel that they have the tools and freedom to succeed at their jobs or the opportunities to move laterally or advance in the company? Employees who *feel* they're at a dead-end — even if that's not quite true — don't stick around.

6. Is there a sense of fairness in your company? Do all employees feel they are and will be rewarded for good hard work? Or is there a sense that only "the big wigs" will reap the rewards of their hard work?

7. Do you offer opportunities for employees to learn and grow in any topic that is even closely related to their job?

Encourage employees to get certified in a skill, even if it's not their current job, if they're interested in knowing about that topic. If it makes them happy and gives them future opportunities in your company, it's all good.

8. Even if no crisis or threat is looming, is the atmosphere in your company one of gloom and doom? If employees feel a crisis is right around the corner all the time, those with marketable skills will take them elsewhere just in case things go awry at your company.

9. Have a heart: do employees tremble at the thought of having to ask for time off or wanting to discuss something that's important to them? Be approachable.

10. Money. Very few people work just to keep busy or just to get me out of the house. Don't forget people basically work for money. Make sure your salaries are competitive in your local market. If not, that could be the source of your talent-drain.

11. Thank you. Such a simple thing to say, but not heard enough by the vast majority of employees on a daily basis.

A small company selling plumbing fixtures and services had a serious morale issue. Of their four full-time employees, only two were truly capable of handling all the customer orders, service requests, and duties such as stocking and ordering. The other two were nice enough guys, but basically incompetent despite years of training and employment experience at this company.

What resulted demonstrates a typical pattern in small businesses where one or more employees have poor attitudes, worth ethics, or are seriously lacking in skills: the owners came to rely more heavily on the employees that they knew could step up to the plate. What happened next is equally predictable: over time, the two capable employees sought jobs with companies where they weren't overloaded and constantly covering for their coworkers.

The loss of its two good employees should have been a wake-up call to the owners; however, another common pitfall reared its ugly head: the owners continued to keep the incompetent employees on board, rationalizing that "at least they're better than brand-new employees would be!"

Wrong, said Walden. Customers, especially frequent ones, know who is and isn't capable of getting them what they need, and if they repeatedly get poor service from you "at least they're better than newbie" employees; they won't come back for more. Walden isn't against giving training and guidance to a new employee or to a person who's fresh to the adult workforce. "If they're inexperienced or misguided, maybe you can [make a difference] but if they're 20 years into their career, no way."

The result of this case was that the owners lost a large portion of their customer base due to loss of competent workers and refusal to replace incompetent ones.

"If you're in a big corporation, you can hide the low performing people better," notes Walden. "In a small business, if you have even one bad employee among your four, that's 25 percent of your workforce." Don't think customers won't notice.

Why don't employers get rid of low performing employees?

- They don't want to deal with conflict.

- It's harder to deal with bad employees than to overload the good ones.

- In some jobs, low performance is harder to measure, and without objective evidence employers hesitate to let an employee go for fear of litigation.

HOW TO ELIMINATE BAD EMPLOYEES

The main reason bad employees stay, said Walden, is because employers are too quick to "lower the bar" at the first sign of trouble, thinking that it will help them get up to par and be productive at a later point in time.

"Don't give poor performers any leeway," advises Walden. "If you don't lower the bar, they'll either fix [what's keeping them from performing] or they'll become frustrated and leave."

When you give poor performers lower standards, you're setting yourself up for failure, notes Walden. "If you lower the bar and then try raising it later, if [the poor performers] can't keep up, they can claim you were overloading them" in an effort to force them to quit. At that point, they may resort to litigation. In short: hold all employees to high standards from day-one. If they can't cut it, cut them from your payroll.

MAINTAINING EMPLOYEES

Create digital files to replace paper employee files to save on:

- Office supplies
- The time required to file
- Possible confidentiality issues (a computer is harder to break into than a filing cabinet)
- Loss due to destruction (a fire, for example, if your computer's files are stored off-site in a secure location)

Be sure to destroy all paper files appropriately and check with your legal counsel to make sure you don't have to keep originals.

Don't waste time and energy on in-depth annual performance reviews, said Drake University Professor Steve Scullen. When you bring up issues with an employee only once a year, the situation can disintegrate into a finger-pointing session. Instead, Scullen advises, take away the element of surprise, which can cause a defensive response, and have regular meetings with an employee throughout the year. Thus you will have more opportunities to see whether the situation of concern is changing favorably or not.[7]

Absenteeism can cost a company greatly in lost productivity. Let employees know that you're tracking patterns of absenteeism. If employees know that there are repercussions, they may think twice before taking time off.

Make work attendance an important part of an employee's annual review and wage assessment. While working hard when they're at work is worthy of praise, they also need to realize that dedicated attendance is required for advancement and higher wages. Conversely, reward high attendance rates. An employee who's considering missing a day might think twice if a small bonus will be lost in the process.

If an injured employee is receiving workers' compensation, have the employee come back to work and perform other tasks that they are capable of. They may receive more income than if they were at home and your costs for workers' compensation will be lessened.

Don't hire a professional to write an updated employee manual. You can buy pre-made templates that will save you freelance writer costs (or many hours of time if you write them yourself). Simply customize and print! One such product that is available for immediate download can be found here: **www.businessknowhow.net/employeehandbook.asp.**

Canvassing Employees

Mom and Dad may know best when it comes to their children, but do managers and bosses always know best in the workplace? Not really, said Allyn Freeman, author of *How to Save Your*

---

[7] Steve Scullen, "Job Tips," January 9, 2006, Asbury Park Press, www.app.com, accessed on January 9, 2006.

Bîz Wîz Says ...

"At all levels of business, [managers] put too much time into trying to fix the bad [employees] and ignoring the good ones"

—Patrick Walden

Company Big $$$ in Small Ways. "It's a truism of business that the person closest to the job knows it better than anyone else," Freeman states, "But unless a company has a method or a process for tapping into their employees' knowledge, helpful suggestions will lie dormant forever." Freeman points to one particularly inventive employee suggestion received by FedEx[8].

An employee in Phoenix was frustrated by the daily sorting of overnight envelopes. The task involved hand-sorting on tables and then putting them into racks for local delivery areas. It took 12 employees two hours to do this cumbersome task, since the sheer number of employees involved created a traffic jam around the table as everybody tried to place their envelope into the proper rack.

A pair of inventive employees discussed the problem and created a prototype of a table with built-in funnels that would drop the sorted items into bins. The prototype, called "The Cyclops Table" reduced the required number of workers for that task from 12 to 9 and reduced the amount of time it took from two hours to an hour and 15 minutes. Their suggestion changed the way things were done company-wide, resulting in great savings.

Here are some other ways to generate those tips from your workforce:

- First, if you don't already have one, start a formal suggestion program that includes more than a seldom-

---

[8] Allyn Freeman, *How to Save Your Company Big $$$ in Small Ways*, John Wiley & Sons, Inc., New York, 1999, page 5.

emptied box on the wall of the break room. Make it simple and proactive. Give employees reasons to submit their cost-saving tips.

- Use your company's current customer-service feedback model for your employee-feedback model. Consider making your suggestion program available to your employees when they aren't at work by letting them submit ideas by e-mail or through a form they can fill out on your company Web site. They can submit ideas when they are fresh in their minds, even if it happens to hit them in the middle of the night.

- Keep it fresh in their minds. Motivate employees to participate by letting them know what their cost-savings will do (strengthen the company, reduce possibilities of layoffs, increase year-end bonuses, for example) without evoking a feeling of "do or die" among them.

Good tips from your employees must be rewarded, although monetary awards aren't all-important. Publicly announce results of your suggestion program, give credit where credit is due, and publicize your savings to the outside world by sending out a press release when significant savings have been generated through the tips of employees. Newsletters, bulletin boards, and personal recognition at company-wide meetings boost employees' enthusiasm for cutting corners.

Accolades for an entire department can often exclude the very ones whose behind-the-scenes work made it possible. When handing out praise for a department's overall achievements, be sure to point out specific employees who worked hard or those whose suggestions assisted in the process.

Money, while not always necessary for motivation, can also be important. Giving employees a bonus proportionate to a percentage of the savings their tip achieved is always appreciated. Other small items such as gift certificates or movie passes can be used for suggestions that create smaller, but still noticeable, savings.

Have your management brainstorm a list of problems that they can see with cost or production issues and present them to your employees. Team them up in small groups and assign them a specific problem. Expect a solution within a time frame and reward the groups for their work in solving the problems.

Make employees aware of specific costs and let them find ways to control, or reduce, those costs. For example, if you hire an outside firm to clean your workplace at night, let employees be more responsible for tidiness so you can reduce your need for the outside cleaning crew.

Since they are the true experts, challenge your employees to solve a problem before calling in an expensive consulting firm. Reward them if they save you that consulting fee!

TEAMWORK AND EMPLOYEES

The old saying that *it takes a village to raise a child* also applies to businesses. It takes all levels, all departments, and all locations working together toward common goals for a business to be successful. How do you inspire your employees, at all levels, to be part of the same team? It's not always easy, but try some of these suggestions:

- Review your company's mission and goals. Don't define what your company is going to be or do but try to define what you *don't* want your company to be or do. Making sure that the owners and leaders of a company have a clear vision is the foundation of teamwork across the board.

- If each department is only working toward its own goals, they may find themselves at odds with each other. Make sure every department's goals are in line with company goals to avoid friction.

- Find ways to build teamwork among all levels of employees and management. If everybody, from the line worker to the CEO, is constantly thinking of ways to *obtain and retain* customers, all employees will see that they really are on the same team.

CHAPTER
5

Productivity Issues

Every employer wants more productivity. But wanting it and achieving it are two very different things. There are many ways to increase productivity, as it can be influenced by nearly every imaginable aspect of a worker's personal life and work life. The more you use your imagination, the more likely you are to succeed in raising the bar on your workers' productivity. Here's how one company did the impossible:

In 2001, nearly every sector of the Unites States economy took a hit for the worse. It was just one of those years. Several factors contributed to the downturn, which will likely always be remembered due to the events of September 11th that year and the beginnings of U.S. military presence in Iraq and Afghanistan. However, many companies were feeling the squeeze long before 9/11 and having to find a way to reduce their costs while maintaining productivity and morale.

Acxiom Corporation is a Little Rock, Arkansas, company that specializes in a variety of Information Technology products and services. Like many tech companies, things were tightening up after the whole dot-com bubble burst.

However, Acxiom had weathered other storms and downturns and felt that it would do fine during this one as well. If they could just tighten the belt a little bit. But how? All the traditional methods weren't really what felt right (layoffs) so the management and HR team came up with a proposal for employees.

A 5-percent pay cut across the board would be mandated for every employee making more than $25,000 per year. Beyond that, employees could elect to take additional pay cuts up to 20 percent of their annual salary. What could entice employees to take additional pay cuts? The same thing that kept employees relatively content over the mandatory pay cuts: stock options. For every dollar cut, whether voluntarily or mandatory, stock options would be given in the same amount.

By keeping employees on the payroll Acxiom was able to maintain their excellent workforce for the future. By giving employees something in exchange for their lost payroll, they were offering hope. But mostly, by replacing salary with stock options, they all but assured that morale would be high and productivity would get Acxiom up and running full-force again soon. Because after all, when that happens, everyone will benefit.

To learn more about Acxiom Corporation, visit their Web site at **www.acxiom.com**.

PRODUCTIVITY AND EMPLOYEES

Productivity starts with management. Make sure everyone in management believes the same things about your company, understands the same goals and works together to create the same productive environment.

Get the log out. *Development Dimensions International* is a human resource firm that sponsors numerous surveys aimed at understanding the work environment from the perspective of the workers. A recent survey discovered that "the majority of employees spend 10 hours or more a month complaining about or listening to others complain about bad bosses, while nearly one third spend 20 or more hours."[9]

Increase productivity on the production floor by hiring energetic managers and supervisors. There's nothing that production employees hate so much as a supervisor who never leaves his desk or cubicle.

Boost morale (and thereby boost productivity) by giving heartfelt and sincere praise throughout the shift. Don't go overboard or you'll sound like a broken record, but train your eyes to find glimmers of productivity in employees and point it out that you see those things. Being praised for being productive can increase productivity.

Handwrite a quick note of thanks and post it in an employee's workspace. Be specific in your praise, put the date on it and sign it. The productivity it might inspire will certainly cover the cost of the sticky notes you use up.

Make sure employees know the manager's vision of the exact needs to be accomplished every day. Have managers use a white-board near the time clock and write clear and do-able goals for each shift. This gets employees and managers thinking of the same goals. Be sure to erase the board daily and put new goals up. If employees see the same thing day after day, they soon won't even bother reading it.

If daily goals are posted, they serve as a reminder of things to be done. It's like this example of a husband's views of chores in one household, according to his wife. "The pile of dishes in the sink that's screaming at me isn't even whispering to him," she lamented. Each person sees different things that need to be accomplished, come up with different ways to accomplish them, and have different timelines in their vision.

Employee loyalty is an elusive quality that all companies want.

---

[9] "Complaining About Bad Bosses Is a Big Time Drain," October 4, 2005, Development Dimensions International, www.badbossology.com, accessed on May 1, 2006.

One way to gain the loyalty of an employee is to gain the loyalty of their spouse or family. It starts with this: *caring* about not just the employee but their family as well.

Boost productivity among workers by allowing them to care for health needs during the day, rather than at specified break times. Diabetic workers, for instance, need flexibility to maintain their blood sugar levels; pregnant employees need to use the restroom or change positions frequently.

Bathroom breaks can become a drain on productivity if they aren't handled properly. Companies have taken different measures to deal with what ought to be an innocuous task. Late in 2005, a Ford Motor plant in Wayne, Michigan, began monitoring bathroom breaks of employees to determine whether a cost-drain was occurring. Soon other automakers issued public statements regarding their bathroom-break policies. DaimlerChrysler stated their intent *not* to monitor bathroom breaks. Some companies require bathroom breaks to be integrated into the regularly-scheduled breaks that occur during a shift while other companies consider them to be a separate matter.

When it comes to bathroom breaks, companies have to balance the perceived morale issue and the actual time spent. Obviously, any employee who is intent on producing as little work as possible may add frequent or extended bathroom breaks to their repertoire of avoidance techniques. Be careful about making the actual frequency or time of breaks the only criterion for determining a worker's productivity.

A number of medical issues may require more frequent bathroom breaks including pregnancy, prostate gland issues, and overactive bladder problems. Find objective means of determining who is truly productive. You may find a percentage of the frequent bathroom users are also nonproductive overall. Those who are still productive despite bathroom usage should not be penalized.

Productivity will decrease if sick employees come to work. Are you offering enough paid sick time to employees? Do they save it up, per chance they will be more seriously ill at another time in the year? Find out why employees come to work ill and do what you can to counter it. Having a sick employee on the job is a hazard to other employees who may well catch a virus or germs from their ill co-worker. Touching the same piece of equipment, such as a telephone, or even a door handle, is all it can take to spread germs. Read more about paid sick time in Chapter 2.

Encourage employees to eat healthier lunches. Eating the wrong foods can cause blood sugar to drop shortly after eating, which causes lethargy and inattention to details.

Encourage all employees to *eat* lunch. In workplaces where there is a full hour for lunch, it's very tempting to spend that time running errands, but not actually eat lunch. Regular meals assist productivity because hunger is a serious drain. Encourage all employees to make the time to eat.

Encourage all employees to *take* time for lunch. Over-zealous employees or those who want to leave an hour early to catch their son's tee ball game or those who scheduled a doctor's appointment and need to accomplish something before leaving may skip their lunch break. But working straight through really may not be good for production. Even if a full lunch break won't fit into their plan, try to make sure every employee leaves their desk and has a healthy snack. The benefit will be increased productivity and overall health and well-being.

Healthier eating and smoking cessation are focuses of an employee wellness program implemented in 2005 at Scotts Miracle-Gro's headquarters in Ohio. The company has put millions of dollars into designing and starting up their program that will likely be followed by many other companies that are looking to trim health care costs.

Smoking is no longer allowed at the workplace. Employees who currently smoke after-hours are given access to smoking cessation programs and support in their efforts to quit. Eventually, they will have to quit—or be fired. However, the company's CEO James Hagedorn, himself a former smoker, knows how hard quitting can be. His plan expects workers to make serious efforts and so long as they are making honest efforts, they won't be fired.

New employees, logically, will have to be nonsmokers as well. And what about that other serious health issue: the bulging waistline? Scotts Miracle-Gro is tackling that as well.

By approaching employees with basic logic—you have to stay healthy so that you live out a full retirement—the company is educating employees in proper eating and exercise habits. A new clinic, a gym, and a cafeteria are part of the big picture that the company hopes will add up to a smaller healthcare bill for Scotts Miracle-Gro, and companies that may soon follow suit as well.

Hunger is a big drain on energy, as candy bar TV commercials point out. But instead of candy bars to combat mid-day blahs, pass out a healthy snack to employees (apple slices, carrot sticks, grapes). A bushel of apples might reap you at least the equivalent value in productivity, not to mention the health benefits of having your employees eat a piece of fruit every afternoon!

Unless it will endanger your product, encourage employees to drink plenty of water during the day. Hydration is important for clarity of thought and overall health.

Safety and productivity can be good partners. Obviously, an employee may suffer loss of productivity even if he isn't hurt badly enough to warrant medical attention or time off. A safe environment leads to a more productive environment.

"Zoning out" is a big productivity buster. Even if they're not involved in idle chatter or surfing the net, employees whose brains are "elsewhere" aren't producing anything. Keep employees mentally stimulated throughout the day and encourage them to change positions and stretch every hour.

Tardiness, whether coming in late to work, sneaking in extra minutes at lunchtime, or leaving a few minutes early, will drain productivity. Remind employees of the benefits of more work done: more income for the company which means job security.

Find a balance between the manager's need to keep things moving swiftly in a production setting with the worker's needs for autonomy and a sense of control. Employees don't like feeling like robots or pack mules, and productivity may drastically decrease if they're pushed so hard that they begin to resent it.

Give workers clear job assignments with timelines and expectations, but allow some flexibility about how the workers want to achieve them.

Add one job assignment to every worker. The increased responsibility may create a sense of urgency and necessity to their jobs.

Find ways to produce more without hiring more workers. Doing so has the same effect on the bottom line as reducing your workforce and expecting the remaining employees to produce the same amount as before, but without the morale slump that can follow a layoff.

Allow workers to form alliances to accomplish work quicker. Some people work best in a team environment. Others prefer to work alone and accomplish more that way. Make sure those who wish to work as a team really do work rather than socializing.

If your company's work schedule can be flexible, offer incentives to high-producing employees such as allowing them to work four ten-hour days if they desire, or allow some work-from-home time.

Let employees know the true value of their product. If you have a big order that your manufacturing department is working on, tell them. "This order will net the company $140,000 in profits! Let's get it done, do it right, ship it out, and get paid!"

Sometimes employees lose sight of what they're really doing at their jobs. Telling them the end result of their work gets them excited to do the work. "Our customers are anxiously waiting for this custom product they've ordered. Let's show them what we can do!"

Make fun a regular part of your workplace. Set aside a few minutes every day for a joke-of-the-day session (clean jokes only) or a show-and-tell session where one chosen employee gets to show off pictures of their children or grandchildren, or tell about their recent vacation.

You need to know how much of a work shift is truly spent on "work." Either monitor each individual or have them log each task they do and how much time they spend doing it. You'll find out who is efficient and who is not. You'll find also that those who are done with tasks more quickly might have a higher rate of defects, and then you'll know why. Doing an annual review of tasks and the time spent at work will increase productivity and improve overall performance.

Get a handle on absenteeism. Absent employees aren't very productive, obviously. Unless you have a company program that uses the paid time off (PTO) approach, you need to have enforced standards that state when your employees may or may not use their paid sick leave. Have a system in place to deal with those who abuse their sick time so that, if it continues, they don't remain in your employ.

Injured employees aren't very productive, either. Make employees more proactive about reducing injuries by creating a team that will take seriously the responsibility for identifying and eliminating the most common causes of injury at your workplace. Unfortunately, you may have to take the same approach to employees who won't use proper safety precautions as you would those who misuse sick days.

If your company has its own janitorial staff, assist them with productivity by providing them with modern equipment. Older equipment is often heavier, even if it still works well, and puts employees at a greater risk for repetitive stress and back injuries. Backpack-style vacuums, sit-down scrubbers, and ergonomic hand tools are good places to start.

Figure out who is in the bottom 10 percent of productivity in your company. Re-train them and see whether their performance goes up. If not, eliminate them. Hint: if you're having trouble figuring out who is the lowest in productivity, ask the lowest-paid and lowest-ranking worker in your employment. He'll tell you.

Five Productivity-Busting Employees to Watch Out For

1. **The Chronic Complainer**: While sometimes an employee's complaints are valid, there will always be that one or two whose complaining is just a way to avoid working, vent unfounded frustration, or simply cause trouble. Complainers not only waste their own time, but the time of all those who listen to them. Constant complaining is like a virus; it needs to be dealt with before it spreads and contaminates other employees' attitudes and work ethics. Chronic Complainers frequently complain about people whose jobs they'd like to have, suggesting, "I could do their job better."

2. **The Worrywart**: This type of employee seems to look for trouble or signs of bad things to come. Every downturn in orders causes fear and trembling that he or she may be laid off. They sometimes worry so much they don't really accomplish much at their job. Worriers need to

learn to focus on the positive, do their job, and leave the worrying to managers.

3. **The Gossip**: This employee isn't necessarily of just one gender, despite popular stereotypes. Some people thrive on creating and perpetuating gossip about others, whether it be co-workers, the manager or boss, or even their own neighbors. The Gossip needs to be confronted about this behavior, which is a huge time-waster and can cause unfounded internal conflicts among employees.

4. **The Instigator**: This employee is not content merely to make up or spread rumors about co-workers and managers but actually strives to create real troubles for them at work. The Instigator can cleverly disguise himself or herself as a "concerned employee" who only has the company's best interests at heart but their ultimate goal is only to drive away anyone that they deem as their competition for a promotion and anybody that they don't personally fancy.

5. **The Comparison Shopper**: This employee never quite gets over their past employment experiences (whether good or bad) and is continuously comparing a previous employer to their current one or rehashing "at my last job…" stories. These recitals are wearing on co-workers who don't really care to hear stories, whether true or not, about a previous employer. Comparers use this tactic to complain about their current job or bemoan their lack of status at their current job.

So many of these employee types have overlapping dimensions. For one, they're all unhappy with their jobs and even themselves to some extent and are using these various techniques to vent their feelings. Employers need to get to the root of these problems and determine if reasonable changes would make these behaviors better. If nothing changes, then it's time to consider releasing these employees to find greener pastures elsewhere.

Contract for your pay. The more an employee accomplishes in their workday, the more they will be paid. If an employee can accomplish as much work in an eight-hour day as another does in a ten-hour day, then reward the faster worker with the same pay as the worker who is getting overtime pay. Find enough workers like that, or motivate enough to become like that, and you're really onto something big.

Everybody works for a reason, and everybody is motivated by different things. Some work to support their family, to provide for their children's education, or to provide a retirement future for themselves and their spouse. Some work because they like the challenge or because they want to save up and travel the world someday. Still others really don't like to work at all but simply want a paycheck.

Determine what level of productivity an employee is willing to give by letting them choose their rate of pay. The higher the rate they choose, the greater the list of demands upon them for maintaining that pay level. If an employee really doesn't want to work *that hard* but is willing to maintain a minimum level of productivity, then the pay rate will reflect that. If the pay rate isn't acceptable, then the employee will either have to kick it up a notch by increasing productivity or quit.

Obviously, this plan requires specific goals, objectives, and measurements of productivity. But give it some thought. You might find surprising results. You may save money on wages by paying the lower-producing employees what they deserve: less than the high producers. You may pay more in wages but greatly increase productivity because workers are motivated to stay at that pay level.

The following 10 Topics on Motivating Your Employees and Increasing Productivity are explained at **www.motivation123.**

com/employee-motivation.html.

1. **Employee Motivation 101.** A primer on what motivates and how to instill motivation.

2. **Four Steps to Driven Employees**. Have employees who are charged up from the minute they walk in the door till they walk out at the end of the day.

3. **The "secret" motivational tool** you might never think of on your own!

4. **Master _all three_ important aspects of motivation,** not just the first one as your competitors are doing.

5. **What's the #1 mistake** made by those who want motivated employees? Make sure you find out so you can avoid it!

6. **Get your FREE Motivation Quick Tips pack** from **Motivation123.com**.

7. Another **FREEBIE**: A motivation newsletter delivered weekly.

8. **Motivational Quotes** page for a bit of quick inspiration.

9. **The Six Keys of Motivation.**

10. **A Money-Back-Guarantee** on a motivational book sold at this site, _The Motivated Mind_ by J.M. Gracia.

PRODUCTIVITY AND TECHNOLOGY

A Smart Move L.L.C., a Denver-based company that has one of the most efficient Global Positioning Systems (GPS) in place for people who are relocating, uses numerous technology-based items to perform their services at top-notch reliability with a reasonable cost.

In addition to their High Density Polyethylene (HDPE) containers that are very strong and easily secured with the customer's own padlocks, Smart Move's containers have a translucent roof, allowing sunlight inside so you can see while you're loading, and straps to secure layers of boxes so that they don't shift or crash into other layers.

But the technology is really in the GPS installed in each SmartVault that allows the item to be tracked. It can't be opened by strangers or employees, and it can't be stolen without being easily tracked. Customers can track their SmartVaults across country by simply logging onto Smart Move's Web site at **www.gosmartmove.com**.

Smart Move teams up with United Parcel Service of America, Inc., (UPS)-owned Overnight Transportation to bring the SmartVaults to their new location. This partnering enables Smart Move to use the technology of UPS without having to try and compete with them.

In 2005, Smart Move provided SmartVaults to secure and transport items for the Professional Golfers' Association (PGA) International Golf Tour. They have been widely used by individual homeowners when selling a home. Real estate agents often do what's referred to as "staging" a home. This process entails removing excess furniture, moving boxes, and other clutter from the home to make it more presentable for open houses and showings. SmartVaults make the ideal temporary and provide a safe storage place for the home's owners, and can also be kept on-site for the actual move after the sale of the home.

Finding a way to use current technology and giving new options to those who are faced with the arduous task of relocating, Smart Move takes advantage of technology and smart partnerships to operate a highly productive and busy industry-leading company.

Technology has done wonders for productivity in many industries.

However, sometimes it takes plain old common sense in the *use of* technology to make the difference.

One of the most recent booms to productivity has been the advent of wireless networks, commonly referred to as Wi-Fi systems.

VoIP, which stands for Voice over Internet Protocol, can greatly reduce the need for people or systems to route calls within your organization. Plus, the costs are competitive and could generate large savings for the right companies. There are many vendors coming into the market so be sure to do a lot of comparison and investigation before choosing one for your needs.

VoIP can help company divisions that aren't geographically nearby to increase communications and the sharing of data and other mutually beneficial information.

Increase productivity of employees who receive e-mail. Have them check e-mail only three times a day. Leave the e-mail program off so that you don't get a notification every time you receive an e-mail, eliminating a constant distraction .

Invest in faster Internet connections so downloading time for e-mails or necessary files isn't wasted by the employee staring at the screen and waiting. The more work your employees do using the Internet, the better your connections need to be.

Restaurants have some pretty high-tech devices available to them now that improve productivity dramatically. Imagine a waiter being able to place your order *as you* place your order with him. He can do it now, thanks to PDA-type handheld wireless devices that are connected to a central computer in the kitchen. And at the end of your meal, he can print your receipt and handle your electronic payment right at your table as well.

Look into hand-held devices for your workers who are in the field, such as repair personnel and salesmen. Wireless laptops, text messaging on cell phones, and other technology can speed up the process from order to shipping to payment.

Purchase, or hire a programmer to create, software that can analyze your data and create variable pricing for your customers based on their history with you.

Technology, ironically, can be a huge productivity-buster. Having all the gadgets and gizmos can be a distraction to workers, especially those confined to a desk or those who actually use their computers and Internet for their actual work.

Unfortunately, technology has its downsides when it comes to productivity as well. Computers have made the workday much easier for many employees, but these awesome machines also pose great threats to getting real work done because there's so much more than work to do with them!

Eight Technology-Related Productivity Busters to Be On the Lookout For:

- **Internet.** Granted, there may be valid reasons for an employee visiting the Internet, but this virtual candy store is so tempting that many employees surf the net at a rate that would be downright alarming to their bosses.

- **E-mail.** Using company e-mail for personal messages on work time can quickly become a very bad habit that's hard to break.

- **Games.** One of my employers actually went so far as to have the pre-loaded games removed from every desktop in the office because one employee was found to be using them constantly. Even simple games like solitaire can become a serious temptation if an employee is trying to avoid work.

- **Communities.** Online communities, such as Yahoo! and GeoCities, have made it possible for people to communicate with each other anywhere as long as they have access to the Internet. Time spent at these sites is time that isn't used working.

- **Chat.** Online chat and instant messaging are also serious threats to productivity.

- **Cell phones.** An employee who has some freedom could be text messaging all day long on their cell phone and nobody would be the wiser.

- **Computer viruses.** Obviously nothing's going to shoot your productivity quicker than a computer virus. Make sure you have the best protection for every computer in your company that's hooked to the Internet or the network.

- **Out of date computers.** Computers that are slow to complete tasks, load screens, or save files may be giving your employees time to play those games, do that chatting, or read their personal e-mail.

In times past, employees who felt nonproductive found creative ways to waste company time. Doodling, making things out of paper clips, balancing their checkbook, or sleeping at their desk were common issues. The advent of computers and Internet in the workplace have given unmotivated employees opportunities to waste time with increasing ease, speed, and secrecy.

How do employers combat the misuse of company computers, especially in regards to the Internet? They fight fire with fire. Use your computer network to your advantage. There are several software packages that can be purchased that track every employee's computer usage, including the web sites they visited, every word of their instant messenger conversations, keystrokes, downloads, and even those programs they accessed on the computer's hard drive.

Even when not using the Internet, employees may be using their work computer for personal reasons, including printers. Having the ability to record all documents printed is another feature that is helpful to employers.

Just one such company that offers these software packages is Computer Monitoring Software at **www.computer-monitoring. com**. Their NetVizor program is specifically designed to monitor all employee actions in your company network. The monitoring can be done from one secured computer, and it can be set up to block access across your network to any nonwork related web sites and activities. Visit **www.computer-monitoring.com/ employee_monitoring.htm** for an idea of what a powerful tool monitoring software is.

According to Computer Monitoring Software, 75 minutes of every work day is spent by every employee in nonwork related Internet usage. That adds up. Additional statistics provided on their Web site include:

- Nonwork related Internet surfing results in up to a 40 percent loss in productivity each year at American businesses. —Gartner Group

- 85.6 percent of employees use office e-mail for personal reasons. —NFO Worldwide

- 70 percent of all web traffic to Internet pornography sites occurs during the work hours of 9 a.m. to 5 p.m. —Sex Tracker

- 92 percent of online stock trading occurs from the workplace during work hours.

- 64 percent of employees have received politically incorrect or offensive e-mails at work. — *Business Week* magazine

- 30 percent of American workers watch sports online while at work.

- 24 percent of American workers admit to shopping online while at work.

- Employees use company high-speed Internet access to visit sites such as Broadcast.com and MP3.com more frequently at work than they do at home because of the high-speed Internet access at work. —Nielsen Ratings

- 30 to 40 percent of Internet use in the workplace is not related to business. —IDC Research

- 37 percent of workers say they surf the World Wide Web constantly at work. —Vault.com

- People are spending more time surfing the Internet at work than they are at home, mainly because home web connection speeds pale in comparison to the faster connections that companies give their employees. —ZDNet Interactive Investor, 2/18/00

- 77.7 percent of major U.S. companies keep tabs on employees by checking their e-mail, Internet, phone calls, computer files, or by videotaping them at work. —American Management Association

- 63 percent of companies monitor workers' Internet connections and 47 percent store and review employee e-mail. —American Management Association

- 27 percent of companies say that they've fired employees for misuse of office e-mail or Internet connections, and 65 percent report some disciplinary measure for those offenses. — American Management Association

You can check out the Employee Monitoring pages on Computer Monitoring Software's Web site at **www.computer-monitoring. com/employee-monitoring/benefits.htm**.

The pages include full articles about the topic, statistics, and suggestions on how to implement a monitoring program and disclose it to your employees.

PART II:

The Departmental Element

Cutting Costs Related to Specific Departments or Processes

"No country can sustain, in idleness, more than a small percentage of its numbers. The great majority must labor at something productive."

— ABRAHAM LINCOLN,
16TH PRESIDENT OF THE UNITED STATES

Doctors Foster and Smith. Are they characters on a daytime hospital drama? The latest diet gurus? Advice columnists for your teenagers? Actually, none of the above. If you're a pet owner, you may very well know who these veterinarian doctors are. And they are real, not like Betty Crocker or Sallie Mae.

In the early 1980s, Doctors Foster and Smith were just three Wisconsin veterinarians who wanted to provide quality pet care items to their customers. Today, the remaining two are the owners of the largest mail and Internet order pet-supply company in the country. How did they achieve this status and what makes this small Midwestern company thrive?

Doctors Rory Foster and Marty Smith began with four animal hospitals that showed early signs of forward thinking and a true caring for animals. They were the first in the United states to offer free rabies vaccinations and free spaying/neutering of pets. In 1983, Doctor Race Foster joined the team and that same year, the first flier of products available for order was printed. Only 1,500 customers received the first Drs. Foster and Smith 16-page catalog.

Within two years, the business was growing so quickly that the doctors had to expand, moving all the mail-order and catalog production processes into their own facility in Rhinelander, a small town of about 8,000 residents. Despite losing Dr. Rory Foster to Lou Gehrig's disease late in the 80s, the remaining doctors pressed forward with their joint vision of responsible pet ownership and appropriate education for all.

Within a decade, the mail-order business required round-the-clock attention, so a third shift was added, speeding up order lead times dramatically. Another major milestone in the first decade was the opening of their current building that houses customer service and the warehouse.

But just selling pet supplies at reasonable prices isn't really what it's all about. Doctors Foster and Smith dedicate parts of every customized catalog to articles about pet care and education. They want pets to have the best possible life, and they keep this in mind when choosing the products that they offer and the advice that they give.

Their customer service philosophy is one that gives "World Class Customer Service," said Gordon Magee, the company's Internet Marketing and Analysis Manager. "The idea is one internal to the company, to drive us all in our decision making and actions to take better and better care of our customers."

Nationally recognized for their mail-order catalog business, Drs. Foster and Smith found it only natural to add an Internet presence to their lineup. In 1998, they began the process of starting two web sites to cover all the needs of their customers. Their complete mail-order business can be found at **www.DrsFosterSmith.com.** Their complete inventory of educational articles about care of every pet is located at **www.PetEducation.com.** This free information resource is widely used by the Discovery Channel's pet health site at **www.AnimalPlanet.com.**

The doctors are also widely read due to their "What's the Diagnosis?" books on pet care. Doctors Foster and Smith have been at the forefront of the pet mail-order business, and now are at the top of the pet Internet-order business as well. Becoming a leader in e-commerce wasn't really a goal as much as providing their customers flexibility in ordering.

The company employs more than 600 people in Rhinelander and 94 percent of them are full-time employees. With over $200 million in sales, the company is obviously doing something worth emulating.

Gordon Magee believes that their focus on what he calls "Balanced Efficiency" accounts for much of their business success. Rather than making cuts to budgets and processes, the company seeks to find both *balance* and *efficiency*. For instance, he notes, "We want to be sure that we take care of our customer needs and to do so, the right mix of personnel and equipment is needed." That is the *balance*.

"Efficiency," said Magee, includes a focus "on what is best for the long term." When you also keep an eye on the balance, you find ways to bring the two philosophies into line and accomplish your goals.

Another important aspect of Drs. Foster and Smith's success is "to manage by present need with a constant eye to the future, as opposed to managing by some preconceived assumption," according to Magee. He points out the fact that their company has no "vice-presidential" management layer. The company decided that even with sales in the hundreds of millions, they neither need nor desire a layer of management that would operate at arm's length and mostly through delegation.

Instead, he notes, "Departmental managers basically function at that level, but without the VP title." The result is that mangers become "very hands-on in the day-to-day operations," — ultimately better for meeting their customers' needs.

"We aren't separated into independent VP-run business units. Instead [departments] work as a collaborative team, in many instances, cross-departmentally receiving and giving suggestions for handling operations or tasks in our or another's department."

This model of balanced efficiency is present in the everyday work lives of the employees as well, notes Magee. New employees soon see that doing things efficiently "makes them more fun regardless of one's department or responsibilities," said Magee. "There is a buy-in all along the way, in that efficiency is the focus, not cost cutting. And everyone loves efficiency since it will make their lives and working environment better."

Employees are given opportunities to advance within the company, giving Drs. Foster and Smith a cutting-edge in customer service as well. When a person is moved up in the company, they are given the training necessary to learn their new job and an opportunity to show their value in a new area. The company allows for growth and flexibility of the employees who soon learn that growth and opportunity aren't just for the benefit of management.

Cost cutting has been simplified as well. One question: "Do we need it?" is usually all it takes to determine if something is an asset or a liability to the company. Remaining a healthy, profitable company seems to be as equally uncomplicated as everything done in the Doctors Foster and Smith way.

One way of looking for costs that have got out of hand or simply not been reviewed is to have each department question everything they do, every item they order, and every process they use to do their daily work. Like the managers of the departments at Doctors Foster and Smith, you must ask the obvious, "Do we need this?"

6 Production Costs

Your production costs are only one segment of your final product cost, but every aspect of a product's final cost must be scrutinized to make your company stronger. Ultimately, the goal of every business is to produce its product cheaper, better, and faster than its competition.

You also want to offer better customer service with a superior warranty or guarantee and have greater visibility of your product in stores, making it more readily available with value added for the same money that your competitors charge.

That's a hefty order, and a large portion of that stems from what? Well, the product itself. It's important to keep that in mind; your product will speak for your company, so you need to be able to evaluate all parts of the production process and look for ways to trim away costs.

PRODUCTION COMPONENTS

- Determine the actual labor wage *vs.* labor cost for your production. It might not be salary alone that's too high, but the cost of training, supervision, errors, and other considerations that are adding to it and pushing it up.

- If raw materials for your product are available cheaper in another location (or cost of shipping them is cheaper from another locale) then consider moving your production facility closer to the materials to reduce costs.

- Recycle some parts of your production process for use in another department. Bic, maker of ink pens, uses a centrifuge to remove contaminants from oil that is then reused in some of their machinery. They used to send the oil out and use new oil.

- When you want to create a premium-quality product that will bring top price, don't skimp on the cost of raw materials. Those who would pay top dollar often can tell when inferior quality materials have been used. A reputation of skimping is *not* where you want to go!

- Find out if all the bells and whistles on your product are really used or desired by customers. You may be able to reduce your production costs by eliminating features that aren't used by customers.

- If your product requires batteries to run, don't include them. If customers need to see how the item performs in the store — use demonstration batteries that have less power.

- Determine what features you can eliminate without reducing your customers' willingness to pay the same price.

- Determine what features you can add for a small cost that will increase your customers' willingness to pay more for the product.

- Use target-costing when considering a new product. First, determine what your customers would be willing to pay for it, then work backwards to find components and build it while still making a profit at the acceptable price.

- Share components among the products you produce. Maybe something that was used in a previous product line would work for a new one, rather than have engineering invent a whole new piece.

- Be sure you do the proper planning so that when you do share components, you work out the bugs before beginning production. Make sure the parts fit.

- Don't assume that the way things have always been made is the only way to do it. Keep your creativity flowing and constantly look for components that will creatively replace something else.

- Not only might a different component be less expensive, you might find that it actually improves the product's quality.

- Don't replace a quality component with a cheaper one of inferior quality unless it doesn't affect the overall quality of the finished product.

- Find new ways to use previously purchased technology or capital investments, getting double use for the item since it's already bought and paid for. Pull something out of storage and take it to a department meeting and challenge people to come up with a new use for it.

- Make your production floor more flexible to changing product lines or improvements by not permanently affixing anything (including walls and dividers, machinery, or assembly lines) to the floor. You can rearrange to suit new product lines or become more ergonomic without major work to un-attach everything.

- Speed up your operating cycle, so that you use components very quickly after receiving them and have the finished product shipped out quickly for sale.

Nowhere in American industry is this concept carried out than at Dell. This computer giant has perfected their cash conversion cycle and now stands at a *negative* 39 days![10] Translation: Dell has sold their computers 39 days before the payment is due to the vendors who supplied them all the products to make the computers.

How do they do that? Very carefully. Dell keeps inventory for only four days, on average, before it's built into a computer. By having a state-of-the-art supply chain system, they are able to have in stock only what they need. And because they build the computers *after they sell them*, they can count the income even before the item is shipped out the door. Because of this system and the fact that they pay every payment right on time, Dell has been able to demand the very best terms from their vendors and suppliers. For the vendors and suppliers, it's like money in the bank, even if the terms are extremely generous toward Dell.

It's a slick method that has proven a winner for Dell and makes them the envy of almost every other retailer in the country. Only one other American retailer is believed to have the power to leverage the very best terms from its vendors and suppliers: Wal*Mart.[11]

PRODUCTION PROCESSES

- Spring clean all year long. Even if you've reviewed your

[10] "Summary of Dell, INC. Form 10-Q," June 3, 2005, http://biz.yahoo.com/e/050603/dell10-q.html, accessed on May 1, 2006.

[11] David Harper, "Advanced Financial Statement Analysis," www.investopedia.com/university/financialstatements/financialstatements6.asp, accessed on May 1, 2006.

processes in the past for redundancy and waste, do it again in a systematic fashion (so long as this process doesn't become redundant). Small costs can creep in over time that you won't notice until you're looking specifically for them.

- Create teams of review to do this task and make sure you include employees who are not content with the status quo in the mix. Those who aren't thrilled with their job may be motivated to find better ways to do it.

- Develop nonfinancial indicators of performance that may be more meaningful to your production crew. Some examples are a goal of reducing downtime and measurable reductions in waste. While these often aren't listed on the balance sheet, they do affect the bottom line.

- Reduce your waste disposal cost by finding ways to use less of everything in your process. Even small amounts, when tallied throughout the week, month, or year can add up to big savings.

- Reduce your energy costs by turning off machines not in use and turning off lights at the end of every day. In large production facilities, electricity is a large expense that's easy to reduce.

- Simplify. Use the same brand and model of machinery for reduced maintenance costs.

- Teach workers to do some of the basics of maintenance, freeing up maintenance personnel for more serious tasks and reducing waste from poor quality products because workers can fix the problem as soon as it happens.

- Use machines properly. If a machine can do the job faster than a human, let it. Reassign workers to other tasks and decrease your need for hiring as machines do more.

- Cross-train employees so that production doesn't slow if an employee becomes ill or suddenly quits.

- Before making drastic changes to your product at a high cost, be sure customers really want or need the changes. Sometimes the changes are more desired by the engineering department or management.

- Reduce warranty costs (replacing or repairing defective items) by reducing defects during the production process.

- Reduce production costs by reducing errors that aren't necessarily related to product quality but nonetheless require an employee's time to undo the error. Even if nothing got ruined in production, the error cost time.

- Reduce production costs by having a well-rested workforce. Keeping overtime low will cut wage costs and afford employees time to recharge.

- Make sure your processes are up-to-date and flexible enough to keep up with product life cycles and changes in trends. If you're unable to change courses fairly quickly, you'll be left in the dust.

- Use Activity-Based-Costing (ABC) to pinpoint unproductive and redundant activities in your process.

- Use teams of employees to produce products start-to-finish, as opposed to an assembly line where each worker may only be concerned about his part.

INVENTORY

- Reduce your holding time on inventory, even if by just a few days. Keeping inventory costs money.

- Shorten your supply chain to reduce inventory by streamlining what you order and how much. Specialized software can be purchased or created for this task.

CHAPTER

Advertising and Marketing

Advertising and marketing can often seem like hit/miss adventures that can either pay off big for your company or simply drain away your revenue. How do you decide what to do in terms of advertising? How much of your profit should you spend on this activity? Do you hire an ad agency? Do you try the do-it-yourself approach? Are traditional newspaper ads the ticket, or should all your advertising dollars go into the Internet?

There are no easy answers to these questions that plague small business owners all over the country. What works one time may not the next month or even the next week. What brings the customers to you may not provide any new contacts for another business. But there is one thought that all business owners must keep in mind when it comes to marketing and advertising.

According to entrepreneur.com you need to determine who your ideal customer is. This is vital because "the greater clarity you have with regard to your ideal customer, the more focused and effective your marketing efforts will be."[12] Find your customers. Target them. Sell to them.

---

[12] Brian Tracy, "Determining Your Ideal Customer," January 17, 2005, www.entrepreneur. com/article/0,4621,319591,00.html, accessed on May 1, 2006.

How do you define these ideal customers? Ask yourself these questions, similar to those available at **www.entrepreneur.com**, to help you find them so you can get to the next step: targeting them.

- What does your ideal customer think of your product or service? What need in their life does your product satisfy?

- What is the age, education level, or occupation of your ideal customer? What is his or her financial status?

- What features of your product or service are most important to your ideal customer? Why?

- What geographical location does your customer live in? Where would your customer go to purchase your product? Are the two within range of each other?

- When does your customer make purchases? Year round? Holiday seasons? Seasonal?

Targeting your customer: write up a description of your customer including all the characteristics of the questions above. If you were to place this description in a newspaper where your target customers reside and you wanted only your target audience to respond to the ad, would they recognize themselves by your description? If you haven't yet determined who might be your customer exactly enough to describe them adequately, your advertising and marketing efforts likely aren't going to be effective.

Biz Wiz Says . . .

"Take the time to analyze sales dollars vs. ad dollars."
—Patrick Walden

A retail shop had slick radio ads that were fun to listen to and played on the local Top-40 station. These ads were costing about $8,000 per month; eating up 80 percent of the business's monthly advertising budget.

But the owners weren't seeing a huge influx of customers. Why? Surely the ads were pleasant and played frequently enough. When consultants were brought on the case, they decided to find out where this shop's current customers were coming from. A simple survey handed to every customer on the way in the door promised a tasty treat upon completion and entry into a drawing for a gift certificate. All they had to do was reveal where they'd heard about this business and whether they were a new or repeat customer.

Nearly all the customers coming in the store for two months filled out the survey. The results were startling. The radio ads, which amounted to 80 percent of the advertising budget, was pulling in only 5 percent of their customers! The vast majority of their new customers were finding out about the shop via the good old yellow pages and direct mailings.

After completing their contract with the radio station, this business stuck with the "oldies but goodies" from then on!

Why do businesses make mistakes in choosing their ad methods? Walden believes it amounts to one of these three things:

- They don't know where their customers are coming from.

- They don't take the time to determine what portion of their sales is directly related to their advertising.

- Their emotions get caught up in TV or radio ads. Face it, they're "cooler" and more enticing; who doesn't want to see their storefront on TV or hear a catch jingle with their company name on the radio? But the bottom line is that these exciting advertising venues often don't bring about the anticipated bang for the buck.

ADVERTISING

Ad campaigns are most effective when targeted to a specific audience. When ad dollars are scarce, don't take a broad approach to your marketing efforts.

- Free samples, a free consultation, or the chance to win a free prize are just a few of many ways that you can draw people to your product. Distribute the samples at a place where your customers typically gather such as trade shows and conventions.

- When it comes to the freebies with your company logo, don't put your name on items that are flimsy and worthless. Invest in a decent quality item, or one that will truly be used and not tossed in the trash or given to children to play with. Better to have 1,000 of a decent item than 20,000 cheap ones to give away.

- Is your company logo easy to understand? Does it make a lasting impression? Is it too wordy or too vague? Having a good motto, slogan, or logo is very important. If yours isn't adequate, consider working with a graphic artist to create a new logo.

- What about your company's phone number? You can check with your phone company about getting a number that could correspond with a word that relates to your business, such as a glass company whose number is: 994-5277 (99G-LASS). If you're concerned about all the company information with your current number, consider keeping two numbers and phasing the first one out over time. Having a number that comes to mind quickly can gain you customers who don't want to page through a phone book.

- Save company logo pens and notepads for use outside the company only. Don't use them for in-house office supplies, as you don't need to sell your company to your own employees. Do so, of course, if you've obtained these items cheaper than you would obtain ordinary office supplies.

- Find a combination graphic advertising and printing company. Dealing with just one vendor may yield savings over using two different companies.

- Try using freelance artists or writers recommended by the print shop you frequent.

- Use syndicated broadcast commercials as opposed to having one made specifically for your company. These pre-fab commercials can be tailored with your company's name, logo, and other choices.

- If there is an art school or a university with a graphic arts program locally, see what talent you can gather from those sources. The students will get experience and you'll get reasonable labor costs and fresh ideas.

- Barter your services with an ad agency or radio station in exchange for air time, Maybe they need some of what you produce?

- Scrutinize your advertising budget, and try cutting it 10 percent or even 15 percent. Creativity can actually increase if you have less to work with. Necessity really is the mother of invention.

- Try cinemeetings. Check out **www.cinemeetings.com**. This is just one source for meeting with customers and others all over the country at once using local cinemas and state-of-the art equipment to broadcast your presentation, take questions, and answer them in real-time.

- Word-of-mouth advertising is as cheap as a sample you give away to a customer.

- Press releases only cost paper, ink, and the time it takes someone to write them. You couldn't buy the same amount of space in the newspaper for that amount!

- Have creative and informed employees or managers contribute articles and editorials to trade publications.

- Having too many different product lines can cause huge advertising budgets. Cut down your ad budget by reducing the number of product lines you make/carry.

- To shore up your fourth-quarter earnings, target your marketing toward your most profitable customer base for the entire quarter.

- Create your own advertising discount. Buy ad space after the deadline has passed. Sales people may be willing to give you a break just to fill space. Have your ad ready and in-hand to show you're serious about placing the ad with a discount.

- You can also share the cost of advertising by partnering with another company for a joint venture. If your floral shop is next door to a candy shop, have a sale the same week and share the advertising costs.

- Do good. Wal*Mart and other retailers have made no bones about displaying the results of the good they do in their communities. Bulletin boards, located right at the front of the store, display thank-you letters, statistics about how much money their local store has raised, and where the money has gone. Not to say you should do good just for the publicity and sales it may generate. But doing good certainly never hurts business.

- When looking for some good to do, partner with local radio stations, TV stations, or other media sources. You'll get a lot more coverage with the media if you're partnered with one of them.

There are times when it is beneficial to cut back on your advertising budget, and other times when doing so may sink the ship. New companies who need to inform the public about their product and services are those whose ad budgets are most needed. Don't skimp too much or too quickly when you're a new business.

Wording your advertising, whether in print, on television, or announced on a radio, is crucial. Nobody will deny that. Make the most of every word you pay for regardless of the media being used. If you have the mindset that every word is crucial, you'll say only what you need to say and your offer will be enticing to customers.

MARKETING

Choose your retail outlets wisely. It may be cheaper to sell exclusively to large national chains than to small local outlets. The streamlined nature of national chains often makes the whole process smoother.

- Balance your product line between these two goals: uniqueness and variety.

- Understand the economic forecast. Wall Street reports and reality may not always mesh here. If your business is derived from mostly local sales, take a look around town. How many houses are for sale? Businesses? Rental space? Is there an excess amount? Having your finger on the pulse of the local economy will help you plan your marketing strategy in the future.

- Market your company through networking. Trade shows, conventions, and even local events can offer your company a great chance to market your product or service to the general public or a specific group of potential customers.

Six ways to network, from **www.entrepreneur.com** [13]:

- Go where your customers are.

- Don't try to pass out a thousand business cards so much as try to make fruitful contact with everyone you encounter. Get their card in exchange!

- Remember that even if someone doesn't seem like a good fit as a potential customer, they might know someone who would. Make sure they have your information to pass on to those they want to refer to you!

- Be people-oriented. When you are speaking to someone, whether a potential customer or potential referrer, give them your undivided attention.

- When someone gives you their card, take down information about them that will help you recall who they are after the event is over.

- Don't forget to follow up every contact within a short time. The best way to follow up is with a handwritten note. If that's not feasible, at least hand-sign any printed correspondence.

Time spent marketing can reduce the need for advertising costs. Do you have a product or service that's geared toward a small segment of the population? If so, then you could run a full-page advertisement in a newspaper, or run spots on television or radio stations and just hope that the people you want to reach read the paper or see and hear the ads.

Or, you can take the ads to them. It may actually be cheaper to print a flyer with a special deal or coupon on it and distribute them by hand. If you're on a tight budget but have some time to invest, this might be just the ticket.

---

[13] Laura Clampitt Douglas, "Networking Basics," January 15, 2001, www.entrepreneur. com/article/0,4621,285396,00.html, accessed on May 1, 2006.

Bíz Wíz Says...   "Simple methods work."
—Patrick Walden

You don't have to get fancy to get results from your marketing efforts, said Walden. One method of marketing often overlooked is direct mailings. They can require a little elbow grease up front, but for small businesses they can reap nice rewards.

For example, a contractor in any of the building trades could go to the courthouse and peruse public records for people who have recently requested building permits and then mail them a flyer about your services, whether it be carpentry, plumbing, electric, flooring, drywall, painting, or windows! So many industries could be using this method, but don't.

By going directly to the people you know may be needing your services, those with full intent to remodel at least part of their home, you are saving yourself from the expense of advertising to every person in your town via radio, television or the newspaper. And if the potential customer doesn't need your particular service right now, they may very well keep your flyer or at least remember your company's name for future reference. A flyer, unlike a radio ad, can also be passed on to someone else who may need it.

Following up with a phone call is also a good idea, although nowadays you might be inciting the wrath of uninterested parties who may see you as a telemarketer of sorts, so be diplomatic and extremely polite.

Other simple ideas:

- Make sure your yellow pages ad contains directions and hours of operation as well as good contact information.

- A simple Web site isn't expensive. At the very least it's important for your Web site to contain at least as much information as your yellow pages ad.

- Look at where national companies in your industry are marketing their product and follow suit. Odds are their deeper pockets have some knowledge about where the customers are.

- Co-op marketing: share the cost of an ad with a company that does complementary business; for example, a store that sells fax machines and a company that refills toner cartridges. Use coupons and send business to each other.

- Nontraditional advertising: specialty newsletters from local businesses like a health food store, for example. "Freebie" newspapers, and college newspapers may target a specific audience for you.

Where are your customers? Are they teenagers, who can be found by the hundreds at your local mall? Do you service musical instruments? Then find a way to get fliers to all the band students at the local high school. Do you provide a service that new homeowners would be interested in? Call your local realtors association and ask about inserting a flier in their monthly newsletter sent to all members. Realtors can then pass the flier on to customers who might need your service.

By going directly to your customers, you can target your audience and save a bundle vs. telling the whole town about your business.

Don't rule out referrals. Traditional newspaper, radio, and television advertising has its place: even if everyone who sees your ad doesn't specifically need your product or service, they can refer their friends to your company.

It's been said that the most powerful word in advertising is free. People can't resist getting something for nothing. The cost of a sample is small compared to many other methods of obtaining a new customer.

Wal*Mart does it, Target does it. In fact, check the ads of all the national chain stores in your Sunday paper this week. You'll see they all do it! "Price leaders" is a concept as old as marketing. Second only to the word "free" is the lure of getting an item so cheap you'll drive across town to a store you normally don't shop at just to take advantage of that sale!

That's what a price leader is: one item, usually featured prominently on the front page of a national chain store's ad, that is priced competitively. Very competitively. Sometimes below normal retail. Whenever you see such an ad, it isn't a misprint; it's a lure. And customers love it.

But small businesses don't take advantage of price leaders often enough, believes Walden. There are a few preconceived or wrongly felt notions about price leaders that can get in the way of a small business's successful use of them:

- Negative attitudes: just because it works for Wal*Mart doesn't mean it will work for me!

- Fear: to get an item to sell that cheaply, you have to negotiate a steep discount with your vendor — not easy for some people to do.

- Pride: some business owners chafe at the thought of lowering their margin on any item, however temporarily, regardless of how many customers might come through the door and purchase other items as well.

These can all be roadblocks that should be eliminated to take advantage of this worthwhile marketing tool, said Walden.

The Internet has spawned a whole new way of distributing a great deal of information easily and cheaply. E-books, especially those with viral marketing built in, can generate thousands of leads in a very short time. To learn more about how to use e-books to your advantage, read about it at **www.entrepreneur. com/article/0,4621,324604-1,00.html** or visit **entrepreneur.com** and search for the article titled *"How to Use an E-book to Promote Your Business."*

If your in-house advertising or marketing team is looking to pinch a few pennies, one way to do so is to get the best deal possible on stock photos. There are a number of stock photo sites on the web, but one of the fastest-growing ones is **www.BigStockPhoto.com**.

This company, started in the fall of 2004, has been growing faster than a speeding bullet. With the average price of their photos under $2 and no more than $2.50, they are swiftly beating out the competition that charges $40 or more for a single photo.

It isn't just photos that make this site unique, however. They allow photographers to upload their personal stock photos for free, and then pay a commission rate for every time their photo is downloaded. Featured photographers are shown on an attractive sidebar on the site as well.

Photos are purchased by a system of Download Credits which are purchased with a credit card. If you purchase 100 "credits" each photo will cost you $1.40 each. If you only purchase one "credit" your photo will cost $2.50. This ingenious system allows the company to upsell their larger "credits" packages; however, the overall deal is still great for the purchaser who only needs one photo.

Users can also refer new photo buyers to the site and receive a nice little commission for themselves. Company Web sites can join the affiliated craze and earn credits by directing new customers to BigStockPhoto's site. They also offer licensing rights for reprints beyond the scope of general usage. Creative marketing has definitely played a role in making BigStockPhoto a success that is not often seen in such a young company.

CHAPTER

8 Sales

Sales. This is what it's all about. If a person who starts a business doesn't know how to sell his product or service, the business won't last long regardless of the superior quality of that product or service. Business owners realize that without sales, there is no business.

So how do you get the most from your sales tools or sales department? Try some of these suggestions for streamlining and pumping up your bottom line:

The data that is generated by your sales, or sales department, is crucial in managing your inventory and thus your supply chain. Do you get daily data about sales? If so, do you review it and use it for making important decisions about inventory and cash flow? Getting your goods from your warehouse to your buyer faster creates faster payment to you, leading to timely payment to your creditors. The sales team, then, is a vital segment of any company.

In addition to reviewing frequent data and using it for those timely decisions, here are other ways your sales team can boost your profits and cut costs:

- Set up an online ordering system for your established customers who know their pricing scheme already.

You cut transaction costs if they can go to your site and enter their order that will be sent directly to the correct department for filling it.

- Even if you don't sell your products directly through your company's Web site, have your products and features displayed to save the salesperson time because the customer is already familiar with the products and has an idea of what they want.

- Your company's Web site can be a valuable tool for sales personnel in the field too. Use a password-protected portion of your site to list account information, product and pricing information, and even your competitor's information so that the sales department can refer to it simply by gaining access to the Internet.

- The newest cell phones to hit the market are being equipped with GPS. For salesmen or employees in the field, they are handy for getting driving directions while on company business. And the home office can keep track of their employees on the road. The technology is a little expensive at this point, but time will do a lot to change that.

- Save your not-so-creative salespeople's time with instant sales letter templates. Get them at **www. businessknowhow.com/store/Templates.htm**.

- If your company has several divisions or product lines, make sure you aren't sending several different salespeople to the same location. Instead, train salespeople to cross-sell for other product lines or divisions.

To whom is your product being sold? Directly to the end-customer? Through middlemen? Both? What will bring the most profit and how? If you can answer these questions, you may find a way to sell differently and boost profits.

Alienware isn't a space-age set of dishes, but one of a handful of high-end computer manufacturers who got their start by knowing exactly who would buy their product. In the late 1990s, computers were coming down in price so that nearly every household could easily own one. Companies like Dell were shaking things up in the industry with their no-retailers approach that brought customers directly to the manufacturer for their computing needs.

In the same time frame, Alienware founders Nelson Gonzalez and Alex Aguila also wanted to make and sell PCs, but they wanted to go against the grain. They wanted to charge more than the going rate for their computers. But in return, they would make a custom computer packed with power and built especially for computer gaming, an industry that was booming as well.

Computer gamers have different needs for their machines than the average family of four who want to play solitaire, read e-mail, and maybe track their stock portfolio. Gamers need lightning fast speed, massive power, and superb graphics.

Alienware gives gamers all that, and at a cost above the major computer manufacturers. But gamers are a unique breed of computer users. Demographically they are more often men, and when they want the ultimate, they are willing to pay for it. The average PC with good gaming capacity will run a customer between $3,000 and $4,000. The ultimate system loaded with every extra could easily run $10,000.

When deciding how to sell to their customers, Alienware borrowed the direct selling technique from competitors such as Dell. You can't buy an Alienware computer in any retail store; only from them. Cutting out the retailers allows Alienware to offer excellent customer service because their customers don't have to try and figure out where to go for help: the retailer or the manufacturer. Their customer service has been praised as highly as the quality of their PCs.

While Alienware has broadened their horizons a bit in the past couple of years, making less-powerful product lines and even doing some custom work for the military and the United States government, they still sell the vast majority of their machines to gamers.

This company knew where their market was. They knew what the customer wanted, and they sold it to them. That's a pretty simple process, but in reality it's not always as easy to determine those things for your company. However, it's something worth finding out.

Don't resort to corporate spying, but do keep your eyes on your competition. Use all publicly available information to find out where they are taking the company. It may give you some good ideas on where to go — or where not to go!

Have your sales people use software that tracks their clients' transactions, quotes, discounts, preferences, and more. This way if a salesperson is on vacation or needs emergency time-off, his or her clients can still be serviced without interruption.

Even though you may pay more in the long run, it will assist in cash-flow if your salespersons aren't paid their commissions until you receive payment for the sales they make. To make this arrangement more agreeable to your sales force, offer them a higher commission in lieu of their time spent waiting. (Bonus: they will be motivated to get the customer to pay on time or sooner!)

If you can consolidate office space among employees who don't use it full-time (such as sales reps), you may be able to sub-lease it out to another company that just wants a place to park their briefcase. Don't make your sales rep's offices too cushy. They might want to sit in there all day instead of beating the pavement.

If your sales are directly related to bulk e-mails, then you may wish to invest in Yahoo! or American On Line's (AOL's) newly planned services to ensure your business e-mail gets delivered. Bypassing junk mail and spam filters and hoping your potential customer will receive your e-mail is not a particularly effective way to go about e-mailing. With these new services, your company would be charged a small fee per e-mail (one fourth cent to one cent each) but you would be guaranteed delivery to the inbox. Now if only they could guarantee it would be read...

16 Selling Tips for When the Market Is Cool:

- Don't necessarily stick with the same sales pitch. Just because it's always worked doesn't mean it always will. Review your pitches and techniques every six months.

- Focus your efforts on repeat sales.

- Call every new customer within two weeks of their purchase to discuss their level of satisfaction, gain input about the product, and see if they want to buy again.

- Make connections with companies that sell complementary products. If you sell lawn décor, offer some free display units to greenhouses in exchange for a small sign by the display telling customers where they can obtain the same items.

- Offer to share customer lists with other sales people at these complimentary companies.

- Always give your business card in duplicate: one to keep and one for the person to pass on.

- Make sure you refer your customers to other businesses that you have faith in, and remind them to mention your name when they patronize the other business. You may earn some referrals in return.

- Offer money-back guarantees on all products.

- When loyal customers are tempted to shop around, lower

prices enough to retain their interest and make it worth their loyalty (because you're such a trusted business with good customer service and honest policies).

- Use slow times to do that prospecting you're always meaning to do.

- Don't let customers see any fear or panic in your demeanor when sales are slow. If you appear desperate, they may wonder if the entire company is in trouble.

- Follow every written contact with a telephone call or professional e-mail.

- Have the best "service after the sale" in your market.

- Offer add-ons, such as extended warranty, at a reduced price.

- Always ask customers what your company can do for them. Perhaps they'd like a service that you don't already provide or have a suggestion for improving a product. If you don't ask, they may not offer their suggestions.

- Be on the lookout for new uses for your products and new customer groups that you aren't currently selling to. Sometimes a slight modification can rally interest from a whole new demographic.

Your sales team will often be the most familiar with your competition and can help your company determine how to set your pricing. Obviously, pricing your product correctly can have an impact on your profit. If you charge too much, you'll lose customers to the competition. If you price too low, you might sell a lot, but you'll also lose out profit that could have been earned at a higher price that still would have been competitive.

An introductory pricing strategy might entice new customers to your new product line, but it might also give the perception of lower quality. You can't control how your customers will perceive your strategies, so be sure to balance your pricing with a strong marketing plan that will emphasize the quality and durability of your product.

Another common error made with pricing a new product is to overprice it to recoup your investment quicker. Over-pricing decreases demand, resulting in your investment's taking longer to recoup. Avoid the temptation to overprice an item. On the flip side, a higher price might carry a high perceived value for your product but make sure you give customers a great value for the higher price they pay for your product. Giving excellent "service after the sale" is one way to achieve that goal.

Pricing your product in the mid-range may be a good strategy, but remember that all pricing strategies do contribute to your company's image. Be sure to cover all these issues with your marketing department, and do the appropriate market testing so that you don't confuse customers and the public. Once you've established an image as a low-cost leader, a high-end full-service company, or a reliable middle-of-the road operation, stick with it. There will always be customers for every type of company, even if their products are very similar.

Bíz Wíz Says . . . "Opening a small business doesn't mean you know all about selling—or vice versa."

—Patrick Walden

Too many times during his years as a business consultant, advised Walden, he saw people open up their own business after years working for someone else. They knew their job, probably better than their former boss, but that didn't guarantee they knew about business.

One case that sticks in his mind is that of a top salesman at a local car dealership. He'd been in sales for years and had built up a reputation as a persuasive salesman, recalls Walden, "But what he didn't know is what it took to get the customer to the lot. All he did was close the deal."

Eventually this salesman decided that he'd rather keep all of the profit from a sale, not just the commission. He opened up his own sales lot, had a nice sign, and nice looking vehicles displayed. Finally, he'd be making the big bucks, with nobody but himself to pay!

There was just one problem. He had no customers. When the business obviously wasn't going to turn a profit, he sought help from the Small Business Development Center whose contracted consultants informed him that he needed to learn how to do more than just close the deal. He needed to learn how to actually run a business.

The salesman turned businessman didn't have a happy ending to his story, however. He just couldn't switch gears and see that his mere presence on the lot wasn't going to bring the customers in. His refusal to get any training to learn about all the other aspects of business ended his business-ownership dream pretty soon thereafter.

- **Lesson #1**: Don't assume that because you are a good salesman that you can run an entire business. Get training to learn about accounting, advertising, and all the other aspects of business before investing, and possibly losing, your life savings.

- **Lesson #2**: If you have the opportunity to get some consulting from some place like the Small Business Administration, do it before you find yourself in a serious bind. The best time to start getting help is before you even open your doors for business.

E-COMMERCE

Selling with e-commerce is a great option. Customers the world over can do a simple Internet search for a specific product and come up with sellers all over the globe. Why don't you have your items for sale on your Web site?

Six Ways to Make E-Commerce Easier and Increase Profitability

- **Auto responders.** This is a little bit of software that will e-mail your web customer to verify their order, let them know their order has been shipped, or inform them of any delays in processing their order. They save time and make customers feel like they're in the loop—a great way to garner repeat orders.

- **E-books.** These can be purchased on your site, and they don't cost you a penny to ship them. In fact, you can use an auto responder system to e-mail the file (or the password to enter a portion of your site) to the customer.

- **Checkout.** This is an area that is often frustrating to customers if they feel like they have to jump through too many hoops to check out. Keep it simple.

- **Shipping.** Streamline your checkout process and provide the shipping costs very early on. Some lookers want to compare shipping, not just the price of the product, so don't hide that information at the very end.

- **Order confirmations.** Customers appreciate having a confirmation number, especially if this is the first time they've ordered from you. Either display a number after they've checked out, or have an auto responder send one with the order confirmation.

- **Payment options.** If your company already has the ability to process credit card payments from customers you won't have to worry about setting up payment options for your e-commerce sales. However, if you don't want to get involved in credit card payments, look into a merchant's account with PayPal or other services, such as **www.mycheckfree.com** or Western Union's MoneyZap service, where customers can pay you directly from their checking account.

CHAPTER

9

Shipping, Receiving, and Mailing

CUSTOMER RETURNS

It's been estimated that one out of every ten products is returned to the retailer where it is purchased. Returns can pose numerous problems, especially if your product is carried at stores nationwide, or if you sell items via the Internet.

There are a few options that will make handling returns easier, short of simply not accepting them. First off, look into the programs offered by all the major shipping companies. UPS, FedEx, and the United States Postal Service have programs in place whereby your company can send pre-paid return labels to customers, and then either you or the customer can arrange for pickup by the carrier.

Simplifying the process for your customers will make them happier and more likely to return the favor by purchasing from you again. It is important that you receive your merchandise back in like-new condition, and when you are paying the cost of shipping, the customer is more likely to package it more securely and carefully than if they were concerned about making the package's being too heavy with extra packing materials.

For companies whose products are sold nationwide, sometimes

the retailer who sells the product will accept the return. Retailers such as Wal*Mart will accept most items back within 30 days, with exceptions and restrictions. But what happens to the item then? That depends on the retailer.

Rather than having a stream of returned products coming back into your production facility, many companies are turning to outsourcing their returns to a company that tests for defects and refurbishes those products that have a minor issue. These refurbished items are frequently sold at Internet auction sites and other liquidation-type retailers.

Companies that deal with returns as a business are called Returns Management Solutions (RMS) providers. RMS providers may be able to link to your order and returns systems to get the information to you quickly when a product is returned so you can credit your customer's account quickly. New, nondefective merchandise can be routed back to your facility for restocking.

Many retailers who sell through catalogs or Web sites try to deter returns by imposing a restocking fee. Others try to discourage returns by noting in the product documentation or assembly instructions "call us first" if there's a problem. By simply supplying the missing part or replacing a broken piece, many companies have been able to reduce the number of returns as well.

However you handle the issue of returns, getting the item back to you is going to cost some money because of the time required to process the customer request. Look carefully at your data regarding customer returns, however, and make sure that your returns aren't an indication of an inferior or defective production.

IN-HOUSE SHIPPING AND RECEIVING

Every aspect of business, even shipping and receiving, is becoming more high-tech than workers 30 years ago could have imagined. The technology that made bar codes commonplace pushed supply chains into a new era completely. Now, another technology is doing for this process what bar coding did in the 1980s. Radio Frequency Identification (RFID) operates with tiny radio transceiver chips that can be attached to shipping containers and tracked using GPS tracking.

This technology will eventually be used on a much grander, but smaller, scale. It could theoretically be used to track every single item as it moves through a supply chain, not just whole containers of items. Gone will be the bulky electronic tags on high-end items in the stores, or the ink-filled tags that will destroy an item if you try to remove the tag improperly. Eventually, if an item is shoplifted, the thief may be tracked using GPS. How's that for "James Bond" tactics?

However, the initial and most cost-efficient use currently is for accurate and fast tracking of items from production to shipping to supplier to customer. Technology has a way of spawning whole new ideas and ways of completing a task, so watch this technology closely and be sure to incorporate it into your business as soon as you can afford to do so.

Look at your process for duplication, wasted efforts, or inefficiency. A small change can generate big savings. For example, at the Phoenix FedEx location (see story, Chapter 2), two employees created a special table to filter sorted items into bins. The new setup required fewer employees to perform that task every day, resulting in $32,000 in savings at that location that year.[14]

Set up a place on your Web site where customers can see their order status and, if it's shipped, the date it shipped—cutting down on calls to your customer service department.

Consider outsourcing your shipping to a large freight company

---

[14] Allyn Freeman, How to Save Your Company Big $$$ in Small Ways, John Wiley & Sons, Inc., New York, 1999, page 5.

who will come to your site and perform this function for you. It may be cheaper.

Reduce your costs by sending nonurgent items in the mail as opposed to using company vehicles to hand-deliver them locally.

Check around for lower shipping rates. Often you won't get a lower bid from your current company unless you have a bid from their competitor on your desk.

Even if the customer doesn't pay separately for shipping, find out when they truly need the product and ship accordingly. If they're in no hurry, choose a cheaper method that is only slightly slower.

Become your own shipping insurance provider by banking the insurance paid by customers and building a fund from which to pay occasional claims.

Stay ahead of changes in international laws, treaties, and regulations. Shipping an item to another country only to have it refused at customs (or have it left idle at a port) costs you money in unsold inventory.

Packing Materials

Cheap packing materials can be produced by shredding your office paper with nonconfidential material printed on it. Junk faxes, photocopier goof-ups, and out of date employee handbooks make great package stuffing.

Store and reuse packing materials that come in shipments of components or raw goods. Or, if they aren't usable by you, resell them to someone who will use them.

Obtain inexpensive shipping material from local newspaper publishers. They may sell "end rolls" which are the leftover amounts of unprinted newspaper. They change the roll before it runs out, often leaving 20 feet or more of paper on the roll. Many newspapers will sell these for a reasonable cost. Better yet, barter for them!

If your company has an industrial type of shredder, you can even shred cardboard for packing materials. Imagine shredding and reusing all the boxes your components and goods arrive in!

Pallets

Keep pallets that are broken for parts to repair others to cut down the cost of buying new ones. A few minutes and a hammer and nails are all that's required to fix a pallet.

Join a co-op for your pallets. This way, when you ship things on a pallet, you haven't lost it if it goes to another co-op member. You'll get a credit for it.

Sell your broken pallets to a company that recycles them. Check your yellow pages or do an Internet search for companies.

Company Trucks

Consolidate loads to fill up your trucks when at all possible, as long as the customers aren't inconvenienced. To avoid customer annoyance, build in a little extra time in the shipping process to allow for this practice. If trucks fill up faster, customers get their items faster than expected and are even more pleased.

Have your company trucks pick up merchandise from your own suppliers and vendors on their way back, saving you some shipping costs.

Mailings

- Contact your local post office for help in streamlining your mailing processes and reducing postage costs. They're happy to help!

- Learn all you can about the bulk mail program and use it to your advantage. It doesn't take hundreds and hundreds of pieces to qualify for bulk mail.

- Using the postal service's online program, click-n-ship, saves time. You don't have to go to the post office or wait in line. It has some freebies included, such as free tracking and delivery confirmation for certain mail classes!

- If various departments send several pieces of mail to the same company daily, have the mailing department set up a system to gather all mail in one location and package it in a large envelope. The cost of shipping the large envelope will likely be cheaper than sending all the smaller envelopes individually, and the savings could even cover the cost of the larger envelope and any soft-dollar costs involved.

- Consider using postcards for brief and nonconfidential correspondence. You can even purchase cards pre-printed with postage on them for a reasonable cost at the post office.

- Find ways to determine who actually reads and needs the regular correspondence you send — newsletters and reports — and who uses them to line their birdcage.

- Encourage departments to send correspondence via e-mail if possible.

- If you send out catalogs to customers, encourage them to sign up for a program to receive e-mail links to online catalogs instead. E-mail specials and notices to customers keep your company name in front of them in the same manner a catalog used to. Be sure to remove the customers who sign up for online catalogs from your mailing lists.

- Use a digital postage scale to determine exactly how much postage is *truly* needed avoiding underpaying postage, wasting time by having the item sent back to you, or worse yet, being delivered to your customer with a *postage due* notice, and it saves on overpayment of postage.

- Get a postage meter. Some companies even let you pay for additional postage online. No more waiting in line at the post office for more stamps. If an item weighs one ounce or less, fold it and put in a standard #10 envelope rather than sending it flat (unless, of course, it truly needs to be flat).

- Avoid using odd-sized envelopes and postcards, as they can cost more in postage even if they meet the one-ounce weight requirement. Standard specs are available at the post office's Web site **www.usps.com**.

- Create postcards from standard cardstock, four per sheet. Simply cut a sheet in quarters, or use a program (such as Microsoft Publisher) to fancy them up a little.

- Make sure your mailing lists are current. Don't waste postage sending mail to people who don't ever open it. Think about all the personal mail you get every day and toss into the trash without opening it. Does your mail get the same treatment?

- Be careful about sending things "overnight." If the second day would be sufficient, you have at least two options: 2nd day air and Priority (U.S.P.S.), and the rates are much easier on the budget.

- When you use Priority Mail, be sure to use the free envelopes and boxes. Create an account at **www.usps. com** and have them shipped to you for free as well!

CHAPTER

10

Accounting

Your accounting department plays a crucial role in cost cutting. Not only do they facilitate the flow of income in and out of your company, but they often generate the very reports you need in order to find out if your methods are being successful. They assist in budgeting and interact with nearly every other department on a daily basis.

Use your accounting department to identify leaks in your revenue stream. Just like the pipes in a very old building, your system may have small cracks where money can slip through undetected. Experts believe that the slippage can account for 1 to 10 percent of all revenue. Tighten up your pipes by identifying the weak spots. Whether they are due to uncollected accounts or improper invoicing, complicated checks and balances, or communication gaps, these leaks need to be located and fixed.

BASICS

All companies need an accurate and reliable accounting system that's been in place since the day their business began. Keeping track of every penny is important. When you must cut costs, you know where every penny has gone.

When deciding on where to spend your pennies, keep in mind

that the best use of your money is to make money. Spend it on things that will ultimately add value, productivity or revenue to your company. Doing so should be an attitude that remains in your company long after it has become profitable. Being frugal doesn't end just because you start turning a profit or just because there is a good economic forecast.

Accounting Tips

- Review your chart of accounts. Is it detailed enough to give accurate information about where the money is actually coming from and going to?

- Is your chart of accounts so complex that your staff is performing coding errors, resulting is additional time to fix them later?

- Are all transactions entered into your accounting software promptly? A backlog not only is time-consuming to fix but can cause misinformation in reports.

- Use cash for items that give no return or, conversely, borrow only for items that do give a return.

- Set transfer prices at market rates, when possible. But even if not possible, be sure that your company's transfer price policies ensure that managers will make decisions based on the best interests of the entire company, not just their own division or department.

- Make sure all nonfinancial managers understand and use the company's established costing procedures correctly. Skewed numbers from using different methodology can be confusing.

- Keep things friendly between the accounting department and the managers who supply them the information they need to do their job properly. Managers can see the accounting staff as bothersome or nosy about details.

Department or division managers who don't trust the accounting department—or don't agree with their reports—may be keeping a parallel accounting log of their own. Not only is this a waste of time because their log can't generate accurate reports and it's a duplication of work already being done, but it fosters distrust and bad feelings between the two groups of employees. You must not tolerate parallel accounting systems.

"Eliminate checks and balances that add no real assurance or security," said James Powers and Michael Conner of Meridian Consulting in Boston. Another tip they offer is "to put a halt to momentum spending—outlays that continue long after their rationale has vanished."[15]

These are examples of what Powers and Conner call "Quik-hit" cost savings: small items that can add up if consistently located and eliminated. They identify these additional ways to find quick-hit savings:

- Unnecessary paperwork that's a duplication of something someone else already does.

- Layers of procedures required to accomplish a relatively simple task.

- Clarify the company's procedure for receiving and routing invoices.

- For retailers, reduce the number of physical inventories taken each week.

When you find these and other little nooks and crannies where antiquated procedures and duplication lurk, root them out and toss them out!

---

[15] James Powers and Michael Connor, "When It Makes Sense to Cut Practices, Not People," January 27, 2002, http://hbswk.hbs.edu/item.jhtml?id=2697&t=operations, accessed on May 1, 2006.

Ignore sunk costs, according to David W. Young, author of *A Manager's Guide to Creative Cost Cutting.* An example, Young notes, is that of people who "refuse to sell a stock until its price returns to the level at which they bought it." Why do people do this? Because, Young points out, "Ignoring sunk costs is something that is hard to accept emotionally."[16] In short, if you have a product line that's performing very poorly, ignore your sunk costs and get out before you lose more on it. All the money you've already spent is just that: already spent. Nothing will change that.

- Deposit, deposit, deposit. The sooner money is deposited, the sooner you earn interest.

- Lower fees at your bank. Very few banks have fees that are not negotiable. If you have an excellent history and a reasonable amount of money in your accounts, ask for lower fees on check processing and other items. Be prepared to shop around; you may find a better deal elsewhere.

Bíz Wíz Says . . . "You're collecting the data anyway. All they're doing it is entering it and spitting out reports and income statements."

—Patrick Walden

"Small businesses often use an accounting firm to do their books," noted Walden, but a heavy reliance on a CPA firm is a serious drain of money. His suggestion: "Learn to use QuickBooks or Peachtree; these are easy-to-use programs with tax tables, payroll packages, and more." Training can even be obtained through the Internet from the software's maker.

---

[16] David W. Young, A Manager's Guide to Creative Cost Cutting—181 Ways to Build the Bottom Line, McGraw-Hill, New York, 2003.

Some basic training in understanding reports and income statements can usually be obtained right through your local college or university, or online.

PAYROLL

Switching from a weekly to bi-weekly payroll cuts a number of costs. Preparation time, printing costs (including the actual number of checks used), and bank costs. Monthly payroll yields even greater savings, but is often not well accepted by employees.

Get all your employees to sign up for automatic deposit (or require it).

Make a policy (and enforce it) that no overtime is allowed without prior authorization. Even a few hours sneaked in here and there can mess up the budget.

BUDGETING

While a large corporation wouldn't dream of operating without a budget, many small businesses don't put as much emphasis on this aspect of their accounting work as they should. The day-to-day running of the business, obtaining and servicing clients, and managing their few employees becomes all-consuming. However, a budget is just as important for these businesses as a large corporation.

A small business budget may not have to be complex or even exactly accurate. But they should be thought of as an item that should be referred to frequently to gauge the business's health. Thinking of a budget as a static and unchanging document is often a mistake.

Budgets, for small businesses, help investors and financial institutions see clear goals for the business and then determine if they met those goals within the monetary requirements set by the budget. Income and expenses that are accurately reflected show those outside the company that those running the company are working toward the company's growth.

A good budget will allow you to project your numbers at least a year out. Find out what things are going to cost in the next year by having ongoing conversations with suppliers and other vendors. Make sure you account for all possible income sources so your reports aren't skewed. Doing a little research into your competitors may also help new business owners to project accurately.

Profits should also be projected for at least a year out. Then compare your actual monthly profits with the budgeted amounts to help pinpoint things that are working, things that are not and help generate new ideas for maximizing profit.

In short, when a new small business sets up a budget, it can avoid many pitfalls such as unexpected results from expenses. Many new business owners can't conceptualize how much their expenses will dig into their profits until they see it on paper. Having a properly prepared, realistic budget will help alleviate some of the inevitable shock.

Even though budgets are usually limited to one year, small business owners should review them monthly, or even weekly, to compare their projections with actual numbers. The more familiar they become with how their business works, the better they will be at budgeting in future years.

Larger businesses often have the assistance of a CPA, or their own in-house accountant or accounting department to prepare their budget for them. Even with the input and oversight of management and owners, the research and detail work is easier with the assistance of professional help.

Here are some tips for all companies, with larger ones in mind:

- Give each department manager their own budget to work

within, rather than giving them actual overhead. Having to meet their own budget might inspire creativity in them that will result in further savings.

- Putting department managers on a "financial diet" is good, but make sure you don't starve them. Give managers enough to work with so that quality doesn't suffer as a result.

- Have managers track costs and income as their own "profit center" to see where money is leaking through the cracks. (Note: Managers are not to keep their own secretive parallel accounting system.)

- Avoid duplication in the budgeting process by having managers involved early on, rather than presenting them with a budget and trying to rework it after their input is given.

- Don't waste money by going somewhere (in terms of short term goals) that doesn't coincide with the company's long-term goals. It might sound exciting and profitable right now, but it could become a costly mistake if you have to backpedal.

ACCOUNTS PAYABLE

The number-one strategy to increase your interest revenues is by paying your accounts payable on the exact date they are due and not a minute before. In essence, keep your interest-earning monies in the bank till the very last moment.

Setting up all your vendors and suppliers to receive payments through an ACH will generate time savings and let you manipulate the system (see tip above) by paying on the very date an item is due.

And for those you can't pay via an ACH, mail payments on a Friday if the due date falls on a Saturday or Sunday. You'll gain a sort of "float" that way rather than mailing so the check arrived on the Friday, since many businesses close their week out by depositing all income.

Create digital files for all customer invoices and destroy the originals. Savings come from reduced office supplies (folders, tabs, labels) and reduced time to file or locate later, assuming you have an efficient computer filing system in place, and a secure storage—harder to break into a computer than a filing cabinet.

Have your accounting manager do an audit of your accounts payable to locate duplicate invoices. It happens. Get refunds from the vendors and suppliers who got paid twice. You can also hire someone who specializes in this service.

Make sure your accounts payable are all in your favor: get the most attractive terms you can from your suppliers and vendors by stretching it out as long as possible.

Lower your transaction costs or your cost to process an invoice by avoiding invoices that are smaller than your transaction cost. Use petty cash instead of getting an invoice for those small purchases.

Thieves love to use pre-printed checks to rob your bank accounts silently. Keep your printed checks in a very secure place where very few people have access to them, and put safeguards in place to prevent misuse.

ACCOUNTS RECEIVABLE

The counterpart to the number-one strategy of Accounts Payable works in reverse for Accounts Receivable. Get your money from customers as quickly as possible. And when you do get it in the form of a check, deposit daily to maximize interest earnings.

If a customer comes to pick up an order in person, ask them to come prepared to pay for their order at the time of pick up, saving you the cost of billing and increase interest revenue by depositing monies faster when you get paid faster.

Create a system of invoicing customers via the Internet/e-mail. You can drastically cut these costs:

- The paper you normally invoice with.
- The ink to print the invoice.
- The envelope to send the invoice in.
- The stamp/postage.
- The employee time to create, envelope, and mail the invoice.

Set up a system so that your customers can access via the Internet, such as at your company's Web site, to pay their invoices through an ACH. The savings are numerous:

- The cost of opening envelopes and entering payments, coding, and depositing will be saved.
- The time waiting for check to clear is eliminated.
- A system that is used by a fair percentage of your customers will pay for itself, possibly within a couple of years.

Speaking of invoices, if your customer changes an order after it's placed and the change is made correctly in the outgoing order, was the invoice properly changed to reflect that? If not, your customer may have received more than they paid for. An extremely honest customer might inform you of this discrepancy *if* their accounting department is aware of it. They may not realize the error until inventory time, or never.

Accounts Receivables Tips

- Manage your financial cycle properly so that accounts receivable items are collected in a timely manner so you can pay debt payments in a timely manner.

- Decrease the time it takes your customers to pay. Make sales people more responsible for on-time payments by tying their commission to the payment—no payment, no commission yet.

- Are sales personnel responsible to generate invoices for orders they take personally? If so, make sure you have a system set up so that the accounts payable department is aware of the invoice and can follow up if necessary.

- Shorten your accounts receivable with the exception of your very best customers. (Give them the best terms.) Slow paying or nonpaying customers should have their terms reviewed frequently.

- New customers should always be subjected to a credit check unless they are set up to pay cash. Not giving credit to those with a questionable history will earn a payback.

- Demand payment in advance or a C.O.D. for customers who have been slow payers in the past or who are in a line of business that's unstable at the moment. If the potential customer won't agree to those terms, let them *not* pay someone else.

- Offer a discount for those who pay in advance or pay C.O.D.

- You can even build in a small discount for those who have terms. For instance, if a customer has a term of net 30, consider offering a 2 percent discount if they pay within 10 days.

- Charge late fees. Be clear with customers with terms. They are expected to pay within a time frame, and if they do not, a late fee will be assessed which is either a flat fee or a percentage. Just make sure all terms are fully disclosed. And if a customer is late, impose the fee, either bringing them into line with prompt payments or causing them to take their slow-paying ways elsewhere.

- Be aggressive with unpaid accounts. Certain occupations, such as real estate appraisers who do work for mortgage companies, need to be careful about their unpaid accounts. If a mortgage broker goes out of business, small bills like those from appraisers are apt to be left unpaid. Not collecting on unpaid accounts is like working for free. Pointless.

- Use credit insurance for new overseas customers until you are certain they are prompt and reliable customers. Pass on the cost of credit insurance to the customer with the understanding that it will be eliminated after certain criteria are met.

- For companies in the service fields, reduce the cost of billing your customers by equipping your service vehicles with a wireless laptop and basic printer. The service personnel can use templates to generate an invoice or call headquarters to have one generated and e-mailed to the laptop, print it out, and collect payment right away.

- Take it one step further and have the service person collect payment through your company Web site using a credit card number.

Remember, "work in progress" becomes an accounts payable item as soon as it is finished and billed. Always keep your accounting department appraised on the exact moment an item becomes billable.

REDUCING CUSTOMER DEBT

Reduce your bad debts from customers: stay on top of accounts that are past-due. Your customers' debts are yours until they're paid.

- Offer incentives for customers to pay you promptly to avoid their becoming nonpaying customers.

- Be willing to renegotiate terms with customers in arrears to give them an incentive to pay. You might consider reducing interest owed or giving a rebate.

- If an account isn't large enough to warrant going to court, send it to a collections agency instead rather than give up on it.

- In some circumstances, you may be able to repossess an unpaid item, such as high-end durable goods or large machinery.

- Send unpaid accounts a letter informing them that they will receive a 1099 form at the end of the year, meaning that they must pay income tax on the amount of goods they received from you because if they refuse to pay, you must consider the goods a gift that is taxable to them. If they respond by paying the bill, you will now have to pay income on it, but if they don't, you can write it off as a loss—in which case, don't forget to follow up with the 1099!

REDUCING YOUR COMPANY'S DEBT

The easiest way to keep from having too much debt is to avoid accumulating it. Weigh your business risk carefully to determine the financial risk you can afford.

- Consolidate. Restructure your debt by consolidating your

short-term loans and lines of credit into one longer-term loan with lower interest.

- Arrange a "debt-equity trade" and sell off stock to pay off debt.

- Have a garage sale. Well, not quite, but reduce debt by selling off assets.

- Reduce dividends on stocks and use the cash to reduce debt.

- Reduce future debts by leasing new equipment instead of purchasing. Plus you can often upgrade quicker and cheaper when you use leased equipment.

- If you have dormant lines of credit, either begin using them or close them. You may have lines of credit that are being charged an annual fee even when you have not used them.

If you don't have any lines of credit, check into getting some with attractive terms, especially if they don't have annual fees. Use them wisely, but save them mostly for times when you are temporarily short on cash. Using a credit card (which many small businesses do) can cost a lot more in the long run if you can't pay it in full by the end of the grace period.

Paying Less Interest on Debt

When you pay interest on debts related to your business, they may be tax deductible; be sure to explore this option come tax-time.

- You'll always pay less interest on your debt if all your debt is consolidated into one loan. Or, take out only one loan at a time.

- Shorter term loans may have a slightly higher interest rate, but if you are able to pay off sooner than the established payback time, you'll likely come out better in the long run.

- Make sure any loans you take out don't have a pre-payment penalty.

REPORTS

Do a complete review of your accounting practices and reports. Does your accounting system generate reports that tell you what you really want or need to know? If not, then your system may be obsolete and need some tweaking.

Monthly accounting reports may be too generalized to give you details about costs. Assign someone to break the costs down into specifics. For example, you may have a dollar amount spent each month on office supplies, but which supplies, exactly, are heavily used and why?

Make sure your reports are generated and reviewed by the controller in a timely manner. If the report is generated a week early, but reviewed two weeks later, the information is not the same anymore.

When reviewing reports, pay close attention to accruals and keep them in check.

You may be able to get double-duty from a report that you're already generating. Survey all managers and others who read the accounting reports to find out what they really want to know or what they'd like done differently. You may be generating reports that aren't really necessary or, by simply modifying one report, you can eliminate others.

When management needs to request a special report or special data from the accounting department, does it throw them all in a tizzy? If special requests result in chaos, perhaps your accounting department isn't being run efficiently or isn't staffed as professionally as it should be.

Give all managers a training session on the company's accounting structures so that they will understand the reports and their contribution to the system.

When you've done all you can to try and locate and stop leaks but feel that your efforts have not produced the proper results, it may be time to call in a professional. Companies such as Sentori, Inc., produce software that specializes in leak-detection and prevention. While Sentori targets the telecommunications industry, there are companies that provide these services for others as well. The results suggest in almost every case, leak-detection projects pays for themselves.

Inventory and other financial reports are a hassle. If you must close a retail store for a day or hire an inventory company to come in and take inventory, the added expense might seem like a quick way to cut a cost—by not doing it. Don't give in to this temptation; how do you really know what you've sold or still have on hand without it? You may never be too sure.

Taxes

Internal Revenue Service. Audit. These words strike fear in the heart of every small business owner. What's the best way to avoid an audit, keep the IRS happy, and pay as little tax as possible? Use a CPA every year to compile your tax forms for you, advises Walden.

But wait? Earlier in the chapter, you advised *not* using a CPA. What gives? Small business owners, said Walden, try to save themselves money by doing their own taxes but often the end result is just the opposite. He recalls one business whose tax strategy had them barking up the wrong tree.

A husband-wife team operating a dog-training business had a regular clientele, taught hunting and obedience lessons, and traveled to various venues to showcase their services. But when it came time to file their taxes, they were far from successful. They unknowingly claimed dog food for their pet dogs as a business expense and made a few other blunders, causing the IRS to flag them for an audit. The results were disastrous and, not knowing what else to do, they paid the interest and penalties, resolving to do better next year.

By the next tax season, Walden convinced them to have their taxes done professionally. A CPA knows tax law better than any business person who isn't trained in taxes. Their CPA found them legitimate business expenses that they hadn't even considered claiming previously. He helped them differentiate what was personal or home expenses versus business expenses and even found some errors in the previous year's audit which allowed them to file an amended return for that year. All told, the $300 bill from the CPA netted them more than $4,000 in legitimate expenses that they hadn't known to deduct before.

Even though you may still be audited if a CPA does your business's tax forms, a CPA knows how to avoid items that often cause deductions (audit flags) and will be successful in defending their choices in deductions if audited.

CHAPTER

11

Purchasing, Vendors, and Suppliers

PURCHASING BASICS

Today's economy is a global one on a scale that nobody could have imagined a century ago. And even though it may seem like an advanced system, having products or components made on the other side of the globe and shipped to you is not always the most reliable or trustworthy system.

As your company considers becoming part of the global marketplace, you'll likely be buying goods from overseas, not just selling them overseas. Components, raw materials, and even finished goods are imported into this country at a growing rate. It can be tricky to find established and reputable sources of materials and goods, so be sure and invest in the time to find reputable suppliers. Saving money by dealing with someone whose prices are just too good to be true could be a costly mistake.

Comparison shopping may seem time consuming, but make a habit of doing it for everything you buy. Use the wealth of information available on the Internet to read reviews of almost anything that's made these days. Many sites will give you side-by-side comparisons of similar models of an item. Not only will be you educated so that you won't fall for a slick sales person's personal opinion, but you may find alternatives or items you never knew existed.

You get what you pay for. Before purchasing twelve cases of industrial lubricant that's half the price of your current brand, do some investigation. Obtain some samples from the manufacturer and have them tested on your equipment first. It may turn out to be a great deal, or maybe not.

Form a co-op by banding together with other local businesses to buy the things you all use in bulk.

When purchasing items for your company, establish the salesman's rock-bottom price first. Then negotiate the perks, such as an extended warranty or at-cost replacement parts for a year. The salesman often won't offer these perks; you have to ask for them.

Don't buy the extended warranty; negotiate it as a perk. Simple logic tells you that if they didn't make money on them, they wouldn't offer them.

Use your bully power. That's right—the larger your company—and "large" can be relative, based on where you live—the more likely you can get a lower price than another company of smaller size. Use your business size to reduce your costs for materials, components, or other goods.

Barter with other companies. You want ten boxes of letterhead printed at cost, and the printer wants some of what you produce. You don't have to spend cash, just inventory. Trade, so long as the values are equivalent. Be sure to pay attention to any tax ramifications there may be in bartering.

Search out equipment and supplies from companies that may have the item and are not currently using it. Buying it used may generate significant savings.

Review the policies for purchase orders. Who in your company has the power to sign one? Among those people, who are more likely to approve almost any request? Trim costs by rescinding purchase order privileges.

If your industry has a trade association, join it. Often you can get products and services cheaper as part of your membership benefits.

If your company has numerous branch locations, purchasing from a national supplier may be more cost-effective than having each branch purchase locally.

Don't toss out those mail-order catalogs just yet. At least quickly review them, comparing the cost of items with what you're currently paying from another supplier. If you don't have to have it immediately, you may also save on shipping if you call in your order and ask specifically for the slowest and cheapest shipping method. Some companies' Web sites don't offer shipping options you might get by calling in an order.

Join a warehouse-style store, like Costco or Sam's Club. Business members get benefits, such as being able to shop earlier than the public. For items that you can't wait for a supplier to ship, it may be cheaper than your standard office supply store.

Buy things when they're on sale and buy in bulk.

Keep an open mind about buying online. eBay and other auction sites can net you great savings where a warranty isn't needed on office items such as computer mouse, keyboards, speakers, bulk CD-ROM, or DVD-ROM packages.

Manufacturers' returns may be worth looking into as well. Sometimes a returned item has a very small defect and make a great reduced item when sold as refurbished. The warranty may be reduced, but the reduced price may compensate for that.

Don't rush into buying used software, however, as often it's not legally transferable. If in doubt, contact the manufacturer first.

Consider eliminating the need for purchase orders under $100 because of the cost to process them. However, beware that frivolous spending may result.

Don't just keep buying supplies every time someone says "We're running out of XYZ again!" Take a little time to learn who uses which supplies, how they're used, and whether or not they're being used efficiently. You may find that some secretaries are more frugal with post-it notes while others use them for every little thing. Some janitors may be more liberal with the cleaning supplies than others. Determine an actual amount necessary to do a job and learn to allocate resources that are necessary for a certain time frame, such as a whole week or month. Force employees to learn to use supplies frugally and stick with their allocated amount. You may be surprised by the amount of savings through purchasing less and spending less time doing the duties of purchasing and stocking supplies.

One attractive alternative to buying altogether is leasing. Almost everything you need for an office can be leased. Equipment, furniture, tools, and electronics such as computers can all be leased. There are some advantages of leasing, such as tax benefits. You may be able to deduct your lease fees. Plus, if you want to upgrade frequently you can often do so with the same company.

As with most things, there are downsides to leasing as well. You may have to keep the items for a fixed length of time and if you lease the item long enough, you may have spent more than if you'd purchased it outright. Careful evaluation of all of your lease terms will help you decide the best way to obtain items, purchase or lease.

VENDORS AND SUPPLIERS

No business can operate without building relationships with other businesses. The businesses that you do business with, your vendors and suppliers, can either assist you in running your business well or can drag you down. Consider these ideas about dealing with vendors and suppliers.

Reduce your risk of loss in the case that your supplier has a loss. Ask suppliers for proof of proper insurance so that if their supplies to you are disrupted and you lose business as a result, you can be compensated.

Additionally, any supplier who sells you a part for your product should be able to provide liability insurance so that if their part is defective and caused your product to be inoperable or unsafe, their liability insurance will cover you.

To assure that your suppliers have these insurance coverages, ask for a Certificate of Insurance and the proper information, especially their insurance company's contact information, to verify it. Make this information a requirement before you begin doing business with a supplier and a requirement that it be regularly updated.

Nobody wants to think that their own employees may be defrauding them, but it happens. It also happens that vendors defraud their business partners on occasion.

One of the most famous cases of cheating that's ever been made public is that of the vendors who were caught with their hands in Kmart's cookie jar in the late 1990s. Corporate buyers were taking kickbacks from vendors in exchange for inflating invoices, ordering inferior goods, and for a variety of other reasons.

These practices led to a shut-out of competition in many departments; a single vendor might supply the majority of one department's merchandise for the retail giant. Vendors who were not able to compete (read: honest vendors) were furious with the way things were, but powerless to do much about it.

When Kmart realized its problem was spinning out of control, it hired a consulting firm that specializes in corporate investigations to get to the bottom of it. In addition to weeding out the buyers who were dishonest, this company set up a hotline for vendors to rat on each other, so to speak. Vendors who'd been denied space on Kmart's shelves were all too happy to participate in the hotline scenario.

After the bad buyers, employees, and vendors were weeded out, Kmart began to rebuild its vendor supply. But this time around, all vendors were forced into a compliance program that has helped keep the dishonest ones at bay.

While these measures didn't necessarily fix every issue the retailer encountered in the past decade, it did wonders for the specific vices of vendor fraud. For more about vendor fraud, see Chapter 25: Theft...All Around You.

Visit your suppliers and vendors with a team of employees to study their processes. Improve them so that they can work cheaper. Just make sure they pass some of the savings down to you!

Also consider having your suppliers send people to visit your company. They may be able to give you ideas on how to use their products better to make your product.

When suppliers make cost-cutting suggestions, share the savings with them in some way, either through a bonus or by giving them more of your business in the future, making it worth their time to help you save money.

Renegotiate your standing rates for products and services from vendors. Like you, your vendors are always trying to cut their costs and generate their product cheaper. They may have done so but not passed any savings on to you. Ask for your piece of the pie.

Another way that vendors and suppliers can help you out is by providing you with an annual list of suggested new customers for you to make contact with, based on their own customer lists. If they help you increase your sales, they help themselves as well.

What can you and your suppliers do for each other? You want a lower price for the supplies you need. Do you have anything you can provide in exchange for lower costs? A guarantee of more business? A referral from you to another company they can do business with? Explore the possibilities.

If you can purchase most of your supplies from one vendor rather than three or four, your combined order amount may generate additional discounts for you. However, weigh the value of one supplier against severing relationships with other good suppliers.

General Motors Corporation, the largest automaker in the world, has an entirely outsourced IT structure. Software vendors and others have supplied all the IT services for GM for more than twenty years now.

However, as the company grew and the number of vendors grew, the entire process became very complex. In 2004, GM started working on simplifying dealings with their IT vendors. In the past two years, they have reduced the number of vendor contracts significantly. That move alone has helped make the process smoother.

Additionally, GM is also requiring vendors to sign a standardized contract. The benefit is obvious: reduced legal fees in reviewing hundreds or thousands of contracts. Among other changes in the way they view vendors is a mandate requiring all vendors to work together even though they compete against each other for GM's business.

Another move on GM's part has been to stay in the driver's seat in the relationship with all their IT providers. Since so much of their structure, including the development of all software and electronics that goes into every vehicle they make relies upon the creative energies and technological advances of their vendors, GM naturally wants to retain rights to any advances made by vendors that are used by them. Vendors, however, often think differently about intellectual property (IP) rights.

There has not been any clear-cut legal precedent set in this issue, so for the time being it comes down to a battle of will and wits between companies and vendors.

However, the trend that GM is now participating in, that of having the customer's interests and financial gain be the focus of the contract with the vendor, may very well become the norm in the future.

Reducing the number of vendors can also sharpen the focus of your supply chain, making it more efficient and leaner.

Eliminate some pork from your budget by cutting off *on-time* bonuses for subcontractors. Instead, give bonuses for *100 percent no defects work* done in a reasonable time frame. The on-time bonus often leads contractors to care more about quantity than quality, an attitude that will only cost you more in the long run.

When negotiating with vendors and suppliers, get in writing the exact pricing and timeline that the pricing is good for. You don't want to be hijacked by a vendor who suddenly raises prices before your busy season. If you can't get a guaranteed price through an anticipated busy season, consider buying ahead if doing so will ultimately cost less than paying a price increase.

On the flip side, make sure you clearly understand how much stock you are expected to purchase in a certain time frame. Try to negotiate a "buy as you need it" clause in the time frame, rather than in one lump shipment.

When negotiating payment with your suppliers, ask for terms over the course of six months or a year at an interest rate lower than your financial institution. If the vendor isn't hurting for money at the moment, they may wish to strike a deal and earn a little interest.

Make a contingency plan in case your supply chain is disrupted. The 2005 weather-related disasters in the United States caused all sorts of supply chain issues around the country. Grocery stores posted signs stating that their supply of certain brands of coffee were unpredictable, and one of the country's leading fast-food restaurants had a well-publicized lack of tomatoes for its sandwiches for several weeks. Of course, you can't plan for everything, but it never hurts to try.

Keep detailed records of all promised discounts from suppliers and vendors and double-check invoices to see that those items were given. The sales staff at the supplier may not have properly notified the Accounts Receivable department of discounts, so it's up to you to make sure you receive them.

If you don't have a negotiated and in-writing price from a vendor, negotiate the price on every sale. You don't know what their month or sales quarter has been like; maybe sales have been up or down, which may affect their ability or desire to give you a better price than last time you ordered.

Biz Wiz Says . . . "A vendor's list prices are never not-negotiable."

—Patrick Walden

It was a small retail store with a thrifty owner. In fact, she was so adamant at getting rock-bottom prices for her office supplies that she'd frequently spend all day comparison shopping every office superstore and warehouse store, driving all over town to save a few dollars on paper towels.

But she wasn't really getting as far ahead as she'd like. In fact, her store had a very low margin of sales. Dejected, she sought the help of consultants. While her thrifty ways impressed them, they soon realized that she was making a common mistake that small business owners make. She was "leaving big money on the table" in some ways and focusing instead on the small dollars, those few pennies she saved with comparison shopping for her office supplies, said Walden.

To Walden and the others who looked at this case, it was a no-brainer. They pointed out the obvious: stop spending time driving all over to save a few dollars here and there. Spend that time on the phone negotiating better rates with her vendors who supplied the merchandise she sold in her store. The owner was flabbergasted: negotiate lower rates? What do you mean?

Apparently she was never told—the vendors won't tell!—that the published prices in her vendors' catalogs weren't written in stone. They coached the owner on the three things she needed to know to negotiate properly with vendors:

1. Know how much you buy from each vendor.
2. Know when you buy (pull up your purchasing records).
3. Know where else you can get the same merchandise.

With encouragement, she negotiated a 30 percent discount from her vendors. And while she didn't sell any more merchandise than usual, she made a huge leap in her profit margin. In just a few months it soared from 30 percent to 50 percent which translated to approximately $20,000 more per month in profit!

Why don't many small business owners negotiate with vendors? According to Walden, the answer is simple:

- They don't know that they can negotiate down from list price.
- They don't have the courage to do so or feel that they aren't important enough to demand a discount.
- They don't know how.

CHAPTER 12

Tech Department and Research and Development (R&D)

So much of business depends on the technology used for even the smallest functions. Your company's tech department, whether a single person or a fleet of programmers and technicians, needs to stay on top of an ever-changing world of gigabytes and pixels.

One of the most important duties of your tech department is to protect. They protect your data from corruption, hackers, security breaches, and good old Mother Nature. Lightning strikes and other power failures can doom any system if it's not properly protected. Whether it be from a hacker or cyber-thief, or the result of nature's fury, every company is vulnerable to loss.

10 Ways to Protect Your Systems and Data.[17]

- Losses come in many forms. Some are data loss, downtime, or hardware or software corrupted or physically destroyed. **Have a plan to deal with every possible loss.**

- **Any loss could easily lead to loss of revenue.** Determine at what point it would be critical for you to get up and running again in the case of any loss.

---

[17] "101 Top Tech Solutions," August 4, 2005, https://www.entrepreneur.com/article/0,4621,322744,00.html, accessed on May 1, 2006.

- **Your recovery plan should be in phases.** Mission-critical items should get priority. Then you can worry about restoring less critical functions.

- **Make sure you keep your plan current.** Changes in hardware or software and updates in technology can cause your plan to be unworkable if it's not current.

- Smaller losses, such as identity theft, can be devastating. Even businesses are scammed. **Encrypt all sensitive data** to avoid losses.

- **Video surveillance** monitored via Internet can be a target. If you use these systems, make sure you use the password protection features to avoid online spying on your surveillance.

- **Power supplies.** For critical areas, consider investing in Universal Service Program (USP) devices which can supply your computers and equipment with enough power in the event of an outage to save files and properly turn equipment off.

- **Power surges.** Be sure that if you have systems hooked up to a traditional phone line that you run the line through your surge strip as well. A lightning strike can travel through the phone lines and fry your modem and even your hard drive.

- **Backing up business data.** The larger the company, the more complicated this process can be, but it must be done. Even smaller companies should back up their data daily and keep copies of the data off-site. External hard drives are becoming very economical. Electronic tape systems are reasonable in cost and easy to use. Putting your data on a CD or DVD is also an economical choice.

- **Online data storage.** There are now companies online that will store your data for easy retrieval in an emergency. These subscription-based companies can vary in price and service, but you must check out their security first.

WEB SITES: COSTS AND MAINTENANCE

Web sites. Everybody wants one, many companies have one, but the real question is this: do they actually bring any value to your company? How do you get the most value from your Web site, whether in actual numbers or otherwise?

To begin with, look back and think about what happened when your Web site first went online. Who put it there? Web site developers, likely. But once they set up the site, made sure all the links were operating and updated the site occasionally, they left the picture.

To get the most from your Web site, consider hiring an Internet solutions provider. Companies that specialize in not just designing and maintaining a site, but that incorporate your company's very business into the site will bring better results because Web site developers don't specialize in web marketing. Why have a Web site if it isn't going to further your business in one way or another?

Search engines are important, but do you invest a lot of money into getting your search term at the top of the engine? Consider trying for second or third place. Some Internet solutions providers actually believe that second or third is preferable.

Don't leave your site unattended. Visitors to your site want to see up-to-date information. Be sure to leave a "date last updated" easy to locate, so visitors know the information they're seeing is current and accurate.

Think of your Web site as another sales avenue, and measure its activity — sales generated from the site — the same way you would any other sales avenue.

Turn your Web site into a power-selling machine with mass customization! Everybody loves to get just the right product. If you have a product that is built to order for every customer, then use your Web site to facilitate that process. Hat World, Inc., is a fairly young company that sells custom-embroidered hats in malls, airports, entertainment venues, and street-level stores. Customers can see the hat styles, pick them up, and feel them.

But what about people who like to shop online? Hat World wasn't about to be outdone when it came to their Web site. Using LiquiFire Dynamic Imaging Products software by LiquidPixels, you can custom-design every aspect of your hat and visualize the finished product before finalizing your order. Hat World realizes that mass-customization is the only way to go, and that a customer, not being able to touch and feel a hat and flip through a book of graphics, has to have something better than just their own imagination. They create your own concept with full visualization at their site, **www.lidscyo.com**.

Find ways for your Web site to facilitate mass customization and you, too, may find your own power-selling machine!

Generating traffic on your site is important, even if not every visitor becomes a customer. Beyond Internet search engines, here are 17 suggestions for planting your company's Web site into the minds of your customers and the general public. The idea is that you want every person who knows about your company to remember your company's Web site address just as easily as your company name.

- **Company invoices.** Put the web address on them especially if you offer the option for invoices to be paid online through credit card of ACH.

- **Payments you make to your suppliers.** If your suppliers can check your site and learn more about what you do, they may come up with ways they can do more business with you!

- **The company letterhead.** All correspondence should include your company's Web site, especially sales letters!

- **Company e-mail.** Create a custom signature line for all employees that includes your company name, Web site address, and slogan, logo, or other information you want everybody to share. Most e-mail programs will insert signatures automatically.

- **Your own Web site.** Build a place in your Web site where visitors can enter the e-mail address of people they think would be interested in it. The system then generates a link to your site and e-mails it from the visitor.

- **Make me an offer.** Offer something of use to visitors to your site, such as a newsletter, product updates e-mailed to them, or a chance to be in a drawing. Pair it up with the "tell a friend" option so they can refer others to do the same.

- **Tell me something I don't already know.** Turn your company's Web site into a library of articles and information about your product and your industry in general. Someone performing an Internet search might find your article quicker than your product. Keep an archive on your site of all past information.

- **Stay in touch.** If you can get visitors to your site to give you their e-mail address and sign up for e-mail product updates, newsletters, or other freebies, be sure to contact them regularly with new offers and information to keep their interest level up. Make sure the e-mail contains a worthwhile deal such as a coupon or online-only special.

- **Links.** Place links on your Web site to the sites of companies that provide compatible products and services if they will provide the same on their site.

- **Your company logo.** Find a way to work your Web site

address into your logo. Maybe it's time for a complete logo makeover?

- **Your slogan.** For decades, companies have been building their phone number into their company slogan and now you can do the same with your Web site address.

- **Your advertising.** Every print ad should absolutely contain your company's site address. Television ads can use scrolling marquees and other eye-catching effects to display the address. Radio ads can be combined with a catchy song featuring the information.

- **Internet advertising.** Always include a hyperlink to your company, not just the address.

- **Viral web marketing.** This sounds like something that shouldn't be passed on, but don't let the name scare you. Viral marketing is simply an ad, a video clip, a cartoon, or something else created by your ad team that is so funny, amazing, or unbelievable that people will e-mail it to their friends, who in turn forward it to their friends. While this type of advertising isn't easy to track, it can create brand awareness.

- **Business networking sites.** Join sites that allow you to display company information. Not only might you learn something from others who are using the site to share tips and leads, but you'll be creating awareness for your own company.

- **Become a blogger.** If your company or product is unique, generate interest by becoming a mini-expert. Those blogs that are heavily read and generate a response can create a media buzz. Obviously, every entry in your blog should include your Web site address. To find a place to blog, you can start your own—a simple Internet search will give you many sites—or offer your services to a site whose readers would be likely to use your product. Blogging has become a hot new trend, so be sure and get in on it!

- **Books.** Write articles about your industry, product type, or something related to the use of your product. Offer it at no charge to e-zines, online newsletters, and other local media sources.

Protect your Web site from vanishing into cyber-space! If your hosting company has a disaster and their system is entirely wiped out, your site may be as well. Verify with your hosting company that they backup and properly store all data. You may wish to ask for a CD-ROM with your Web site's code on it as well.

New Stuff: Equipment and Technology Upgrades

Consumers who are in the market for new stuff can find no lack of technology to buy, and for businesses, it's no different. But what new stuff do you really need and where do you get it? Those are questions that, if not looked at systematically and logically, can cause your company's IT budget to balloon out of control. If your company's systems are a like a quilt of many colors, patched together but not really coordinated, you may be in for some expenses down the road to undo and redo that mess. Save yourself money in the future by fighting the urge to customize all your systems. Instead, look to standardize and simplify.

If You Want It, But It Costs Too Much, Build It.

Southwest Airlines did just that when they pioneered ticketless boarding in the early 1980s. Southwest's ATM-like machines that allowed passengers to buy a ticket right on the machine with a credit card were expensive: $50,000 per machine! To be able to offer these machines at all their sites, their in-house technology department decided to build a machine themselves. The result: the same basic machine now costs $14,000. The savings were huge! [18]

Nobody lives the adage, "Necessity is the mother of invention" better than the R&D department. In fact, necessity is more like a rabid stage-mother, forcing its child into the spotlight at every turn. So here's an important tip about saving money: if you need it but can't find it, invent it. Not only will you save money over hiring someone off-site to invent or develop the product, but if the need extends beyond your own company's uses, you may well form a whole new profit center for your company.

River Steel in La Crosse, Wisconsin, found a way to avoid outsourcing some work and actually created some extra income by becoming the outsourcer instead. When beams for certain projects are fabricated, sometimes the requirements call for cambering them, meaning to slightly bow them. Then when the beam is used in a building, the bowed portion is placed upwards and when that cambered beam is required to support weight, the weight on top of it forces the beam back to a flat position. If the beam had not been cambered, the weight on top of it may have caused it to bow slightly downward. So while it seems illogical to those who don't work with heavy metals, cambering actually strengthens the beam in a weight-bearing usage. This also allows the engineer to specify tighter section sizes, thereby minimizing material costs.

River Steel was spending time and money in heat cambering before they could be properly fabricated to their customers' specifications or they were passed over for some jobs because they didn't own their own mechanical cambering machine. In order to be more competitive and better use labor and reduce energy wasted, shop supervisor Jerry Doll suggested building their own cambering machine. The machines they were considering purchasing couldn't handle their needs in the same way as a custom-made machine could.

---

[18] Allyn Freeman, *How to Save Your Company Big $$$ in Small Ways*, John Wiley & Sons, Inc., New York, 1999. p. 19.

Owner Tim Brennan says that the machine "allowed us to not only be considered for cambered projects, but to become a preferred source for [them]."

Bar-code scanning systems can help automate your supply chain, making it more efficient and producing less overhead for inventory of supplies.

Supply-and-demand software can analyze your systems faster and more accurately than humans can. Reduce your inventory holding times and avoid excessive inventory. Software can even predict demand based on a number of factors, helping you to streamline your ordering of raw materials.

Wal*Mart and Dell, Inc. are often cited as industry-leaders in their use of technology to help cut costs. They both invest heavily in hardware and software of cutting-edge technology to predict their needs and reduce their supply chains.

Before investing in new computer systems, determine what functions each computer in your company *really* performs. You might be able to get away with much less than you think. Buying a bare-bones computer and having only what you really need put on it is cheaper than buying pre-packaged deals with lots of bells and whistles. Computers needed only for inventory tracking software don't need a full office suite, a DVD-burner, and a host of free games. In fact, plain-Jane computers may actually perform better when not bogged down by extra components and software.

Technological advances in computer scanning now allow manufacturers to scan their products for defects, thus saving money on product liability issues.

Use technology creatively to shorten your product development cycles. Get the input of all your component suppliers by e-mailing design information or posting to a secure portion of your Web site. With widespread access to the particulars of the problem, everyone can begin working on solutions right away. Vendors can view orders online in a secured area of your Web site and predict what you'll need for components or raw goods.

Tracking your customers' statistics can allow you to personalize their experience with you. For example, customer calls from highly profitable customers can be routed directly to a designated customer service rep. Other customers can be routed to voice mail or to a menu of choices before speaking to a customer service rep. Customers who call for quotes but never actually order can be referred to the online quote system on your Web site. When he starts ordering, he'll get to speak to a person. While this type of segregation of your customers is controversial, it can save you time and money by letting you focus your attentions on the customers who help you make money.

I recently called a large national insurance broker whose agents sold life insurance policies to my husband and me. When I dialed the toll-free number, I assumed that I'd get a receptionist or a menu to choose options from. Much to my surprise, my call was answered by the same sales rep that we had dealt with all along and whose opening words were "Hello, Mrs. Russell. How can I help you today?"

My mouth dropped open in surprise and I couldn't help but ask how it was that he answered the 800 number and how did he know I was calling? He chuckled and replied that their system is set up to recognize incoming calls from their current customers (by their phone number) and route the call directly to their sales rep. Before even picking up the phone, the sales rep is notified about who is calling. Their computer opens up the customer file and *voila!* — instant service!

Keep up on new software applications that can automate tasks and find creative ways for them to be used in your company. The company who used software to route phone calls no doubt found savings in the number of receptionists or customer-service reps they had doing that job previously.

No matter how amazing a software application is, don't expect it or any technology to fix all your company's problems if the problems stem from internal communication issues or other internal problems.

Technology often brings with it the need to create new procedures or items such as manuals and training sessions. Don't hesitate to get those things in place immediately so the technology can do the most for you right away. Otherwise, you'll just be draining your resources while waiting to get things up and running properly.

In fact, Erik Brynjolfsson of the Massachusetts Institute of Technology believes that for every dollar spent on new technology, a company invests another $5 to $10 in setting up efficient processes for the technology and training employees to use the technology correctly.[19]

OLD STUFF:
MAINTAINING WHAT YOU HAVE

Some of what you have may be older but still quite usable. Computers, for instance, can get bogged down by the amount of data storage that's necessary for accounting programs, customer files, R&D documentation, and just plain old stuff that's on computers.

Your older computer systems may benefit from having a pooled storage, referred to as a storage-area-network, or SAN. These systems aren't cheap, but if storage is a problem or will soon become a problem, SAN is a solution. Many systems use a modular concept so that you can continue to expand as your storage needs grow. Find a system that allows for expansion rather than spending money on a whole new system a few more years down the road.

---

[19] Jon E. Hilsenrath, "Adventures in Cost Cutting," *The Wall Street Journal*, May 10, 2004.

Reduce your data storage costs by evaluating what you are storing on computers. Let employees know that storage space isn't free. Computers run slower when storage is used up, and if it's used up with non-business junk, your employee will work slower due to the slower computer.

Look to the future for technology that will make all processes in business faster or more convenient.

Six Current and Near-Future Technologies to Keep Your Eyes On:[20]

- **VoIP-to-mobile services** are on the drawing board.

- While Wi-Fi is still a relatively new term to some portions of the population, the *next generation of Wi-Fi* is being planned. It may soon replace all fixed cable DSL and T1 line systems.

- Wi-Fi snoops may be foiled with new standards in security. One such *encryption standard, 802.11i,* is something to watch for if your employees need to use Wi-Fi services while on the go.

- **Mesh networking** is an up and coming system that will give greater flexibility for Wi-Fi in areas, such as large office complexes, where these systems often have difficulty.

- **Wi-Jacks** are another way to provide full Wi-Fi coverage in buildings where it's extremely expensive or difficult to set up a traditional wireless network.

- **Just one inbox.** Look for new services that will route your e-mail, faxes, and voice mail into one inbox, including the ability to "hear" your faxes using text-to-speech technology.

---

[20] "101 Top Tech Solutions," August 4, 2005, https://www.entrepreneur.com/article/ 0,4621,322744,00.html, accessed on May 1, 2006.

Keep a sharp eye out for new technology and if it will help you do business faster, smarter, or cheaper, as soon as your company can afford it, get it.

RESEARCH AND DEVELOPMENT/ NEW PRODUCTS

When your R&D department is working on a new product, be very careful about cutting the budget here. Creating successful new products is what drives companies to stay competitive and profitable. Not to say that staying lean and mean isn't wise, but make sure that this department has what it needs to do the job you've asked of them.

To make sure you get results from the money you're pumping into R&D, make sure you follow these basic steps:

- Determine if your proposed product fills a unique or immediate need in the marketplace. If it won't improve, change, or affect the life or work of your customer in any way, why should they purchase it?

- If there are already numerous companies making a nearly identical item, then find your niche. Can you make it easier to operate than the competition's product? Does it have more features that are desirable? Will yours be more durable than the other guy's?

- Pricing must reflect your product's quality as well; if you are going to ask a higher price than your competition, your product quality had better be up to snuff. Building quality into the product right from the get-go is crucial.

Determine a "break-even" time for all new products developed. This is the time at which your product's sales have paid off the development costs. When you have this information, you can find a mix of long-term and short-term payoff products.

Find out what the market wants versus what your customers want. If you survey customers, they might say, "Improve your product work." But the market may say, "We want a totally new product that does a better job than the current product." This difference will help you decide which vision to pursue.

Doctors Foster and Smith found a way to give customers what they want and help the environment at the same time. Knowing that there was in influx of interest among hobbyists in saltwater coral reefs, concern arose over the decrease of saltwater coral in the oceans due to natural disasters and the effects of human interference with the ocean's fragile ecology.

Providing customers with what they wanted: saltwater coral, demanded that their R&D team come up with a way to give it to them without harming **or** harvesting from the world's oceans. The Doctors wouldn't have it any other way.

Out of that customer need came what's believed to be the largest domestic coral farm in the United States. Considering this company is located in the north woods of Wisconsin, that's quite an amazing achievement. On their Web site devoted to live coral and fish, **www.LiveAquaria.com** customers can view actual pieces of coral being grown in Rhinelander and purchase it in a WYSIWYG (what you see is what you get) format.

When R&D departments are working with suppliers and others during the development of a new product, the whole process could take months or years. Use the Internet to cut that time down substantially with these services:

- **Instant messaging.** Not just for teens and geeks, instant messaging can help those collaborating at opposite ends of the globe to converse in near-real time. Free services online abound, and there are even services that will let you cross platforms if you're using one IM software and the other party is using a different one.

- **File sharing.** Another wonderful thing about the Internet is the ability to share files via e-mail. Look for secure servers to avoid having your files lost in cyber-space!

- **Start a wiki:** No, a wiki isn't some crazy junior high stunt played on your friends. It's a file that is built through contributions of many different people. You can set up a spot on your company Web site with passwords and allow your suppliers or others who are assisting the R&D department to contribute. Who knows what the results will be when everybody can see what others are thinking, collaborating on, and working toward!

- **Use your company's Web site.** Find ways to build communication into your company's Web site.

- **Chat.** Like instant messaging, chat is near real-time and allows users to hold a conversation almost as easily or as well as a phone. But a chat is the conference-call version of instant messaging. If you have several people in various locations who are all working on one portion or another of the same project, chat is a great way to share the information all at once.

13 Travel and Entertainment

When times are tough, a freeze on all travel is often one way to achieve some quick hit savings in the company. Entertainment expenditures are also an easy target for the axe. So what do you do with visiting dignitaries and high profile clients if you have no entertainment budget? Be creative, mostly!

Don't be too rash, however, as sometimes there is truly a need for travel. When you want to go meet a prospective client, review their business, and try to seal a deal; you should probably make a personal visit. Consider also what your competitors are doing — if they're wooing the same client *in person*, you'd better be doing that as well.

Set up meetings with other potential customers in the same city. Do some cold calling after you finalize plans with the customer you're meeting so you can offer definitive times to meet other prospects. The trip could pay for itself this way!

Although established customers often are willing to meet via technology, if you're working on a new contract, a bigger deal, or a joint venture you might want to do it live. It just all depends on the circumstances. At any rate, don't rule out travel altogether, just start thinking of it as a luxury for the *really important* times.

Videoconferencing has come a long way since its introduction in the 1990s. And while the quality is exceptional, a potential customer will probably be more interested in your demonstration if he can not only see but touch and try out your product himself. This, too, may be a case when travel is truly necessary. Or perhaps you can ship only the product and videoconference a demonstration while the customer follows along on their own demo product. No doubt your product can fly cheaper than you can.

Items that are generally handled only at the very top level of a company, such as mergers, might be better discussed in person than via the telephone or a videoconference, especially if there are details that might be confusing or require clarification.

Meeting with prospective investors can be complicated, but is it always necessary to do so in person? That would depend on how far you have to travel, whether these investors have experience with your company, and the amount of investment you're seeking from them. As with prospective clients, getting to demo the items or having yourself, the business owner, in person might make a bigger impact. For local travel, encourage employees to take subways, buses, trains, or other local transportation rather than hiring a private car or taxi.

Conventions that are must-attend functions shouldn't be eliminated from your roster. However, check the entire schedule and determine what items are the most important for you to attend. You may be able to skip a day at the beginning and at the end and save yourself the hotel and meal expenses. You may also be able to get a cheaper flight in or out, rather than when most of the participants are arriving and leaving.

Set a realistic budget for a business trip and inform the employee who's taking the trip of the budgeted amount and what that includes. If the employee wishes to stay in a cheaper hotel and eat less, he can keep the excess amount in the budget. If he chooses to stay in the pricier hotel and eat well, he can use up all of the budget. If he runs over, it's at his own expense.

Traveling with technology is becoming easier all the time. Laptops are becoming more powerful and lighter, and a new line of ultra-small, lightweight laptops is being created especially for the business traveler. Spending money on necessities for doing business on the go will ultimately save you money.

While it may not sound cost-conscious to have the newest gadgets on your cell phone, these extra features can pay off when you're on business travel. Being able to take a photo of a prototype and e-mail it back to the office through your phone is very useful. Conventions and trade shows, too, are places where you are gathering information and may want to relay it quickly back to the office.

Having access to your e-mail while on the road has never been easier. Cell phones, Blackberries, and PDAs have allowed business travelers to use their time more wisely and stay in the loop when traveling. They also save the hassle of locating an Internet café or other place to access your e-mail.

DRIVING

- Drive instead of flying, especially if there is more than one person going and you can carpool.

- Reward employees who choose to drive rather than fly, above and beyond reimbursing them for their mileage costs. For local travel, it may be cheaper to pay the employee mileage costs rather than to pay for a taxi.

- Postpone anything low priority. Use another method, such as videoconferencing.

- Use all discounts from professional organizations or associations you belong to, or join a travel club for discounted rates.

- When planning for travel, check into package deals that include airfare, hotel, and rental car for one low price.

FLYING

A direct flight will generally cost more than a connecting flight to the same location, so you can save if you're willing to endure a layover or change planes—usually not a problem if you have only carry-on luggage

If you're willing to wait until the last minute to book flights, you can often snag a good fare if the airline wishes to fill the plane.

Use online booking sites that get lower fares by negotiating with airlines for last-minute deals. It might take you a bit longer to get there but at substantial savings.

Even the airline's own Web site might have online-only deals. Be sure to check these out before finalizing plans with any other travel service, agent, or site.

The time of day can affect the price of the flight. If you need to be in your destination city in time for a lunch meeting, flying out first thing in the morning may be more expensive than taking the same flight out the evening before and staying in a hotel. You'll be better rested for your meeting, too.

Look for fares that offer a price-break for a weekend stay. Perhaps you can schedule meetings on Friday afternoon and Monday morning, and you'll have the weekend to relax and explore your destination.

Require all frequent-flyer miles earned through company travel to be used only for company travel. In fact, you can even set up a pool so that company travel miles can be used for any company travel, not just for the person who earned them.

Flying to and from for a one-day meeting can be both exhausting and expensive. Check for other options, such as staying overnight. You may get a lower fare the next day or a different time of day.

Consider train-travel rather than flying. While it may not be any faster overall, most trains allow passengers to use cell phones and laptops while in transit so that the employee's time may be more productive.

HOTELS

- If more than one person of the same sex is traveling to the same destination, insist on hotel-room sharing, regardless of seniority issues, as long as the room is double occupancy.

- Hotel costs can be reduced by contracting with one hotel chain for a discount.

- Use frequent-stay programs and require that all earned rewards be used during company travel.

- If you have friends or family to stay with, be sure to treat your hosts to a nice dinner or some other appropriate compensation. Odds are it will still be cheaper than a hotel in a large city.

- Stay in touch with Wi-Fi hotspots. Many hotels are now offering them for guests, but make sure you ask if there's an extra charge for use. Patronize hotels that throw this freebie in with your stay.

MEALS AND TRANSPORTATION

- Reduce the cost of ground transportation by taking shuttles instead of a cab or limo from the airport to your hotel.

- Reduce costs on meals by setting a per-meal limit and

having a clear policy on what the company will not pay for, such as alcohol or prime rib. The policy may have to be flexible because a hamburger in a city will cost several times what it does in a small town.

COMPANY VEHICLES

Weigh the costs of company vehicles against their true necessity or convenience, and include in your assessment what you'd lose if you didn't use your company vehicle. For instance, a florist may be able to pay a local delivery service less to deliver flowers than to have their company van with paid driver do the same errand (when they factor in all the costs such as mileage, wear and tear on vehicle, the driver's wages and insurance). *But they'll lose* the free publicity attracted by their van with the company's logo. Just seeing a florist make a delivery is something that brings a smile to people's faces.

If your company supplies vehicles to sales people who don't use the vehicle to transport high-profile customers, then use subcompact cars with low maintenance and great mileage. Companies in Japan are revolutionizing the salesperson's vehicle. Some of them come with e-mail on board too! Even with some frills, the vehicle may cost less than a plain version of a larger vehicle.

14 Customer Service

Save money simply by keeping customers. It is generally true that it costs more to develop a relationship with a new customer than to keep current customers happy. Keep this idea in mind and make customer service an important part of your business, from the boss on down to the janitor.

Tim Brennan of River Steel in La Crosse, Wisconsin, has some common-sense wisdom to share about customer service. "Too many companies are focused on their bottom line and on creating wealth for their stockholders," he observed. "I think that while companies need to be profit oriented to perpetuate their own existence, too many companies run their business as if it were a contest or a game. In a game, it's not about perpetuating what is good or about maintaining and developing relationships. It's about winning and losing—trying to be the last one holding all the chips."

He wisely notes that he runs neither his personal life nor his business life as if it were a game. By treating everyone in his business day with respect and fairness, from employees and vendors to customers, he is building a respectable company. That's not as common as one might think.

About his approach, Brennan said, "It's not winner-takes-all. But [this approach] does afford the opportunity for a win-win result." As a final thought, he adds, "It also affords me the opportunity to sleep a little better at night."

One big mistake that companies in cost-cutting mode make is to cut items that directly affect the customer. Making cuts that reduce your quality, speed of delivery, or make it harder for your customers to receive good customer service isn't wise. While companies recite a variety of mantras about customers being important, they must live it and continue to offer great customer service at all times.

Your company Web site can be a great tool for assisting your customers with simple requests like your phone number, address, directions to your location and other frequently asked items. Make your Web site's home page user friendly with links to all the needed information clearly marked.

However, don't fail to include information on how your customers can locate a live human being to speak to. Specific questions sometimes can't be answered via a Web site. Being able to locate and speak to someone quickly will gain your customers' appreciation, especially if they do business through your Web site, rather than simply reading about your company. A site that displays no information on how to contact you may be appear suspect, as though you are trying to hide from your customers.

A customer who experiences a difficult time trying to purchase something on your site may not bother returning. With the efficiency of Internet search engines, it's very easy to locate another online retailer to do business with. Low prices notwithstanding, customers on the Internet are no different from those who walk through a business's front doors: they want to be treated fairly, with respect and efficiency.

Having an online customer service department may not be enough in some cases. Waiting for an e-mail reply is as annoying as being put on hold or having to wade through a series of phone options before getting to speak to a live person. Therefore, if your site relies on an e-mail based customer service team, be sure to advise customers on how long they should expect to wait for a reply to their inquiry.

Some companies have taken online customer service to a new level, offering live chat-type sessions with a customer service representative right on the site, bridging the gap between phone and e-mail customer service. An efficient employee could handle several conversations at once in this type of format.

This type of setup could be especially beneficial for those customers who want instant information about your product to make a decision to purchase it. If they can't get fast information from you, but they can from someone else, they may buy from your competitor, even if your price is lower. Especially when it comes to impulse purchasing of nonessentials, getting the sale at the moment the customer looks at the item and starts imagining it as "theirs" is crucial. Snag that opportunity by having an information source readily available. Learn more about Web site performance factors at **www.gomez.com**.

Gomez's mission is to "help companies achieve and maintain high-level performance of their mission-critical Internet applications," according to their site.[21] The company tracks the performance of the top 25 online retailers, monitoring uptime, speed and consistency, among other factors.

Their annual review of retailers during the critical holiday seasons has shown that in 2004, the top online retailers lost out on sales due to problems with their Web site or flaws in their online customer service, resulting in hundreds of millions of dollars lost. In the 2005 shopping season, which was projected to show an increase

---

[21] "Holiday Shopping 2005: Reveals if Retailers' Web site Performance is Naughty or Nice," November 16, 2005, www.gomez.com/company/press_releases/20051116.html, accessed on May 1, 2006.

in online spending by 20 percent, Gomez predicted that online retailers would lose out again to the tune of millions of dollars for some of the same reasons. Quality of customer service was noted as one reason that online retailers retain or lose customers.

Take a page from e-commerce history and set up a place on your company Web site where customers can leave feedback about their transactions with you, much like they do on popular auction sites such as eBay. Making your customers' responses public will encourage new customers who can see the results of your hard work.

When a customer needs a form, a brochure, or a manual, try e-mailing it to them instead of mailing it. Therefore, the cost of printing is borne by the customer, saving you the postage, and the customer can have the requested item in their inbox before they even hang up the phone! Obviously, some customers don't have access to e-mail or a printer, but make a conscious effort to use this option as much as possible.

Warning: Don't make this mistake. Recently my bank needed my signature on something and called to ask if I had a fax machine. I do not, but suggested they e-mail me the document which I would sign, scan, and return to them immediately via e-mail. They did so, and I thought the matter was closed until three days later I received the same form in the mail, requesting me to sign and return it. When I called, I was instructed to disregard the mailed form, as they already had a signed form on file. Not only did they waste my time, but it was a flagrant waste of the bank's own time and resources to print out, stuff, and mail the very form that they'd received long before mailing this one!

Take this a step further by having common forms, documents, manuals, and brochures available on your Web site. If customers go there to locate your phone number or e-mail address, they will locate what they need and save your customer service department the time to answer a call and generate an e-mail.

Reward customers for visiting your Web site by posting "Web site-only specials" or coupons they can print and bring to a retail location. Forms and documents that you don't want available to the public can still be stored and accessed via a Web site with password protection.

Give your customers a chance to help you save money. An excellent example of this is shown by the international grocery chain store Aldi. With more than 5,000 locations around Europe and the United States, Aldi refers to themselves as "an international brand leader in grocery retailing."[22] Their no-nonsense style is evident in the warehouse-style shopping. Items are set out for easy access, often on pallets or right in the cases. There are no bag-boys, no checks allowed, and no grocery bags. You bag using your own bags or a box you can pick up at the checkout stations. But in addition to saving money by having a no-frills environment, Aldi also put their creative savings in effect outside their stores.

Anyone who's ever shopped at an Aldi location will remember at least one thing: you must rent a shopping cart. Yes, outside of every location is a machine that will "rent" you a shopping cart for a quarter. And when you return that shopping cart to the same machine at the end of your shopping, a quarter will be returned to you.

This, according to the company's Web site, helps "customers participate in the savings process." Not only does this free them of any customer complaints about loose carts that are clogging parking spaces or damaging vehicles, it eliminates the need for their employees to round up the carts regularly. If someone is lax and unwilling to return a cart for their quarter refund, you can bet the next customer to come along will swoop down upon it like a hawk on a leaping trout and save themselves the rental fee.

Have you ever asked your customers who *their* customer is? If you take the time to find out, you may learn something about

---

[22] www.aldi.us, accessed on May 1, 2006.

how your product affects the end user. The end user may even have some suggestions for you.

To cut down on the number of product returns, many companies are now placing notices in their products with a statement similar to this one: *If there is any problem with this product, please do not return it to the store where you bought it. Call us and we'll assist you directly.* If your products don't have such a statement, consider adding it at the beginning of the owner's manual or assembly instructions. Often a very small issue can be resolved and avoid a product return.

Determine what the actual cost to your company is to process a warranty claim. Consider giving salespeople the authority to make adjustments directly for those claims where the warranty amount is equal to or less than the actual cost to process a claim.

However, if your company has a large number of calls, use that information as a catalyst to improve your production process. Review the records of all incoming calls about new products with problems to find places for improvement.

Excellent customer service is the ticket to having repeat customers when you are competing against larger stores and national chain stores, notes Walden.

For example, a men's clothing store might sell the same quality and

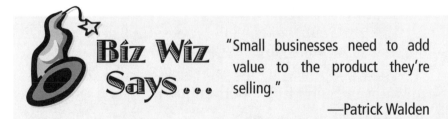

Bíz Wíz Says . . . "Small businesses need to add value to the product they're selling."

—Patrick Walden

similarly priced items as a department store, but where they'll fill a niche is by having a team of excellent employees who can give appropriate advice on what fits properly and why, what colors or styles work best with the customer's needs. "Most men don't have a lot of fashion sense," admits Walden, so when you need to have a professional image and want clothing of good quality, you are willing to pay a bit more for your clothing if you also receive excellent advice and suggestions at the same time. That's what is called "adding value to your product" and it's crucial!

If you run a retail business, another way that you can serve customers well is by training your employees to spot the clues a customer gives by just walking through the door. Some customers want suggestions or help with their purchase. Others consider it an invasion of their privacy even to be approached uninvited.

Sometimes, a sales staff develops a habit of waiting until the customer asks for help. No doubt they've encountered more than one customer who seemed to resent their presence. However, some customers want to be waited on by the sales staff and don't feel they should have to ask for it. How's an employee to know what to do?

Train employees to approach every single customer, even if from afar. They can make brief eye contact and merely say, "Let me know if you have any questions" and still keep their distance. Then, based on the reaction of the customer, they can decide if they should approach for further contact. A willing customer will say, "Well, actually, I do have a question…" or "Thank you. I will!" An unwilling customer will likely say nothing, ignore the sales person or say, "I'm just looking."

Have a brainstorming session with all sales staff to compile a list of all possible customer reactions and appropriate responses. Then practice approaching every customer until it becomes second nature.

"If a customer can get the same thing at a big chain store, they need value added to it to make it worth their while [to buy from you]," said Walden. Make certain your customers never leave your store frustrated because they didn't get any valuable advice, help, or even friendly offers of such from your sales staff.

PART III:

The Specific Element

Cutting Costs for
Your Specific Industry

"Happiness lies not in the mere possession of money; it lies in the joy of achievement, in the thrill of creative effort. The joy and moral stimulation of work no longer must be forgotten in the mad chase of evanescent profits."

— FRANKLIN D. ROOSEVELT,
32ND PRESIDENT OF THE UNITED STATES

When Y2K dawned over east central Wisconsin, Stephani Halderman had just one thing on her mind: soap. More specifically, the business of soap making was foremost on her list of New Year's resolutions in 2000. Since she and husband Dave were planning to have children in the future, she had a goal: to build up a business now so she could earn an income while being home with children someday. With that in mind, Sunshine Garden Soapworks was born.

Many people turn a hobby into a business just as Stephani did. For years, the recipients of her handmade soaps had been encouraging her to go into business. She believes this is one of the tickets to success. "Make sure that you love what you will be doing," she cautioned. "If you don't love it, the fun wears off really fast." Six years later, she loves making soap as much now as she did then. "I loved the product and making it, so I wanted to find a way to keep doing that but not end with too much soap," she recalls.

To prepare for this venture, Stephani, whose career paths included that of software tech support personnel and web designer, took an accounting class at a local university to learn how to keep books for a small business and filed the necessary forms to become "official." She created her company's Web site, **www.sunshinegardensoap.com**. Additionally, she planned out a product line, a company philosophy, and expanded the hobby-sized workshop in her basement to accommodate the larger-scale production necessary to sell her items on her Web site and to other retailers such as specialty shops.

But as anybody who's done this same thing knows, just having everything in place is no guarantee of success. It takes a lot of hard work and dedication, and a fair amount of doing without. For the first year and a half, Stephani continued with her other job part-time while building her customer base and wholesale accounts. "Make sure you think about the money you might need while you are getting your business off the ground," she said. Don't forget things like health insurance and retirement, either. "Many times its necessary to keep your current job (as well), but if you're determined, it pays off," she believes.

Eventually she gave up her job to focus just on the soap making business, even though the income was lower. Going without that regular income was an adjustment that some small business owners aren't able to grasp and handle, but Stephani's business survived.

"Working from home is significantly cheaper than running a business from a store front," she notes. That cost-savings helped her stay afloat when others might have sunk into debt.

When the couple's two children came into the picture shortly afterwards, Stephani found herself pulling double-duty, but she was also able to combine many things in her day so she could care for her family and run her business at the same time. "I can update my Web site, answer e-mail, or plan new products while my children are running around me." Being able to manage both duties at once also presents Stephani with cost-savings by avoiding day care, which would be necessary if she worked at her previous job.

There are drawbacks, however, to having young children around when your business is in your home. Interruptions and noise from playing children can be awkward while making business phone calls, for one thing. Stephani also notes that "you have to be disciplined to keep at your work and not get distracted by other things." Her husband holds down the fort some evenings while production in the basement workshop is in full swing.

In the six years since starting Sunshine Garden Soapworks, Stephani has streamlined some of her processes and found other ways to cut costs or boost her profits. Because she buys most of her supplies in bulk from wholesale suppliers, she has learned to compare shipping rates when the cost of the items is equivalent from one supplier to another. "For example," she notes, "I had been buying my sea salts from a supplier out of New Mexico. It was costing a lot for a 50-pound box to be shipped." To cut her shipping costs, she found a supplier closer to her, since shipping companies factor the distance into their costs. This move alone "cut the shipping cost in half" for that item.

Another way to achieve greater savings on the items she needs to make her product is to participate in a co-op of others who make products similar to hers. When all the individuals in the co-op combine their orders, they are able to leverage a better discount. Even when she is simply purchasing items on her own, Stephani always tries to buy as much as she reasonably expects to use to gain the greatest discount.

"If the saying holds true that time is money, then I've definitely saved some money by organizing my workspace, creating labeling and packaging that is quick to put together, and finding tools to create and fill products more efficiently," she said. In addition to finding ways to make her product better, she's learned to use QuickBooks to spot spending trends and locate ways to save money in her purchasing and production costs.

Designing and printing her own product labels have been big money-savers as well. With basic software and the help of a nice color laser printer, Stephani can create beautiful labels that add a personal touch to her products. She also uses her Web site to her advantage, by offering a monthly giveaway and the opportunity to sign up for an e-mail newsletter which customers could even pass on to other friends, hopefully resulting in free publicity and referrals. Of course, having the ability to maintain and update her own site is a one item in her budget that doesn't have to be outsourced.

Wholesale customers have their own login-access to a portion of the Web site designed just for them. In addition to selling directly from the site and to other retail outlets, Stephani also attends craft shows before the winter holidays and sells direct to shops in her geographical region who feature locally-made products.

Her Web site and newsletter are her main marketing media at this time, although Stephani also has used Google's AdWords program as well to drive traffic to her site. She's submitted her site's address to every free search engine and feels that she has a reasonable amount of exposure for the amount of business she can handle at this time.

While running a business from your home, especially one where you do most of your sales via the Internet, can be a solitary venture, Stephani has used the resources of professional trade associations of soap makers for networking. Being a member of a trade association gives her the right to display their logo on her Web site, lending credibility and a sense of professionalism to her business.

Additionally, membership fees can be deducted as a business expense, and the associations "work to promote the industry and the members in general," she notes. She has the opportunity to attend annual conventions where workshops and seminars educate members on the latest processing methods, marketing trends, and business advice.

Even with professional support systems from trade associations and her network of fellow entrepreneurs, the future of Sunshine Garden Soapworks is dependent on a continuation of sound business decisions coupled with the needs of her family. Stephani has plans to grow her business when her children start school full-time in a few years. The plans include the possibility of building a workshop and storefront outside of her house but still on the family's property which can be seen and accessed from a busy highway.

Another possibility is to expand her other avenues of selling. "I'd love to see my business expanded with my products in more wholesale locations. I'd love for this to be a larger part of our income," she said. However, she also realizes that unless she's willing to take the leap into becoming an employer to others, her growth will always have to remain manageable. "I don't want to grow to where I'm so busy I don't have time to do the fun things and participate in my children's lives," she said.

Do what you love using basic business knowledge and a whole

lot of creativity has been the right philosophy for Stephani Halderman to turn her soap making dream into her dream business.

The home has been a place of business for as long as people have been buying from and selling to each other. Yet it's just one of many categories where we've assembled tips just for you: the home-office dweller, the manufacturer, the restaurateur, retailer, or health care provider. Even if you don't operate one of these business types, skim through and you may find something applicable to you!

15

Home Office Environments

Working for yourself, in your own home, can be a very cost-efficient way to run a small business. You don't have to worry about things like employee theft, although your children might pilfer your office supplies if you're not careful. Every day can be casual Friday, and you can do your work at your own speed.

However, most people who operate a small business from home are not millionaires, so you have to be keeping an eye on expenses all the time. You are your own CEO and must be the vigilant one.

Some Ways to Trim Costs In a Home Office Are:

Furnishing a home office can be done cheaper if you get used items. But we're not talking put-together furniture from your local discount chain store. If you want professional furniture, check with office furniture leasing outfits to see if they're selling any leased items to make way for newer styles.

Filing cabinets must be of excellent quality if they're going to last many years. Again, discount store quality often just doesn't cut it. Keep an eye on classified ads for offices that may be getting rid of some filing cabinets. Remodeling, closing branches, or going out of business are all reasons that companies might sell professional quality equipment at rock-bottom prices.

Your office chair must be of good quality and preferably brand new and only used by you. Cheap office chairs take their toll on your body, especially if you spend a lot of time in front of a computer. You'll save yourself many trips to the chiropractor by having a good chair. The good thing about working for yourself is that you don't have to convince your boss to buy you the things you need to work easier or healthier.

For the ultimate in an ergonomic office chair check out Stance® Angle Chair and the TaskMate™ Height Adjustable stand for your monitor and keyboard. You can see these products at the company's Web site **www.plasma2system.com**.

Don't hesitate to check with retail stores that are remodeling or going out of business. Display shelves for clothing can make great sturdy pieces for your office.

When it's time for a new computer, take advantage of the recycling options available at retailers such as Dell and HP. This may earn you a discount on your new purchase and save you the cost of sending it to a recycling center.

If you bill clients for time spent on work directly for them, don't forget to bill for all long-distance calls and factor in their share of the taxes and surcharges, too.

And how do you send your bills, pay your bills, and mail other things? If you are running to the post office, you're wasting time. Invest in a meter machine from a company such as Pitney Bowes, or learn to use Click-N-Ship® from the U.S. Postal Service.

If you don't step into your office from 5 p.m. until 9 a.m. the next morning, then block your heat vents, shut curtains or blinds, and turn off all equipment and lights overnight. Small energy consumption can add up to your home's electric and heat bills even for one small room of your home.

Check with your utility companies to see if you qualify for a business rate on heat and electricity. Beware that these rates aren't always better than residential rates, so choose the most economical option.

Check for the Energy Star logo on all equipment you purchase for your office, from desk lamps to printers. In those desk lamps, use compact fluorescent light bulbs. They cost more up front but provide better light for your eyes and last a lot longer.

Make your office space inviting. Even if you don't have clients into your office, you are there every day, and you shouldn't dread the sight of your employment location!

Seven Low-Cost Ways to Make Your Home Office Inviting:

- **Mood music.** Working from home gives you the opportunity to work with whatever sound motivates you: heavy metal, folk music, Bach, or nature sounds.

- **Mother Nature.** Plants not only bring beauty to your office, but they cleanse the air! Visit a greenhouse for suggestions on what plants would thrive in your office, based on lighting conditions and the amount of care you wish to provide.

- **Fresh air.** Even in the winter, opening a window just a crack for that crisp fresh air can bring a boost in your mental stimulation.

- **Lighting.** A single-bulb fixture on the ceiling might be okay for a bedroom, but your eyes need more than that for serious work. Consult with a lighting design specialist at a home-improvement store or lighting store to find the right amount and type of lighting for your home office.

- **Organization.** Having an office that's neat and organized feels good. Having an office with stuff piled everywhere and chaos is definitely in control makes you groan! Ask friends or family who are good at organizing for help, or hire a professional who can set you up with a great system that will keep things neat.

- **Dust.** Not only does it make you sneeze, but it clogs up computer equipment and just looks awful. Get an air cleaner for your office that will eliminate dust. You'll have cleaner equipment and better air quality to breathe.

- **Color.** Paint manufacturer Behr has several tools on its Web site to help you define what colors inspire you, motivate you, or will give you the atmosphere you desire. Experiment with these tools and find a color for your office that will energize and inspire you! Find them at **www.behr.com/behrx/workbook**.

Small businesses benefit from writing fewer checks. After shopping around, you may want to have your phone, Internet, and long-distance all from the same supplier. Note that bundled packages for phone and Internet aren't always the cheapest options.

Write no checks at all and pay all your bills online at **www.mycheckfree.com** If someone you regularly pay isn't listed on their site, you can suggest they be added.

If you are the only one home during the day and don't generally receive business calls after hours, you may be able to use your home phone number for your office. If you need a second line, just have another residential line set up with your own number rather than an official business phone line. Business phone lines can be considerably more expensive, although they can be a business expense/deduction as well. You can also save on your phone bill by learning to use your computer as a fax machine.

Ask at every local business you patronize if they offer a discount to business owners. This might save you a few dollars, and it will also give you the opportunity to spread the word about your business and perhaps hand out a business card or two.

Speaking of business cards, many small business owners who don't go through thousands of business cards a year are making them using their own computer and printer. Another option is to have the cards printed on a sheet that will go through your printer and you separate them yourself. You'll save money by having them professionally printed. You can even print them up one sheet at a time, or have different designs for different times of the year, including seasons and holidays.

This is also a good idea if something in your business might be changing in the near future, such as a telephone number, e-mail address, or address. You won't have to toss out boxes of unused cards or have them reprinted if you do them yourself.

A good quality inkjet printer can also serve as your own small business print shop. Simple programs such as Microsoft Publisher have templates to create custom fliers, letterhead, and other promotional materials. The templates are easy to revise to fit your style. And, as with the business cards, you can print only what you need at the moment and save the files for later use.

Most home-run small businesses don't have the advantage of an in-house marketing consultant, but that doesn't mean you can't get free marketing advice. Search the Internet for e-zines and marketing newsletters you can receive via e-mail. A simple Google search turns up more than 6 million results, so your odds of finding one you like are pretty good!

While it's not free, a membership in a trade organization such as the National Association for the Self-Employed, **www.nase.org**, will give you access to tax advice geared toward the self-employed, member discounts, and dozens of benefits.

Make sure you take advantage of all the deductions you're allowed as a self-employed person with a home office. Follow all the rules, though, as Uncle Sam can get pretty picky about what goes on in your home office. To qualify, your office must not be used by anyone, for any other purpose, except you and any employees or contractors you have. That includes even the cat. His litter box needs to go. And your children can't play solitaire either, but you can!

Many small businesses that are run out of home offices, such as appraisers and real estate agents, have rules about how long they must keep their files. If storage space is unavailable in your home, you may have to rent it. Shop around to make sure you are getting the best deal. Pre-pay for an entire year if you can get a discount. Don't store unnecessary items, but pare files down so you can rent the least amount of space necessary. Share storage space with another professional who needs to store files and other items.

Eight Ways to Get More Done in a Day

1. **Ignore.** When you don't have other staff to do some tasks for you, you become your own secretary. Every time you answer the phone, you have to disrupt what you're working on. Learn to turn off the ringer and let it go into voice mail at certain times of the day.

2. **Avoid.** Even if you see you have unread e-mail, schedule a time in your day to read and respond. If you only have 30 minutes in your day allotted to business e-mail, you'll be succinct and purposeful in your replies.

3. **Prioritize.** When you have to do it all, from pounding the pavement to filing the bills, you must prioritize to get it all done every day. When you make a list every day, you'll have something concrete to look at throughout the day so you know you're achieving something.

4. **Schedule.** Schedule one day a week to do all your menial chores, such as filing, if that suits you, or file each paper as it comes in, if that's quicker. The key is to find what

works for you and create a system that you can keep up easily.

5. **Play.** Don't let yourself become overwhelmed and frustrated. These feelings, while easy to understand when you're running your own business from home, can be a huge time-waster. To alleviate this, find a few ways to break up your day. If you spend a lot of the day in front of your computer, keep a small box of toys available to play with, such as a Slinky®, Silly Putty®, a set of jacks, an Etch-a-Sketch® or other diversions you can play with for ten minutes. You'll be able to focus better and relive stress and maybe even be more creative during the day.

6. **Eat.** Those who work in offices all day might think working from home would be so much nicer. You'd be able to use the bathroom when you wanted, eat when and what you wanted, and do it all in your jammies. Sure, those are nice perks, but people who work from home often skip meals in an effort to get more work done. You become just as chained to your desk as the guy in his cubicle. Make yourself stop for breaks and meals just as if you were working for someone else. You can be your own "Worst Boss Ever" if you drive yourself too hard, making your dream job a nightmare.

7. **Hydrate.** As your body uses up its store of fluids, you need to replace them. Even if you're not exercising, you are burning up your fluids all day long. Keep yourself well-hydrated for maximum brain power. The best hydration, and one of the cheapest, is plain old water. If your tap water isn't the greatest, buy bottles by the case or rent a cooler!

8. **Exercise.** Yes, get up from your desk every hour and move. Set a timer if you must. Unlike offices where there are noises and constant movement of people in the halls

or around cubicles, you can easily lose track of time in your home office and work for hours on end without realizing it. This is tiring and wearing and can also be bad for ergonomics. Get up and stretch for a couple of minutes every hour.

You may notice that all of these tips have one thing in common: they all instruct you to not work in some form or other. Don't answer the phone. Don't read e-mail. Leave your desk. Play with toys. Sometimes, as the cliché notes, less is more.

Here is a cornucopia of tips that addresses the unique aspects of working from home on a full-time basis. There are many pitfalls and time-traps that you can't really expect when you first start to work this way, but if you can discipline yourself to get past them, you can have a satisfying work environment that won't burn you — or your family — out.

- Start your day the same as you would if you went to an outside office: showered, dressed, and mentally alert. Sure, you're giving up one of the perks of a home office (working in your jammies) but you may find you're more productive.

- Start your day at the same time every day, just as if you were punching a time clock. You'll have a mental "open for business" sign that will get your brain fired up for the day ahead.

- Treat your "work" time professionally. If family or friends drop by or call, gently remind them that you are "on the clock" if you have work to be doing.

- Allow flexibility in your schedule OR schedule yourself daily. People operate well under one or the other of these philosophies. Set a day of the week for each task, or do tasks "as the mood allows."

- Avoid wandering into the living room to see what's on

TV, surfing the net for fun, or getting snacks frequently. Temptations are easy to find at home without a boss to tell you "No."

- Don't let your day run into your evening. It's difficult, but very few businesses will suffer that drastically if you shut your office door at the end of the day and don't go back in until 9 a.m. If you had an outside office, you'd do it, so force yourself to do it for your in-home office.

- Make a goal for every day. Write it down. "Today, if I accomplish nothing else, I will be happy if I do _____." Devote as much time as necessary in your workday accomplishing that one goal.

- Just say "No" to projects, jobs, assignments, or opportunities that, while they may earn you some money, don't fit into your picture of where you want to be spending your professional time. As long as they're not necessary to your immediate financial survival, focus on the meat and potatoes of your business.

- Save your desk for work only. Don't try to relax at your desk; don't eat lunch there.

- Power nap. One benefit of working at home is the freedom to rest when you need to. Experiment with taking a 15 to 30 minute nap in the afternoon. Set a timer to keep you from taking a longer snooze. Some people find naps are very refreshing and give them a great energy boost.

16 Manufacturing Facilities

Manufacturers all across America have one thing in common: the third-world factor. There is very little produced in this country that can't be produced elsewhere for less expense. How do manufacturers compete in a global economy where the standards of living are so diverse? Those who produce goods in countries with a higher standard of living, such as the United States, have to be willing to pay a reasonable wage, provide benefits, and have other expenditures for the good of their employees.

In other parts of the globe, governments and the workers don't demand that companies provide minimum wages, safe work environments, or benefits. This is nothing new; production of goods has been exiting the shores of the United States for decades with no sign of stopping.

Yet the reality is that Americans need jobs too. America's manufacturers have a challenge before them to find the right balance of production done in the USA versus overseas. It's a challenge that is seen differently by CEOs and CFOs than by labor unions and employees.

The objective is not to debate the fundamental necessities of moving operations overseas, but to pinpoint ways for manufacturing firms to remain competitive wherever they do their work.

For those who operate manufacturing facilities in the United States, one way to remain competitive has been by simply choosing their battles. If your company is involved in several different types of businesses and manufacturing, take a close look at each one separately. Consider getting out of low-profit businesses that are competing directly with overseas goods.

Consider getting out of businesses that aren't compatible with your company's main business. If you're a tent manufacturer that acquired a company that makes sewing thread, then you might want to consider hanging on to that division because it's complementary. However, if you also own a company that manufactures lipstick, that division might be worth selling off.

Consider getting out of businesses that you aren't knowledgeable about. This may be best done when there has been a serious house cleaning and a whole new management team comes into power. Perhaps the previous CEO and CFO knew all about running bakeries, nursing homes, and hotels all at once, but if your current leaders aren't as savvy, you may want to sell off rather than lose money trying to do something you can't.

Whenever you consider getting out of certain businesses, be sure you keep the businesses with the greatest long-term potential for profitability, even if it means not following one of the recommendations above. Here are examples of manufacturing companies who have cut costs using technology and ingenuity.

Early in 2006, Toyota announced a redesigned Camry, assembled in the United States, whose engine is faster and lighter weight. It costs less than previous models. How did they do it? Innovation and not ever being content with the way things are currently made or done. To fulfill their vision of a lighter engine, Toyota engineers created the new technology needed. A new process of casting their engine block uses less aluminum. This saves on the raw materials and other affiliated costs. Toyota redesigned the facilities in Tennessee and Missouri that create the engine blocks for the Toyota assembly plants in Kentucky and other locations.[23]

Another company used technology to cut their production costs drastically. Western Trailer, a company that manufactures custom trailers for industries such as agriculture, forestry, and refuse applications, was losing money on some products. It was difficult for the company to create accurate pricing for each custom-built item. Materials weren't always ordered on a timely basis; production delays and engineering goofs drained away profits. Western Trailer turned to custom software from Lilly Software Associates in New Hampshire. Their software has streamlined the process of creating custom products, giving accurate materials lists, quotes and production timelines. The software has reduced money-losing orders from 25 percent to 2 percent and that has resulted in faster turnaround and increased profits that are helping the company to grow.[24]

Many companies are doing whatever they can to reduce emissions and waste. Besides benefitting the environment and boosting public relations, taking green-thinking to the max can also reap huge savings. The planet's largest cosmetics manufacturer, L'Oreal, went green in the last decade and has been seeing green ever since! Everything from energy-efficient lighting that paid for itself in just over one year to a massive recycling program that saved half a million dollars a year have convinced the manufacturer that what's good for the environment is also good for their pocketbooks.[25]

---

[23] John Lippert, "Cost-cutting Renovations Propel Toyota," February 27, 2006, www.canada.com/edmontonjournal/news/business/story.html?id=2a48995c-68f4-44b2-bad3-56aa9674a210, accessed on May 1, 2006.

[24] Lilly Software Associates, "VISUAL Enterprise Helps Trailer Manufacturer Become More Profitable," www.lillysoftware.com/pdfs/WesternTrailer.pdf, accessed on May 1, 2006.

[25] Amanda Griscom, "In Good Company; cutting emissions to raise profits," July 31, 2002, www.grist.org/news/powers/2002/07/31/griscom-emissions, accessed on May 1, 2006.

Everybody wants to make money, and businesses exist to do that by providing a product or service to the public. For manufacturing firms, providing that product isn't always as easy as placing the order, taking the stocked items off the shelf, and shipping them out. In fact, for many small manufacturers, taking the order is immediately followed by the production of the product. This causes lead times, which aren't a good thing to be behind on. So what do you do when you're a small manufacturing facility with a sudden influx of orders. How do you grow without overextending yourself, because you never know if your influx will become a slowdown in six months.

Madison, Wisconsin, based RenewAire, Inc., found the solution they were looking for right in the same town. The University of Wisconsin's Center for Quick Response Manufacturing (QRM) had the answers that RenewAire's owner was looking for. QRM aims to lower lead times and increase flexibility in companies whose production volumes aren't consistent throughout the year. This system is also good for companies that produce a lot of customized products.

To reduce lead time, the QRM process studies a product's MCT, manufacturing critical-path time. This is the exact amount of time it takes a product to go from the moment of order to the customer's own hands. Obviously, the longer the MCT, the more likely that wasteful activities and time loss have snuck into the manufacturing process.

Once the wasteful items have been identified, a variety of checks is put into place to solve every problem in the process so that the product's entire creation is one smooth-flowing activity.

QRM is applicable to many situations, including use in the office portion of manufacturing firms. To learn about QRM visit the University of Wisconsin-Madison's Web site at **www.qrmcenter.org**.

CHAPTER

17

Restaurants and Food Service

THE RESOURCES YOU ALREADY HAVE

There are many people involved in your business besides you who want the business to succeed. Every one of these people is a resource that you can tap for ideas and assistance.

Your food suppliers have a good reason for wanting you to stay in business; you are their customer. If your business closes, so does their account. Here are just a few things they can assist you with:

- **Merchandising suggestions.** Your food suppliers may have suggestions on how to market your products better.

- **Menu assistance.** Want to work salmon into your menu? Have customers been requesting more variety? Ask your suppliers for help; they'll be happy to find ways for you to purchase more from them so you can make more customers happy.

- **Storage.** When you have a menu change, are you certain about all the storage requirements for the new items?

- **Training.** Some suppliers have professional staff to come into your location and train your chefs in new methods or new recipes.

- **Economizing.** Can you cook more portions with the same amount of food? Are there less expensive ingredients that wouldn't compromise the quality?

Don't hesitate to send out an invitation to all your suppliers to send a representative into your business for some on-site training and suggestions.

Your equipment suppliers have the same thing in mind: making sure you remain a customer by staying in business. If you're thinking about a new piece of equipment, contact all your suppliers and ask for proposals that will include the price of the item(s), the training they will give to your employees, and a list of ways that this particular equipment will benefit your operation. Will it reduce cycle time or make things more efficient for the wait staff? Be sure you're convinced that every purchase will add value to your business.

Your wait staff is poised to make your business profitable; their jobs depend on it. However, the wait staff needs to be clued in to the things they can do to help the business.

Three Things to Educate Your Wait Staff About

- **Reducing cycle times.** When the table is opened up, you can seat another customer. When there is a steady stream of incoming diners, train your staff in techniques to reduce cycle time. Proper training will help wait staff to keep the customers moving in and out without offending them or making them feel pushed out.

- **Selling the money-makers.** The most expensive items on your menu may not have the highest profit margin for the business. But wait staff may inadvertently up-sell those items for obvious reasons: larger checks make for larger tips. Educate your staff about the items you want them to sell.

- **Selling the extras.** The wait staff can have a huge impact on how many extras a customer orders simply by the way they phrase things. Rather than, "Can I get you something from the bar?" they might say, "Will you be having beer or mixed drinks tonight?," thereby suggesting that the customers are going to purchase drinks. They may not have been planning to, but sometimes the mere suggestion can spark their interest.

Your food prep and other staff may not have the contact with the customers that the wait staff has, but they have plenty of good ideas. Encourage them to share their ideas and reward them appropriately when profit rises, losses fall, or productivity increases because of their idea.

Even your dishwashers might find ways to reduce the use of dishes. (They have a vested interest in doing so—to cut down how many they wash!). Your hostesses may have tips that they personally use to keep customers content while waiting to be seated. Make sure that those tips are shared with the entire staff of hostesses so that your service is consistent across all shifts.

Tap into the incredible power of your employees to make your operation run smoother and more profitably.

Your customers know what they do or don't like about your restaurant. If you don't ask, most of them won't bother to tell you.

Six Things Only Your Customer Knows

- **The view.** Your staff may be too busy to pay attention to the details. Is there dust hanging off your ceiling vents? Are your high chairs clean enough that you would put your baby in them? Even a restaurant whose kitchen is spotless and whose buffet line is immaculate can overlook the things that a customer may see.

- **The value.** Do your customers feel that they are getting a good value for their money? Where else to do they frequently dine out and what brings them to your establishment on any given day?

- *The variety.* Are your customers pleased with the menu or buffet choices? Is there something (such as nutritional information) that they'd appreciate having available to them?

- **The vibe.** Do your customers feel welcomed? Are the staff friendly and helpful or do they feel abandoned once they've placed their order?

- **The variables.** What image do all the combined elements create? What do your customers think when they hear your business name on the radio or see it in an ad? Does it conjure up images of a negative experience or make them want more?

- **The vote.** One local restaurant our family frequents often includes a postcard-sized survey with mints at the end of the meal. It has several questions regarding the various aspects of your visit such as the food quality, the friendly service and the facilities. At the very end, they ask this question: *If you could change one thing about this restaurant, what would it be?* A customer, even a relatively content one, will rarely take the time to seek out a manager and make a small suggestion that would make them happy. But when given the opportunity to influence the service or product, customers will often oblige and be pleased that they were asked.

WORKING WITH SUPPLIERS

Having enough food on hand, or the right food at the right time, can be a serious headache for some restaurant owners. Suppliers who are reputable will work with you to make sure that supplies are there on time with orders that are complete and accurate. If you are a good customer to them, they will be a good supplier to you.

However, that doesn't mean you don't demand quality at an acceptable and fair price. Don't let suppliers walk all over you, but also do not try to walk all over them. View your relationship as a partnership whereby you are both working together for the same goal: feeding your customers to make a profit.

A good supplier will ensure that orders are shipped and arrive when promised. If you can't do it yourself every time, assign one staff person to check in every order, comparing all paperwork to be sure it's accurate. Having consistency in this task will save you money by not accepting inaccurate or unacceptable items. Over time, your staff person will be able to manage this task efficiently and become very knowledgeable about what quality is acceptable.

CUSTOMER SERVICE

Reduce your "cycle time" to serve more customers. If your wait staff can get people in and out the door faster, you can serve more people in the same hour. New technology is creating ways for this to happen including wireless order-taking systems that can transmit an order from the waiter directly to the kitchen so that no one has to go to the kitchen or to a terminal to enter the order.

Another way to reduce cycle time during peak hours is to have a limited menu. This will free the kitchen up to cook faster by having fewer things to prepare. The menu can change daily, or you can offer a build-your-own system where customers can choose one entrée from a list, then their choice of side dish, dessert, and drink for one low price.

Don't eat alone! If your business has a friendly atmosphere, allow strangers to share a table. Set up a large table with plenty of room between chairs and invite single diners to share the common table. If they opt out, then by all means give them a private table. Perhaps they have some work they need to accomplish during their lunch hour. If they agree to share, then you've freed up another table for the next group that comes in the door.

Repeat customers can be one of your greatest word-of-mouth advertising partners. Be sure to spend a little more time and effort in making repeat customers feel welcomed and special. Try doing some of these things for your special customers:

- **Keep track.** Create a simple form that you ask repeat customers to fill out voluntarily, including names of family members and their birthdays and anniversaries, their preferences in seating or food preparation or their favorite menu items. Use that information in any creative way. Mail a birthday card with a coupon for a discount on their next meal. E-mail them when their favorite items are the "special of the day." Your imagination and thoughtfulness will pay off.

- **Reservations not needed.** For the most special of customers, keep a table or two in a prime seating area available at times when they are most likely to come in. Let them know that they have a special status and don't require a reservation. This alone may prompt them to choose your restaurant over other places where they have to reserve or wait in line.

UNIQUE ANGLES

Restaurants with uniqueness can endear themselves to their patrons in a way that will keep them coming back. What might be unique for a bar-restaurant might not work for an elegant dining experience or a family-oriented establishment. Research some of the finest examples of unique restaurants across the country to get ideas for your business.

Would you like your dessert at a different table? For a full-service formal dining establishment, dessert may be more commonly purchased than at the casual eateries. Give your customers an extra special experience by offering for them to "retire to the library" for their dessert and coffee. Have a separate room with a quieter and more intimate atmosphere simply for savoring the experience of a luscious dessert.

Make yourself a reputation for being quick and efficient in getting the orders placed and the food on the table, especially if you serve a steady lunch bunch needing to be back to their desks on time.

If your dinner hour is characterized by a fair number of families coming to eat, then make your mark by being child-friendly. Here are some things that are important to parents but may not be obvious to owners and managers:

- Functioning seat belts on high chairs.

- Disposable bibs provided.

- Comfortable places to change diapers.

- Crayons and something to color on or small toys to play with.

- A child-proof atmosphere; no priceless art on the walls above the booth!

- Specially equipped tables without temptations like sugar packets or peel-top jelly.

- A tray of healthy finger foods for hungry children delivered immediately.

- Free meals for children, "children's night," and healthy options on the child's menu.

- A willingness to make things "special" for children who are finicky.

- Patience of the wait staff in accommodating and cleaning up after children.

Anything that makes the dining experience hassle-free and adds value in the minds of harried parents who also want to enjoy their own food will earn you loyal customers.

It's all about the food. Menu variety and creativity are important but there are other considerations when making customers happy. Do they feel they "got enough to eat" or do they feel they were robbed? One national chain restaurant I ate at recently gave me the same three-egg omelet with the usual sides (hash browns and a muffin) that I've been ordering for years. But they'd recently got new dinnerware. The plate that my meal arrived on was so huge that my initial reaction was that they'd shrunk the size of their portions.

By the time I was done eating, I realized that I'd eaten the same portion size I was accustomed to, but still the image of my meal on that nearly platter-sized dinnerware left a feeling in me that perhaps I wasn't getting a good value for my money anymore. People's perceptions are very important; if I could suggest one thing to that company's corporate office, I'd tell them to go back to their boring-looking but average-sized plates.

If you're interested in a unique reputation, consider being known for serving enough food to fill a lumberjack. While that may not sound unique, it actually is. Serving sizes are shrinking at many restaurants due to the health concerns about obesity. These businesses are trying to bring back realistic portion sizes because the health authorities have tsk-tsk'd about Americans eating too much.

But the reality is still this: health considerations or not, people want to feel that they got enough food to eat. A quick survey of the parking lot at any popular buffet place on a Friday night should convince you of that. Be sure to offer take-home containers for patrons. There's nothing these customers love more than knowing that tomorrow's lunch (or a midnight snack) is available from their leftovers today.

Granted, not every person in America wants to feel stuffed every time they eat out. In fact, there are good reasons to pay attention to those Americans who are doing just the opposite: watching what they eat. Whether to drop a few pounds, lower their cholesterol, or to maintain a vegetarian lifestyle, customers with special eating requirements actively search out restaurants with menu choices that can suit their needs but still provide for the needs of family members who don't have a special diet. Offering such choices can win you a reputation and increase your business through word-of-mouth advertising.

Are you known for some specialty in your town? Having a product that is well known throughout town is a great way to bring in business. But having your product specially delivered to the President of the United States gives you just a little bit more prestige! Mr. D's Restaurant and Bakery in La Crosse, Wisconsin, loves nothing more than to tout their Apple Fritters, and well they should. Locally enjoyed for more than 30 years, these melt-in-your-mouth plate-sized confections have been delivered fresh to Air Force One for the enjoyment of President George W. Bush and his entourage. Several national awards and write-ups in popular magazines have given Mr. D's a stellar reputation. But the people of La Crosse and its surrounding communities don't care about all that; they keep coming back to Mr. D's because of the core items that have made them famous: their cake donuts, muffins, one-of-a-kind bagels, and other creations that are made only at Mr. D's.

A special walk-up window is open starting at 8 p.m. every night for those aficionados who just can't wait till morning to get these fresh hot delicacies. By offering their items for sale throughout the night, Mr. D's offers a unique service you can't get at most donut shops and creates revenue at all times of the night when most businesses aren't earning a penny!

Even customers who arrive during business hours find it difficult to say no to a donut or muffin. You must pass the beautiful array of items to get into the dining room. If you can avoid the temptation to take one along with you to your table, you're going to be further tempted by having a mini donut placed on the plate with your entrée. If that doesn't send you over the edge, you must stop at the display case to pay your bill on the way out the door. This is a unique way to force a customer to say no, in triplicate!

Their breakfast menu is so loved that people don't mind lining up outside the door of the 107-seat facility. Unique combinations make their sandwich menu a delight with truly homemade soups and their own unique dinner rolls that are served with their homemade soups.

If you can't get to La Crosse to enjoy a donut or fritter yourself, at least you can see the photo of Air Force One that is proudly displayed in Mr. D's entryway and read the interesting history of this local icon at **www.mrdsrestaurant.com**.

20 Things Not to Miss Out on For Your Restaurant/Food Service Operation:

1. Get a walk-in cooler with a door wide enough for items on a pallet to be put directly *into* the cooler.

2. Automatic slicers can do prep work beyond what you'd guess.

3. High-tech knife sharpeners to keep your equipment in top shape. Don't toss it. Sharpen it!

4. Cook-chill systems generate great savings.

5. National Restaurant Association membership: get one.

6. Restaurant Direct: a new banking program especially for restaurant owners with lots of cool perks!

7. The Web site **www.tabletoyz.com** creates custom placemats for your restaurant's toddler customers.

8. For another great product to keep children happy while waiting for their meal (without the use of crayons) check out **http://wikkistix.com**.

9. Check out **www.daymark.biz** and view their catalog of some of the best safety products in the business.

10. Several companies are offering or developing self-ordering systems such as those found in some fast-food operations in the Eastern United States and quick-stop chains such as Sheetz.

11. Check out **www.opentable.com**, an online reservation site.

12. Want to stand out in the crowd? Hook your restaurant up as a Wi-Fi hotspot. See **www.wanderingwifi.com** for ideas.

13. The Web site **www.fishbowl.com** creates unique and colorful e-mail campaigns for your restaurant.

14. **www.zebracard.com** is a company that can set you up with a gift card printing system. Get in on this hot trend!

15. **www.commeg.com** has a variety of systems designed to help schedule and track your employees' working hours.

16. **www.rmagic.com** sells Restaurant Magic®, a specialty software meant to help streamline every aspect of your restaurant business.

17. ATM machines are popping up inside or just outside many restaurants.

18. **www.accardis.com** offers bar-coding and weighing systems for liquor inventory.

19. **www.futurepos.com**, an All-In-One software system for

all your P.O.S. needs.

20. Do you want a unique way to present your children's menu? How about letting children look at their options on a View Master®? Are your desserts even more luscious when seen and not just read about in the menu? Create a custom dessert menu on a View Master® reel. Even adults love to look into the viewers and see the 3-D images! Check it out at **www.customviewmaster.com/default.asp**

18 Retail Businesses

Retailers are faced with a myriad of issues that eat away at their profits. Richard Hollinger, Ph.D., is the director of the Security Research Project, Department of Criminology, Law and Society at the University of Florida. Since 1991, Dr. Hollinger and his team have produced an annual, nationwide survey of more than 100 of the largest retail chains called the National Retail Security Survey. Consider these statistics from the 2004 survey (based on data from 2003 surveys):

- The average shrinkage rate was 1.54 percent of total annual sales. All told, that translates into an estimated $31 billion lost to shrinkage.

- The largest offender in the shrinkage phenomenon is the retailer's own employees, who account for 47 percent of the losses through various means of theft to the tune of approximately $14.6 billion.

- Next in line are the shoplifters, whose sneaky ways assist retail businesses in cutting their profits by $10.5 billion in 2003, accounting for 34 percent of shrinkage.

- Administrative and paper errors must take their share of the blame, causing 14 percent of the shrinkage, or $4.3 billion.

- Vendor fraud actually accounts for the smallest share of shrinkage; however, even that 5.5 percent amounts to $1.7 billion.

What do these numbers mean to your retail setting? While these are just averages based on the largest retail chains in the country, and while these numbers may not accurately reflect your experience, there is a grain of truth to be found. Losses happen. And sadly, many of them could potentially be controlled or eliminated.

In addition to the ideas presented below, be sure to check out Chapter 25: Theft...all around you.

CUSTOMER SERVICE

Retailers are focusing on customer service more than they did 30 years ago, but because of the high turnover and the younger workforce in many retail locations, maintaining high levels of satisfaction can be elusive.

Nothing is more of a turn-off to customers as a sales clerk or cashier who is tuned out of their job and tuned out to the needs of the customers. One of a retailer's top priorities is to make sure the customers get the service they need. Employees should be trained to make eye contact with every customer they encounter in the store. Even if they're stocking shelves, they can offer to help. Being ignored infuriates customers as does being deserted. Customers who can't find anybody to help them will get frustrated and may simply leave the store without purchasing anything.

One of the best ways to find out if your customers are happy is to ask them. A number of retailers have offered a toll-free number or a Web site where customers can take a survey and be entered for a drawing. Managers who actively walk through the store and gauge the satisfaction of customers might get good feedback from happy customers. Those who are not happy might avoid the manager or will have already left the store.

When unhappy customers call, the manager should always take them seriously and use the information to change the way you deal with customers.

Technology Boosts

Self-checkouts are becoming very popular at many retail chains. One cashier can supervise six self-checkouts at a time. Even if customers are slower at checking and bagging and don't really get done any faster, the fact that they didn't have to wait in line makes them happy.

Customer returns have become much easier in the past 30 years as well, aided by computerized systems that can scan bar codes and determine whether the item was purchased at their store. To simplify the returns process, KMart is now printing its return policy on every receipt, stating the cutoff date for the return of items made at that date.

While not used extensively yet, biometrics is being looked at as the future of paperless transactions. Biometrics includes electronic devices that scan a fingerprint, verify the identity of the print, and use previously stored information to transmit the transaction to the financial institution of the print's owner.

The savings that can be generated are vast because this process eliminates many types of fraud. A thief can steal a debit card and guess the correct PIN number or steal a credit card that has a signature that's easy to forge. Checks have long been the bane of retailers who forgo checking identity on every one due to time constraints.

Even cash has its drawbacks. Apart from the obvious losses occurred by receiving counterfeit monies, a cash drawer must be processed at the end of every shift, and the amounts must be reconciled to the records accumulated by the cash register. The time involved in counting and reconciling cash would be virtually eliminated if the vast majority of customers used biometrics.

However, even though the cost of the technology has come down to reasonable levels, it isn't being implemented at breakneck speed...yet.

Personalized shopping experiences may become the wave of the future in department stores, where the store personnel still sell to customers on a one-on-one basis. Software can track a customer's preferences, sizes, and past purchases to assist sales persons in suggesting product choices and items to complement other items previously purchased.

One of the nation's largest appliance retailers ran a pilot program in 2003 that allowed an appliance's status to be checked through a remote-access channel, such as through a telephone line. This allows for maintenance issues to be spotted before the appliance begins to malfunction. And web-connected appliances are on their way to being a reality as well. With these futuristic items, you could send an e-mail to your oven and tell it to stop chilling your casserole (that you placed in there before going to work in the morning) and start baking it so that it will be ready when you get home.

Supply chain coordination is a time-consuming job for all involved. Technology has improved these tasks greatly, but the newest one being used could provide cost savings that can't yet even be estimated. RFID, Radio Frequency Identification, is a system of using small computer chips imbedded into pallets or containers of merchandise. These chips, by just being scanned by a compatible system, can give an entire history of the merchandise, where it's been, where it's going, and what's in the container.

If this system can be perfected and accepted by the retail industry, suppliers could drop off a shipment of products without having to go through a check-in process. The goods could be placed on a conveyor that would move the cases and containers past a scanner that would automatically check in the items and route them to their proper location within the warehouse. There are numerous other applications in use and more to come.

An Atlanta, Georgia, company that has spent decades perfecting various RF technology has developed uses that are far outside retail use, but worth noting as applications for their product diversity over the years.

Salto Systems, Inc., has created technology that uses RF technology in the hotel industry. Their innovative product is replacing the magnetic swipe cards used by hotels for the past couple of decades with "contactless" remote "keys". These "keys" don't even have to resemble a key or a card. The technology can be built into nearly anything the consumer wants it in.

So far, this new technology has shown itself to be very useful and reliable. With thousands of clients in Europe, including the French Parliament, Salto Systems has begun offering its services to luxury hotels in the United States. The hotels that use their systems will offer greater efficiency and security for their guests, as the RF "keys" don't have the problems of the magnetic swipe ones. The hotels are also glad to be rid of the bulky box/swiper items on their doors. Luxury hotels see this is a way to improve their décor and the mood of their hotels without compromising security.

The applications for the retail industry for RF technology are obvious, but companies on the forefront of this technology, such as Salto Systems, Inc., will no doubt come up with every creative and unique way for their specialized brand of technology to be used — someday maybe even in your local grocery store.!

Once the merchandise is on the floor and ready for purchase, the technology stops, right? Not quite. The experience of shopping is changing as rapidly as the ways that stores obtain and stock goods. Nearly every major discount chain store now offers scanners at several points in the store for customers to check the price of any particular item. This simple addition to the shopping experience has saved money in numerous ways:

- Cashiers don't have to be dealing with items that are brought to the register and then rejected by the customer who thought the price was different.

- The time and cost to re-stock those items has now disappeared, so long as customers return items to the same location where they found it, rather than just tossing it on the nearest shelf.

- The time and cost to make a price adjustment or refund after the sale has lessened because customers are less likely to read their receipt later and be upset by a price.

Of course, not all customers use these scanners, and there will always be those price surprises to contend with, but by merely sharing their scanning technology with customers, retailers can save themselves time and money in the long run.

The next generation of customer-enhanced shopping is the computer-equipped shopping cart.

Electronic check processing has enabled retailers to continue to accept checks as a form of payment despite the risks involved. However, buyer beware: if you present a check to a retailer who employs this method, you'd better have the money in the bank and available for withdrawal before presenting the check. No more floating allowed here.

The electronic check processing systems are just that: entirely electronic. The actual check never makes its way to your bank; in fact it never even goes in the cash register. A scanning system makes a virtual copy of your check that is sent to a central processing vendor, who instantaneously begins an ACH. So writing a check has now become the virtual equivalent of using your debit card for a transaction.

For retailers, this process allows them to continue accepting checks without the risks. This is good news for customers who don't have a debit card for whatever reason. This is bad news for customers who have relied on the traditional three to five days it takes for checks to clear. Although that time had gone down to 48 hours or less in many cases with the new laws that went into effect in 2004, the time now has gone down to zero. Many retailers who are now using this system have signs posted at their checkout stations informing customers that their check will be processed electronically.

Something that sounds like a sci-fi special effect is on the drawing board for the not so distant future. Called contactless payment, or no-touch retailing, this is a sophisticated system whereby almost anything owned by the customer could be imbedded with a computer chip that can be scanned by a payment station that processes the payment without the customer swiping or signing anything or inputting any PIN numbers.

For example, a customer who takes his children to an amusement park could pay for the admission through his cell phone or by merely holding up his credit card to a payment station at the entrance. Additional payment stations could be placed throughout the park to pay for refreshments by merely waving the card within a specified distance. The time savings in processing transactions could be minimal because those manning the payment stations don't have to make change and can concentrate on handing over the desired items quickly.

While universal usage of this technology is still in the distant future, a few American retailers, most notably the convenience store chain, 7-Eleven, have already implemented these systems, though there are limitations. For instance, the chip-imbedded cards must be within two inches of the readers to operate. Obviously this leaves the customer still waiting in line to pay for their purchases; they can't simply wave their card at a reader on their way out the door.

This technology also brings about the usual security concerns, such as theft of a payment-enabled device and the possibility that thieves will be able to hide scanners near enough to capture the information needed to commit identity fraud. All these concerns are being addressed and will likely prompt yet even more technology to provide the encryption and needed security for these devices. However, if the security concerns and other logistics (such as partnering with companies to create chip-embedded devices) can be overcome, the potential for speedy retail checkout has never been better.

CHAPTER

19

Health Care Environments

ospitals, clinics, long-term care facilities, rehabilitation centers — *every* health care business, whether it be a profit or nonprofit, has to find ways to cut costs and make itself more efficient for patients and staff.

Some of the biggest money savers for the health care industry involve new technology. The problem with new technology, however, is that it's frequently expensive. Technology is definitely one of those *you have to spend money to save money* categories.

While technology is a general term, there is a lot of buzz about Health Information Technology (HIT). Information technology has made big advances in recent years and can be a cost-saver for almost any type of business.

In the world of health care, the faster the information is transmitted and the more accurately it is done so, the greater the savings. HIT requires the use of fewer resources such as manpower, resulting in labor cost reductions. Additionally, it increases safety due to a reduction in errors. Some of the specific ways that HIT is being used are these:

- **Digital systems for film-free x-rays with digital archiving**. The cost of the equipment is staggering, but as with most technology it will likely come down in price as time goes on. However, the savings that it brings in exchange make it worth the investment sooner than later.

The cost of x-ray film is eliminated, as is the space that is consumed in storing processed x-rays and the time spent filing them and retrieving them in the future.

These systems can be linked to special computers throughout the medical facility where doctors can call up the images as necessary—no more file clerks toting them to and from storage!

- **Robotic pharmacy techs.** Every now and then an explosive story on the news captures the fear of every person who has been to their pharmacy recently. A mistake by a human pharmacist has caused a medical tragedy. While sad and rare, these incidents are almost inevitable when humans are processing the materials.

  Robots are now being used in some medical centers to dispense medicines. Bar-codes are used to eliminate confusing names on labels. The robots can even package the drugs for the patient. The savings come in the form of efficiency, speed, and accuracy of the robots that never need a potty break either.

- **Bar-coding.** Medical centers use bar-codes in a variety of ways from ID bracelets on patients, medical charts, and dispensed medications such as IV bags and pill containers. Some hospitals even bar-code their staff, so that every time a nurse administers a medication, the nurse zaps his or her own bar-code as well as the patient's, so that the administration can be tracked along with the other data such as date, time, and treated patient.

- **Wireless devices.** Doctors now use such devices to double check a patient's history, allergies, or any other electronic data. The savings here are generated by the efficiency of data transfer. The doctor doesn't need the physical file on hand at all times if the information can be called up by simply scanning a patient's bar-coded bracelet.

Doctors can even input information directly into these devices, or into networked computers in a patient's room. A new prescription entered into the system can be digitally transferred to the pharmacy and the system will flag a possible interaction with another current prescription.

- **Guided software.** All patient registration staff ask the same questions every time and get accurate information thanks to guided software. Companies such as Cincom have developed new software applications that make changes in insurance regulations and easy application of rules for those manning the registration desks.

  When registration information is gathered properly, there can be a reduction in denied claims due to outdated information in the system. For more information, see their Web site at **http://www.cincom.com/us/eng/ solutions/marketing/healthcare/intelligent-guided-patient-registration/index.jsp?loc=usa**.

- **Software that can scan patient records and make recommendations to doctors.** These applications "consult" the patient's records and indicate the risk factors. Doctors can't recall every bit of information about their patients, and they don't have the time to re-read records every time they see a patient. Scanning the physical record helps, but these software applications can scan for specific things, such as vaccinations that are not up-to-date. If these applications increase overall health and reduced need for health care, they will soon pay for themselves.

- **Remote monitoring systems. Chronically ill patients** can transmit information directly to their doctor from the patient's home. Diabetics can have their blood sugar levels recorded and transmitted; others can have blood pressure, heart rate, and other vital signs monitored and transmitted automatically. This could reduce preventable deaths by allowing the system to notify care providers when early warning signs are present or when a trend is noted by the data being collected.

- **Minimally evasive surgery.** Many surgeries are now being done with the aid of fiber optic cables which have an attached video camera that projects on a computer-type monitor. Not only does this require less cutting, a shorter operation time with fewer staff needed and most importantly, it can reduce recovery time and the chance of infection due to the smaller incisions.

20 Educational Environments

School districts have been feeling the penny-pinch for decades now. They face a dilemma, however, in that they have to be fiscally responsible to taxpayers while still providing a quality education to the children of taxpayers. Creative measures need to be taken, but sometimes just looking at simple things differently can make a difference.

Cutting costs in school districts almost always means losing something such as teachers, extra-curricular activities, or improvements to facilities. Schools are increasingly looking at things that have been around a while, the processes, and what they cost. One process that might be worth looking at in your school is the enrollment process.

Are there forms that could be eliminated for new students transferring from another district or school? How are files transferred for students coming in or out of your school or district handled? Are there too many steps in any of these processes? Are they efficient? Could the Internet/e-mail/file sharing be used in any way to speed up or streamline the process? If it can eliminate enough work by streamlining, a district may be able to avoid hiring additional staff.

What about high school students who need to enroll or register for classes every semester or year? Could this be done via the school's Web site on their own time?

Attendance at parent-teacher conferences is low. Yet conferences must go on. How can you get more bang for your buck in this area? If only 20 percent of parents typically attend, determine how much time is needed for this activity and schedule accordingly. For parents who don't have the ability or job flexibility to attend live conferences, send a report to parents via e-mail, or if you have the technology, have teachers make a brief video report to parents that can be delivered via e-mail. These tasks can be done in the time that was previously scheduled for conferences when the teachers sat idle.

Districts with extreme weather issues in the winter might consider a shorter school week during the peak heating season. Although this may wreak havoc on working parents' schedules, it could cut utility costs during that expensive heating season.

A four-day week has been considered by some districts for the purpose of saving gas in the school buses. With the costs skyrocketing, this portion of a school district's budget has been increasingly tight.

At the very least, a district must evaluate its bus usage patterns. Look at your district's school buses. How full are they? If they're only a third full at any given time, then your routes may need to be compressed or reworked. Especially with rising fuel costs, running more buses than necessary is a huge drain.

According to students, it's always either too hot or too cold in the school. Especially in older buildings with less than efficient windows and heating systems, an upgrade would translate into immediate savings.

Updating light fixtures not only saves electricity, but a higher quality of light may bring a boost of productivity by allowing students to see better.

If portions of a school building are not used at all during certain times of the day, such as the lunchroom that is deserted after lunch time is over, turn the heat in that room or area down earlier in the day rather than wait until the entire school is turned down in the evening.

Utility companies often will do an energy audit to point out inefficiencies and discuss improvements that will make the most sense in reducing energy usage. An independent consulting company may also be a good option. The district can contract to pay the consultant a percentage of the savings made by implementing the strategies outlined by the firm. **Extra tip:** try to determine if there is a consultant whose children attend the district's schools as this may translate into a lower fee or even, if lucky, a *pro bono* consultation.

You don't know what types of work can be done by parent volunteers until you ask. Sure, parents are busy , but there will always be a number of parents who *would* help, but have never been asked. Sending a note home with students or putting a blurb in the newsletter probably won't elicit the response you need for some serious help. Be creative and find a way to get the word out: *We need YOUR help finding ways to cut costs*!

Additionally, parents may also be willing to donate items to offset some of the school's expenses. It's not uncommon today to receive a traditional school-supplies-needed list and see items like packages of notebook paper, boxes of crayons, or tissues to be used by the entire classroom. What other items can a district ask parents to contribute?

Parents have also become accustomed to paying fees for things that were included a generation ago. Fees for using the textbooks not only build up a fund for purchase of newer versions, but they also give parents some idea of the costs incurred by districts to provide books and may translate into students' taking better care of books.

Sports programs also have been asking for fees for the athletes that help offset the cost of teams traveling to "away" games or meets, uniforms, and the costs incurred by locker room usage.

Many businesses who do any type of delivering for their services, such as companies that sell frozen foods door-to-door, the propane delivery companies, and even companies that sell products online have been adding what's called a "fuel surcharge" to their invoices and charges. School districts could also consider such a tactic to help offset the cost of busing.

If school buses didn't exist, parents would have to arrange the transportation themselves or pay a private company for transportation. It shouldn't be taken for granted that schools are going to fund transportation issues forever; parents who think of this as a service the school provides will be willing to assist in paying for it.

A Minnesota school district voted not to impose a fee, which was suggested for students living within a mile of the school only.[26] Concerns had been raised that, if not given a ride for free, the students might be walking to school instead. For

[26] Doug Belden, "$5.6M Cut in School District's Budget," February 22, 2006, www.twincities.com/mld/twincities/living/13929891.htm?template=contentModules/printstory.jsp, accessed on May 1, 2006.

some parents, that is a concern, especially for children in the elementary grades. This demonstrates that public input on any such fees is vitally important and that fees should be mandated across the board. If all bused students in that Minnesota district were to contribute equally, the fee would likely have been negligible.

Taking that line of thinking to the next level, what other parent-contributions could be requested? A $2 per family library fee to fund new book purchases for the year? A $5 fee to build a fund for new computers as they become obsolete? Obviously, school districts need to be selective and not simply hit parents with a slew of new fees at the beginning of the year.

Perhaps the fee could be one simple amount and each year the fee's beneficiary would rotate? This year, the fees will go exclusively to the fund for new library books. Next year, it will build a technology fund. This might be more palatable for parents who are on their own tight budgets, and of course, some parents simply may not be able to pay at all.

Parents aren't the only source of additional funding available to schools and teachers. New Web sites have sprouted up that offer any citizen opportunities to donate to a school or teacher of their *and* decide what the money is spent on. Teachers whose districts can't afford as many new books or supplies as they'd like can apply for grants on these Web sites and then have certain requirements for following up after the funds are received and used. If your district doesn't yet have its teachers working on these opportunities, perhaps you should check out these sites: **www.iloveschools.com** and **www.donorschoose. org**. These programs aren't available nationwide, so be sure to check to see if your schools qualify for the benefits of these sites.

Is budget time something the school board dreads? Does it seem that the public never is satisfied with the budgetary decisions made by the board?

The Madison, Wisconsin, school district took a unique approach to this issue early in 2006. They held week-long sessions where small groups of public members were invited to balance a mock school district budget of $100 and agree on how to eliminate $3.85 from that budget. The district plans to study the priorities identified by these trials to help them understand what's important to parents and others in the district. And hopefully the participants will take away some understanding of the complexity of the decision-making process that school board members face every year when their biggest bugaboo, the budget, needs to be balanced yet again.[27]

Another way to reach the public, whether to let them know what's going on or to get their assistance, is through the Internet.

Last spring, the Seattle, Washington, school district hosted an online survey for parents and members of the public to generate interest in their financial position and determine what the majority of people would suggest doing about their budget shortfall. The community rallied against a proposal that would close several schools in the district, but that change of heart may have to be only temporary.[28] However, their experience demonstrates how using the Internet to reach the public is faster and cheaper than sending out a mailing or sending home slips that get lost in book bags.

---

[27] Sandy Cullen, "Citizens Swing Ax at School Budget," January 23, 2006, www.madison.com/wsj/check/index.php?ntid=69781, accessed on May 1, 2006.

[28] Sanjay Bhatt, "New Test is Closing School Districts' Budget Gap," Mary 31, 2005, http://seattletimes.nwsource.com/html/localnews/2002293514_options31m.html, accessed on May 1, 2006.

Is your district planning to build new buildings? Many small or rural school districts where busing is extensively used are turning to a one location approach. In this manner, they have the district's entire student population under one roof. Separate wings are built for elementary, junior high, and high school students with a central portion used for the support services. Some have separate gymnasiums, cafeterias, and libraries that are age-appropriate.

The cost savings of a system like this are obvious. Busing students to multiple locations is logistically complicated and costly; sending every student to the same location just makes sense. It costs less to build one big building than three smaller buildings at different locations. Support staff can be housed in the same building, allowing for savings in transporting supplies, communicating inter-office, and possibly even needing less clerical staff.

School administrators have been both praised and bashed for allowing companies to place vending machines in their schools for a fee or a kickback on the profits. While any school needs to be sensitive to the nutritional needs of students and provide healthy choices in these machines, other companies are finding ways to get their ad space into schools as well.

Local and national companies are paying big bucks for naming rights to almost any part of a school. Athletic fields, libraries, even entire schools have been named because of a donation on the part of a business. While this practice is still somewhat controversial, it does exist.

Cutting positions is an unfortunate reality of budgeting for school districts. Some districts spend nearly 90 percent of their budget on salaries and benefits for employees. So no matter how creative you get with funding sources and having others kick in a little here and there, layoffs—or downsizing by attrition – that is, not replacing retiring or former employees, often end up playing a big role in cost cutting.

Schools try to avoid cutting teachers because of the move toward smaller class sizes and conflict with union contracts. However, administrative jobs often can be compacted so that fewer people can do the same amount of work. Clerical positions, janitorial staff, and maintenance workers are often the areas hardest hit by budget cutting. While no school district likes to cut positions, it is the harsh reality facing even this large group of nonprofit organizations throughout the country.

PART IV:

Cutting Costs that are Hidden or Overlooked

"Nothing in this world can take the place of persistence. Talent will not; nothing is more common that unsuccessful people with talent. Genius will not; unrewarded genius is almost a proverb. Education will not; the world is full of educated derelicts. Persistence and determination alone are omnipotent."

— CALVIN COOLIDGE,
30TH PRESIDENT OF THE UNITED STATES

In 1908 Henry Ford had pioneered what would become the touchstone of manufacturing simplicity: the moving assembly line. This bold move gave Ford Motor Company the competitive edge for decades to come.

Fast forward two United States Presidents to the last days of Franklin Roosevelt's tenure. Japanese automaker, Toyota, had been a pioneer in getting production parts brought to the assembly line in the right amounts at the right time. But the company suffered the sting of defeat in the thick of World War II, when their famed just-in-time system left quality behind.

Taking a lesson from the father of the company's founder, Sakichi Toyoda, manager Taiichi Ohno recalled an automatic weaving loom invented by the elder Toyoda that would stop automatically when a thread broke. Realizing that this concept, stopping production when a problem was sensed, was needed to bring Toyota's quality back up to par, he began to refine what would later be known as the Toyota Production System.

The Toyota Production System has been studied by numerous professionals for decades, but one pair of researchers, James Womack and Daniel Jones, summarized all of the tools of Toyota's efficiency and high quality into one word: **lean.**

Yes, lean, as in no waste, no fat. Bare-bones. Cut-to-the-chase. Many clichés have similar lines of thinking. Lean is much more than simply a thought. Lean is a full-fledged production philosophy that has been helping manufacturers and many other business types all over the planet emulate the efficiency and high quality of the companies who laid the foundation for these high standards.

Just being popular in terms of improving production, however, just isn't enough. Sometimes it takes a little nudging for a company to decide that they, too, could benefit from trimming away some of their own excess baggage. Understanding the underlying principle of being lean: eliminating waste at every point and applying it efficiently are two different things.

Enter Productivity Inc., a Connecticut-based consulting firm that specializes in implementing lean principles in companies world-wide. One of Productivity's favorite stories is that of Cadco Ltd., a small manufacturer that produces and sells products for the food service industry, such as warming trays, buffet servers, and countertop ranges. Their products are sold at high-end retailers such as Neiman Marcus and the Chefs Catalog.

But despite a successful line of products, Cadco had serious issues with their production. It took too long to get a product built. Holdups were evident everywhere in the process: old-fashioned production lines were pokey, inventory was spotty or overflowing, costs were soaring, and orders went unfilled. Something had to give and fast. But how quickly could being lean help?

How about one day? Just one single day was all it took, with the right expertise. A consultant from Productivity, Inc., put all his energy into the one-day contract he had to turn things around at Cadco Limited.

He started off by studying one production line: the warming tray. He watched as parts arrived on the line, workers worked, and products came off the line, timing every portion of the process and making some mental notes. He talked to people who worked the line and managed the line. Knowing that they needed to increase daily production by 60 percent to keep up with current orders, he proposed a plan: simplify the line.

The warming trays weren't difficult to make. How much more simple can it get? Just because the process wasn't complex didn't mean it wasn't rife with waste and inefficiency. To go lean is to eliminate waste and inefficiencies. The consultant questioned every step of every process in the production line and scrutinized whether it was necessary, efficient, or wasteful.

By moving some people around on the line, timing the delivery of parts to the line better (just-in-time) and giving brief training to the workers on how to work smarter not just faster, the consultant observed as the warming trays began to churn down the line at speeds unthinkable just eight hours earlier.

By the end of the second day (the one-day contract was extended), Cadco's president and managers were convinced that Productivity Inc., had just what they needed to improve their production and product. They achieved their 60 percent increase in production of the warming trays and now wanted to implement lean strategies in other parts of their business.

The next thing that Productivity's consultant tackled was production schedules. Being able to visualize the tasks necessary to complete a function is an important ingredient in any manufacturing process. Therefore, a flexible production schedule was created that also shared all the information about what was going on with the employees. They could see on the schedule what was to be done and get to it without being directed by a supervisor.

Nothing at Cadco escaped the keen eye of Productivity, Inc. The plant's entire layout was eventually updated to allow for more ease and efficiency and to create empty usable space for new production lines that wouldn't have been possible before.

The company was able to eliminate their overtime work and meet all of their production needs in a standard eight-hour day. However, employees missed the lost overtime pay. The company realized that there must be some benefit to the employees to encourage them to continue with their efforts to implement lean strategies.

So Cadco created a bonus program that rewarded quality work on the production lines. The cost savings created by implementing lean practices more than made up for the bonuses paid, and the overall effect was one full of positives.

Production is up. Costs are down. Employees are productive. Everyone is happier. Productivity's lean approach took a company whose troubles seemed to have transparent causes and trained every one of Cadco's employees to become a lean-mean-cost-reducing-producing-machine!

CHAPTER

21 **Growth**

When do you grow? Does it happen automatically, or is it something you plan for and shape as it occurs? Every business intends to grow and most even plan for it. Here are some new ways to think about growth and look for ways to achieve it.

One Midwestern concrete components manufacturer has recently grown because their customers asked them to! Pretech Corporation of Kansas City, Kansas, manufactures components for wastewater treatment but until recently did not manufacture any concrete pipe. Concrete wastewater pipes needed for new construction are very heavy and generally purchased within a couple hundred miles of the work site. Even though there are two other companies in that area that manufacture these items, there was room for a little more competition.

The five million dollar investment has brought Pretech into the concrete pipe market in style, with the best labor-saving machinery and technology that will make them competitive right from the start. And they owe this great idea to their customers.

When you do grow, however, it's important to try to keep costs from following in your footsteps. You don't want to increase your costs just to achieve growth — that isn't progress.

Balance your risks and opportunities, said Lianabel Oliver in her book *The Cost Management Toolbox*. If you are seeing or feeling risks, such as rising interest rates, troubles with your raw materials suppliers, then go searching for opportunities. Shop for lending institutions with better rates or a different supplier rather than just doing what you're already doing and hoping for the best.

Would you be able to grow cheaper and faster by moving to a location where the local economy is eager to have you set up shop? Cities and regions are always trying to attract new industry and some of them offer some enticements for coming to their town.

Pulling from a pool of talented workers at one location might be worth the effort to move. You can't grow without growing your workforce.

Can you serve two segments of the buying public with the same product? Some pharmaceutical companies package the same over-the-counter drugs in two ways: name brand and generic. Since there will always be one segment of the buying public that demands a name brand product and another segment that will always purchase a generic if available, why not get in on both markets and do the same with your product?

Can your product be used for something other than originally intended? If someone has found another use for your product, consider marketing it with that angle. For example, the wax-coated paper known as "freezer paper" is marketed for its ability to keep meats and foods from getting freezer burn. However, years ago quilters discovered its usefulness in making patterns, and it's commonly used by crafters now.

Match your production's growth to the market's growth. While it may be an admirable goal to double your output, it won't do you much good if the market would be flooded by doing so (forcing prices down in the process).

Minnesota—the state that gave us Spam®, Post-It® Notes and

water skiing — has long been the home and a favorite vacation spot for fishermen and water sports enthusiasts. But a new breed of vacationers, retirees, and locals has sprouted up in the past decade: those who want a higher-powered, bigger, or fancier boat than those of years past and have the income available to purchase and maintain these items.

Willey's Marine, Inc., has been serving the watersports population in and around McGregor, Minnesota, for many years, and the owners had built a thriving business in their rural northern county of Aitkin. But when they saw that their clientele was asking them to service and store their higher-end luxury power boats, they realized that the local market had grown enough that they, too, should grow along with it.

An extensive search of luxury powerboat manufacturers turned up the perfect fit for Willey's Marine. In 2006, the company became Minnesota's first, and exclusive, dealer of Campion boats.

These Canada-made beauties go beyond luxurious. They are stunning to look at, with gel-coated exteriors and sleek lines. But the technology that comes along with some models is really impressive. How about an air-conditioned cabin with a flat-screen TV? There's a model that offers fishermen all the gizmos and accessories they want, plus super powerful boats for the water-skiing crowd.

While Willey's Marine probably could have created this new product line years ago, they waited until there was a full market demand and then supplied it. By properly interpreting the market and demand of their clients, they have grown their business in a way that should be nothing but positive.

To grow larger, become smaller. Sell off portions of your business that aren't in line with your main business. Trying to do too many different things at once can blur your focus and hamper growth.

A case in point here is Tyco International, Ltd., a company known for its industrial valves. Over the years, the company expanded and got into other businesses, including healthcare, plastics, coated products, electronics, and security systems. After Tyco's CEO was sent to prison for looting the company, the board of directors was left with harsh decisions about what portions of the company to close to recoup its losses. Late in 2005, divisions that produced plastics, adhesives, and coated products were sold. More might be sold or eliminated as Tyco works hard to turn around from years of mismanagement and abuse.

To grow steadily, don't grow. Don't rush to get into every product line in your general business, especially those whose technology is rapidly changing. You may not be able to keep up with the pack. Instead, continue to grow steadily in the areas where you have a strong foothold.

To grow, ally. Develop strategic alliances with companies whose products are complementary to yours. The company that produces baked goods wants to introduce a new line of specialty cheesecakes with cookie crumb crusts. Who do they ally with? Why, a nationwide cookie company whose customers would try anything that has their cookies in it, of course!

Early 2006 saw the alliance of yet another American company with a Canadian manufacturer. HomeAire, a national distributor of products that are designed to improve indoor air quality, has teamed up with Duo Vac, a company that has exclusively manufactured central vacuum systems for almost 40 years. HomeAire already manufactures numerous products for its customer base, so why didn't they just get into the vacuum business by creating their own vacuums? Some companies realize that they shouldn't try to "be all and do all" in their markets.

And Duo Vac? Why didn't this Canadian company pursue opening their own division in the United States, where there was no authorized distributor?

This is where alliances come to play. Duo Vac wants to get a hold in the central vacuum market here; HomeAire wants to add a top notch, quality and reliable central vac system to their product line. It was a match made in alliance heaven!

This move opens a whole new market for Duo Vac, whose quality and reliability will almost surely make the product a success in the United States.

Try to keep an open mind about near-future technology. How is it changing? Will your products need major engineering overhauls due to technology changes? Will your product be obsolete or have very little demand? Consider the fate of products such as typewriters, cassette tapes or even, more currently, video tapes and players. Don't assume that because your product is well received today that it will stay that way.

Analyze the demographics of the population that your product targets. What will that same demographic group look like 10 years from now? Does the next generation value the same things your current demographic group value? Are you flexible enough to change with the demographics?

Analyzing the demographics of your target population might lead you to uncover new trends based on your findings, opening up a whole new product or line for you.

If your company is going to be outgrowing your physical space in the foreseeable future, don't wait till you're desperate to start looking. Hasty purchases or leases often leave you with the least bargaining power. Start comparison-shopping early and you may peg a deal that will make it worth relocating sooner than later.

If you are building a new location, strategically place it near your largest customers. This will create savings when shipping product to them.

When you make a capital investment, be sure that it will increase production or reduce downtime. If it doesn't really add to your bottom line in some way, then perhaps you really don't need it.

Investments in new product lines or changes to existing product lines are wise only if you have data that shows your customers really need or want these products or changes.

Another way to look at capital investments is to analyze the end goal and then go back to determine if the investment proposed really does meet that goal, or ask yourself "Are there alternatives?" You may find that your goals can be met with a less-expensive device or by modifying a process or item you already have.

When considering an investment in new technology, try to analyze what it will cost you not to invest in it now. If the costs to catch up later are high, it may add more weight to your plan to invest now.

The investment in technology is always important for computer companies such as Hewlett-Packard. Even while the company spent most of 2005 in cost-cutting efforts that included more than 15,000 layoffs, they predicted that their investment in IT technology in 2006 would be substantial. Why would a company invest so heavily, up to $2.2 billion, when it's trying to cut costs? Because they can't afford not to. If HP wants to create and sell cutting-edge technology to its customers, it must be prepared to get some for itself first to meet competition from Dell and IBM.

You may be doing your company a disservice and actually raise costs by failing to invest in more sophisticated inventory and accounting systems. What worked for you as a small company may not grow with you.

If worse comes to worst, you can postpone plans for your new product line. The money earmarked for that can now be freed up for other uses.

If you've already begun a major project, avoid cost overruns by hiring a professional project manager who can be expected to bring it in within budget and on time.

Projects intended to produce growth may or not actually do so. It's easy to get projects started, but they don't always produce the results you were hoping for. When the budget belt needs to be tightened, immediately discontinue all projects that aren't imperative for current needs and those that are showing only lukewarm results. Your project success might be strengthened by focusing your attention on fewer projects.

Funding for projects should be given incrementally. Only fund a project through a certain stage, and then demand verifiable data of the project's worth and stability before funding the next stage.

All projects should have a targeted return on investment (ROI) and a timeline associated with it.

"If you're going to be successful in growing your company," said Walden, "You've got to control the whole dynamic. You have to do things you didn't go into business to do." That means that you have to become a mini-expert in all facets of business."

Why do businesses fail to grow? Two of the largest growth-inhibitors, according to Walden, are these:

1. Failure to bring in repeat customers. One unhappy customer is one more than you should ever want. Bad news spreads fast.

2. Not getting every possible customer in the door to begin with. This can be accomplished by almost every type of business using the Price Leader method (see Chapter 7).

Biz Wiz Says . . . "Successful people are looking at their business in total."

—Patrick Walden

SMALL-SCALE GROWTH

By "small scale" I mean simply growing your company by hiring additional employees, even just one at a time. But having a bigger payroll doesn't make your company grow unless you have additional business to be doing and profits to be made.

Four Ways to Know When to Grow Your Workforce

1. An increase in demand for your products or services that isn't seasonal, freaky, or temporary is a good reason to increase your workforce. Don't immediately jump into hiring, however. Wait until you're certain it is a growing trend you see.

2. Don't wait too long, however, or you'll over-tax your current workforce. You don't want to lose current employees due to an overload of work. That would be counter-productive because it would cause more hiring to be done.

3. You have excess revenue from slowly increasing sales that needs to be put back into the business. Hiring is one way to reinvest in your company.

4. If you're considering a new product line or wanting to expand your current lineup in a way that requires workers with a different set of skills, you can re-train current workers, unless you can't spare them from their current jobs, or hire new ones.

When you do need to hire additional workers, however, don't do it in haste. Hiring people just to have people available to do the work won't always give you productive employees. You may get lucky, but spending time carefully screening and selecting your new employees will give you the most bang for your buck from your investment.

GROWING INTO E-COMMERCE

When your company joins the millions of others doing e-business, you'll find that there are many approaches and different ideas about this new means of commerce. Here are just a few ideas which vary and may even contradict each other. Like most things in life, e-business isn't a one-size-fits-all proposition.

Build your own e-commerce expertise right within your company rather than outsourcing it. Once you're in e-business, you're going to be there for the foreseeable future, so save yourself money in the long run by having all the available talent you need for e-commerce to be successful.

How do you compete in a world of e-commerce? You have to stand out and have something about your company, site, or product that makes people want to buy from you rather than the several thousand other companies that came up on the search engine's results page.

15 Ways to Stand Out in E-commerce

1. **Web-only specials.** Many retailers have deals that can only be purchased on the Web site, not even in the retail stores at that price.

2. **Check-out specials.** Offer special deals on similar or complementary products to what's being purchased, available one-time-only at the point of checkout.

3. **E-mail ads and newsletters** to anybody who will give you their e mail address.

4. **Coupons and codes for discounts** available in these newsletters/e-mail ads will keep them reading and coming back.

5. **Swap banner ads** with another site that sells complementary products to yours.

6. Make sure you're **subscribed on every search engine** out there, even the small guys.

7. **Affiliate marketing** is such a no-brainer; don't overlook it to generate revenue.

8. **Don't get the doldrums.** Keep your site fresh, with new specials, new product announcements, reviews, and anything else that your customer needs to know.

9. **Shopping cart and check-out security.** Don't skimp on the provider for these services; customers may become leery if they're not absolutely certain of the safety.

10. **The need for speed on the Internet is insatiable.** If your site is slow to load, people will move on to the next hit on the search engine's results page. Don't compromise speed for glitz.

11. **Take a turn at ordering from your own site.** You may see things differently when you're on the customer-end of it.

12. **Don't leave people uncertain about your product.** Have sufficient information and photos available for them to make an informed decision.

13. **Comparison shopping.** Offer the ability to compare similar products on your site in a side-by-side format.

14. As with any business, **repeat customers can be your greatest ally.** While you don't physically see them, your systems should be able to recognize them and reward them for their repeat business.

15. **Be exact.** Any errors during the shopping process, from incompatible prices (the price on the page is different than it is once it's in the shopping cart) to informing the customer that the item isn't in stock once they get to checkout, will likely lose you a customer for good. Slipshod e-commerce sites often don't last long.

22

Rent and Building Costs

MAINTENANCE

Be familiar with your maintenance schedule and requirements. Tour your facility and choose a topic of the day, such as polishing floors. Locate all the places in your facility that require this maintenance task and determine how often it's done, how long it takes, and what supplies it uses. Can that timing be spread out a little, saving labor and the cost of materials? If you can reduce every task just a little bit, you might be able to find a way for the department to manage all tasks without increasing department size.

If your company has its own leased dumpsters and pays for disposal on a "per empty" basis, then instruct the waste management company *not* to empty a dumpster until it's completely filled. Have the maintenance department keep dumpsters locked until the preceding one is filled.

If you use an outside company for your cleaning needs, be sure to review the weekly billings and make lists of areas neglected — or not up to your standards — by the crews. Get your money's worth.

Your wholesale or bulk cleaning supplies are only a good deal if they're mixed in the proper ratios and used in a cost-conscious manner. Assign one person to mix all cleaning solutions and keep an inventory of how much is used daily for one month. This should give you an idea of how quickly you go through solutions and help you identify waste quickly.

You may be able to purchase some heavily discounted cleaning solutions from other businesses, especially restaurants, that are going out of business.

When remodeling or building, make sure you choose materials that are easy to maintain and clean.

Buy replacement parts for equipment or cleaning in bulk or ask for wholesale pricing from your supplier.

If your customers do most of their business with you by the Internet or by orders placed through salesmen, be thrifty about your business's décor and frills. An expensive attorney needs a conference room with a mahogany table and leather chairs. Perhaps you don't.

Another way to be thrifty with your furnishings is to have your current items refinished rather than replace them. Check out **www. therefinishingtouch.com** for a look at what one such company does for hotels, universities, and the federal government.

The expensive paint detailing on company vehicles can be replaced by inexpensive decals that stick on and are cheap to replace when they fade or come off.

Tools are important for every maintenance crew. Centralize your tool storage so that all crews and shifts have access to the same set of tools.

Have maintenance personnel officially check out tools and return them at the end of their shift.

Mark your company-owned tools with identifying marks or serial numbers for theft deterrent or to determine who checked out which specific tool.

Be pro-active in inspecting your facilities to stay compliant with government regulators like OSHA or with local building codes. Doing so will not only save potential fines but is good preventive care for your buildings.

If it's broke, do you fix it or replace it? This is a good question that often is quickly answered by "Replace it!" But don't make this an automatic policy. Check out your options. Your building's roof is leaking. But your building sits on leased land. Your lease is up in three years. Do you replace a leaking roof? Not until you've completed negotiations on a new lease, or that money may be lost to the benefit of the land's owners, even though it's your building.

Conversely, there are occasions when it's cheaper to replace than to fix. The cost of outside repairmen, if your own maintenance personnel can't do the job, may be so high that getting a new item with a warranty might be more cost-efficient. However, be sure not to replace expensive equipment that will soon be obsolete. Leasing is the way to go there.

LEASE IT OR BUILD IT?

Whether you lease or build, the same rule applies to commercial ventures as to home owners: location, location, location. Sometimes businesses are successful just because they are in the right place at the right time.

When leasing, you'll pay a bundle for a prime location, but the visibility it can afford may lead to a much larger customer base than a location off the beaten path.

Accessibility is as important as visibility. A beautiful new building along a frontage road might get a lot of visibility from the highway that goes by, but if it's virtually impossible for traffic to off the highway to your building, you may have a problem.

Even extras like the availability of parking, the lighting in your parking lot, and the condition of the lot itself, can send silent messages to your customers. A large retail chain that lets its parking lots become full of potholes and doesn't replace bulbs in their outdoor lights is telling customers, "We are too poor to keep things up" or "We don't care about your safety and comfort." Neither of those is messages you want to send. So if you own the lot, keep it neat, safe, and maintained and if you lease, insist that the building's owner take this responsibility.

Try to renegotiate your rent. If there is a fair amount of available office space out there, your landlord might be willing to renegotiate rather than risk your not paying rent or breaking your lease and moving elsewhere.

If you can afford a long-term lease and are able to pre-pay for it, you'll often be able to negotiate a better deal than if you want a short-term lease or are paying monthly.

Postpone plans to build a new location as a way to cut pre-planned expenses from the budget and boost the bottom line.

Don't pave paradise and put up a parking lot! If your overnight shift generally leaves at 7 a.m. but your a.m. shift is expected to punch in by 6:45, you're going to have a parking shortage because, in essence, your parking lot needs to be large enough to accommodate two whole shifts at once for the 15-minute overlap. Stagger your start-stop times for employees so that there are always employees leaving and coming, thus using the same parking spaces.

If you stagger ending times for the overnight shift so that one-third of them leaves at 6:30 a.m. then one-third of the morning crew can fit into the spaces by 6:45 a.m. At 6:45 a.m., another one-third of the overnight crew leaves, so that by 7 a.m., the second third of your morning crew can use their parking spots. At 7, the last group from the overnight crew leaves, opening up spaces for the third wave of the morning crew to arrive at 7:15 a.m.

If this pattern continues, everybody still works the same number of hours every day but nobody is left running for the time clock because they couldn't find a parking space.

OFFICE SPACE IDEAS

Share office space among employees who are only sporadically in the office, such as sales people or part time employees,. If an employee is using a computer to its fullest potential, there is less need for their own filing cabinet and other things typically filling office space.

Sublet unused or freed-up office space to other companies. And better yet, offer some services to your new neighbor at agreed-upon rates. For example, your day spa might have some unused space that a one-man real estate appraiser might be willing to rent. And while he's away from the office, he could route his calls to your receptionist who would take messages or relay calls to his cell phone at a set rate.

You can rent out even less than a full office as well. In some cities where office space is at a premium, companies can rent out merely a desk complete with computer and telephone line by-the-hour.

A nice conference room can be rented out after-hours to a variety of professionals, such as private therapists, or for educational seminars, community education classes such as first aid or CPR.

BUSINESS INSURANCE

If you pay insurance on a number of buildings your company owns, your insurance company may finance the amount and allow you to pay the premium over 12 months. This can ease the budget woes of having the entire amount available at once.

However, if you can get a better rate of financing from your bank and pay the insurance policy in full, you may be able to negotiate a payment-in-full discount which will further offset the interest paid to the bank.

When budgeting for your company's insurance on items like company vehicles, have your agent determine that your vehicles are properly classified. A simple error in classification could result in your overpaying. If you find you've overpaid in the last year, try to negotiate a rebate or refund.

An annual audit of your insurance may turn up the fact that you are insuring something that no longer exists, including company vehicles, equipment, buildings, or that you are carrying insurance beyond what is necessary.

Additionally, thoroughly investigate just *what* is insured by each policy you have. You may find that you're double-insuring some items that are covered under two policies. This is especially true if you don't have all your policies with the same insurer.

Don't make the mistake of under-insuring anything for your business. Some business policies have a clause that may force you to bear some of the loss when you make a claim if you've under-insured. Be sure you and your insurance company agree on the value of items and properties you own and that you are fully insured.

Another big insurance "oops!" is the issue of rescission. If an insurance company discovers misleading or false information in your application or documentation. Even if the information wasn't intentionally meant to mislead, an insurance company can rescind your policy from the date it was given by simply refunding your premiums. In effect, it's as if you were never insured to begin with. This is a serious matter, so take extra care in all insurance applications and documentation. Rules vary from state to state as well.

23 Utilities and Water

The first place to look into savings on your utilities is the utility company itself. They often will send someone over to go through your building and suggest energy-efficient items or practices to reduce your bills. Also, check with your utility companies to see if you're eligible for any rebates. Often, you have to ask for them to receive them.

- If you have a choice of utility providers, compare their costs and perks.

- Have an ongoing energy management plan.

- Reducing energy costs may have a positive effect on your environmental compliance plan.

- Make employees aware of the utility costs your company incurs by posting copies of monthly bills in lunch rooms or hallways.

Ask employees for their suggestions on how to cut back on energy costs. A quick eye might catch something everybody else has overlooked. Make it fun and sponsor a contest with prizes for the best suggestion to the zaniest suggestion.

PHONE BILLS

- Overbilling is a serious problem for some phone companies. Keep close tabs on yours and find another provider if it continues despite repeated calls to their customer service department.

- Review records monthly and make employees responsible for long-distance phone calls.

- Monitor your company's toll-free numbers to be sure employees aren't receiving phone calls from long-distance friends and family on those lines. A common misconception is that "It's free!"

- Shop around for your company's toll-free rate supplier, as rates can vary greatly.

- Though they make a compelling sales pitch and the package deal seems great, it may not be wise to have all of your telecom needs met by the same company. Ask about individual prices from several different companies. You may be surprised.

ELECTRICITY

- Assign someone to take a walk around the building and double check that all lights and office machines are turned off at night. While it doesn't seem like they *use* that much electricity when not in full operation, it does add up over the course of the year.

- Route all weekend faxes to one machine instead of leaving them on all over the company all weekend.

- Buy inexpensive occupancy sensors that can turn off lights when no one is in a room.

- Replace high-energy light bulbs with low-energy

fluorescent bulbs, which are available in sizes to fit most lamps and light fixtures.

- Relocate lights closer to where they're actually needed, and you'll need fewer lights.

HEAT AND AIR CONDITIONING

- Study your company's energy consumption pattern over each day's period. Install a computer-run system to adjust heat and lights to coincide with these usage patterns.

- If you don't have it automated, manually turn down heat when your buildings aren't in use. However, because it's not always easy to remember to do these things, install programmable thermostats.

- Cover all factory ventilation fans with plastic during the winter to prevent heat loss or cold air coming in.

- Set your air conditioning no lower than 78 degrees for maximum efficiency. While this may seem warm, imagine a 78-degree day. It's do-able. Heat should be set at 68 degrees.

- On hot, sunny days, draw curtains or shades down to deflect the sunlight coming in. This can decrease the temperature indoors as well as help avoid things like fading of office furniture or merchandise due to the sun.

Another item that helps the sun's rays stay away is an awning. Install them on all southern and western-facing windows for built-in shade when the sun hits them. Solar window shades and curtains can deflect the sunshine away from your windows in the summer and draw the warmth in during the winter.

Perhaps two of the most important efficiency tools are your furnace/heating system and your cooling system. Regular maintenance will help them run at their best level of efficiency to keep your bills low.

WATER

Every business uses water, whether to produce their product or merely in their employee restrooms. Water is a scare resource in many parts of the world, and even in some portions of the United States at certain times of the year.

Farming is an industry that requires a lot of water, and even small wineries such as those that dot the map all over California can use millions of gallons of water every year irrigating their crops.

The Green Business Program is a cooperative effort of many federal and state environmental agencies and utility companies in southern California whose mission it is to encourage and teach businesses in a seven-county area to be "Green." A company that wishes to earn their Green Business Certification can work closely with a county coordinator who will help them build a plan for reducing waste and resources and bringing their business practices in line with all environmental regulations.

Companies that "go green" share a commitment to the principles of this program which are:

- Committing to a healthy environment
- Complying with and exceeding all environmental and other laws
- Continuing development and implementation of waste and pollution-prevention practices
- Being an environmental leader in each community
- Striving to improve their own efforts and those of every business

Wineries that have "gone green" have reduced water by

purchasing equipment for cleaning that reduces water usage by replacing a lot of water with high-pressure stream of less water. The job gets done quicker with less water.

Auto repair shops have reduced water by eliminating car washes unless truly necessary, while hotels and motels are encouraged to install water-saving features in their bathrooms. Landscapers who join the program are educated about hydro-zoning, which is simply grouping plants with similar watering needs together in a landscape setting. This helps homeowners reduce water usage by not over watering some plants in a grouping due to the high water needs of a few. They are also encouraged to suggest drought-tolerant plants to reduce maintenance watering by homeowners.

Companies in the printing business have numerous ways they can save water, but one of the biggest ways is to print on recycled content papers. This not only saves a tree but also the large amount of water necessary to turn wood into paper.

Restaurants and retail shops can reduce water in ways similar to hotels: by using low-flow bathroom fixtures. Additionally, it's suggested that you not serve water at the start of a meal unless requested by the patrons.

All business types may qualify to "go green" and there are a variety of ways to achieve this status, but nearly every business can benefit from having a complete assessment done by each of their utility providers. For information about this program, see their Web site at www.greenbiz.ca.gov/index.html.

WASTE

All businesses produce waste, according to the U.S. Environmental Protection Agency. Whether it be paper waste or toxic waste or anything in between, it's still the same: it's something that you generate that you must get rid of. And in many cases, it costs you money to do so.

The EPA has a Web site to help you plan for your business's waste reduction by helping you to reduce it, reuse it, or recycle it. In addition to ideas on how to get started and make a plan, the page contains success stories of companies that have made a significant difference in their waste and created significant savings for themselves in the process. For information abut and links to their waste reduction programs, visit their Web site at **www.epa.gov/oppt/p2home/assist/sbg.htm**.

For companies that are just beginning to evaluate their waste issues, the EPA offers these suggestions:

- Start off small — target one or two materials for reduction
- Focus first on ideas that require minimal capital investment
- Involve all employees in planning and implementation

24 Office Supplies and Office Machines

OFFICE SUPPLIES

Reduce your office supplies and go paperless. Computers can store scanned images and documents, and CD and DVD burners make permanent storage and quick retrieval a cinch. Do not hesitate any longer on your plans to eliminate your filing cabinets!

Going paperless doesn't just apply to documents you've already created and stored. Make an effort to use e-mail for your business correspondence. Although some still consider it tacky, e-mail is quickly gaining a mainstream usage in the business world beyond memos and quick announcements.

However, every office does need to print items. The big question is this: how much paper do you really use? How much does it really cost to print things at your office? How could you possibly answer those questions?

Simple. By using print asset management from a vendor such as Pharos Systems International, you can audit your paper and printer usage, track and record every item printed from every user in your company network. Pharos Systems serves over 1,000 companies in 22 countries around the globe with all their printing management needs.

Employees may not even be aware of what it costs to print a document. What does it cost to photocopy that manual? Companies themselves are not tuned into the cost of printing, so all too often the employees are even less tuned in. Especially when it comes to employees using copiers and printers for non-work related items, costs are ignored.

One spear of Pharos Systems International's arsenal of cost-reduction for printing is their Informed Print technology. This program forces users of the network printers to read a popup box before their item is sent to the printer. The box kindly informs users of the cost to print that job. By choosing not to print the item, once the cost is known, a user can be brought into the company's cost-saving initiative. When employees buy into your desire for reducing print waste, they will modify their printing behaviors.

Making employees informed and accountable is just one part of the process of modifying behaviors at your company. And companies like Pharos Systems International are assisting by putting technology to work for you, not against you! Visit Pharos Systems International at: **www.pharos.com**.

Large corporations that send out thousands of annual reports have been making them shorter, plainer, and even paperless! All the fancy things you put on or in your reports might be costing you more money than you think. Plastic front sheet? Spiral bound? Are all those items truly necessary?

Paper mills may be willing to purchase large quantities of scrap paper of certain grades. If you have some space to store it correctly, why not let it pile up for six months rather than fill your trash cans with it?

Office supplies have a way of slipping out of the workplace, hitching rides in lunch boxes, purses, and shirt pockets. Lock supply cabinets to keep them from escaping!

And you'll never guess where many office supplies hide. Why, in the desk drawers and other stash-spots of your employees. Yes, silly as it sounds, many office workers hoard their favorite supplies per chance there will be a shortage. This doesn't just happen in offices, either, but in nearly every company where supplies of any sort are used.

For example, a teacher I know told me a bizarre story of her first day at a very large, well-funded public school in a major Midwestern city. The school had just been remodeled, all new equipment was ordered and installed, and when the teachers reported for duty two weeks before school opened, their first task was to set up their classrooms.

The principal gave them each keys to their new rooms, which were bare except for the new furniture. There were no supplies of any sort. When she asked where to obtain supplies, such as pencils, paper, glue, crayons, and all the other necessities, the new teacher was directed to the supply room.

When she arrived, the pandemonium inside was something near riot. All the teachers already assembled were grabbing cases of paper, whole boxes of glue, scissors, tape, stickers—anything they could get their hands on, and running pell-mell down the halls to their assigned room, depositing the items and returning as quickly as they could for more.

Only later did she realize what this was all about. The school district was known to order supplies at the beginning of the year and expected their teachers to ration it out and make it last all year. Teachers who had been in this district for years had developed a system of grabbing everything they could up-front and bartering with each other throughout the year. I'll trade you two bottles of *my* glue for thirty of *your* pencils. It didn't matter so much that they had a balanced amount of all supplies, so long as they had a stash of *something* that they could barter with later.

Now, it doesn't take much to see that this school district's system of ordering office supplies was not working. If, to take advantage of bulk discounts, they ordered only once a year, so be it. However, they failed to set up a system where the supplies were doled out over time. This lead to a very human reaction: hoarding. Luckily, this system has since been obliterated by proper controls.

The lesson here is this: even if you buy 10,000 Post-it pads at once, don't put them all in the supply cabinet. And if you do, by all means don't leave it unlocked and unaccounted for! Even if employees don't take them home for personal use, hoarding will ensue, and you'll be left with what appears to be a shortage.

Even employees who aren't intentionally hoarding can accumulate vast quantities of supplies over time. Here's a good exercise for your office. Hand out small boxes to every office worker with a desk and instruct them to empty their desks of all office supplies except for a minimum necessary, such as a few pens and a few note pads. You'll be amazed at what is pulled out of desks that can be returned to the supply cabinet for use by all.

Encourage employees to reuse items like large envelopes and file folders. Designate spots in your office for collection of such items, the same as you'd collect soda cans for recycling.

Do you really need to *print* a report or memo to distribute it? Find ways to use your internal network to distribute items that will be read once and disposed of. Or you might print one copy and then have it circulated. Have everybody who reads it initial it so you know who's seen it. Items that are printed for internal use only should always use both sides of the paper.

Reports that are normally sent to customers or investors can be posted on the company's Web site instead of being printed and mailed.

When you are printing something for internal use only don't worry about making a hand-written change to a typo. Office policies should allow these types of items for internal use.

Unwanted mail contains also paper that you must recycle or

get rid of. A good site with information on how to eliminate unwanted business mail can be found at: **www.ciwmb.ca.gov/ BizWaste/OfficePaper/MailReduce.htm**.

OFFICE MACHINES

The technology of office machines is rapidly changing. What was a novelty a decade ago is now either a necessity or a dinosaur. Use the services of an appraiser for your office equipment to be sure you're not overpaying taxes on it.

When your office machines are replaced by newer items, don't junk them. Believe it or not, somewhere on the planet there's someone to whom that item may be very valuable. Sell old office equipment at an online auction site or through a dealer in used office equipment. Another option is to donate your old office equipment to a charity that will either use it or sell it themselves. Be sure to get a receipt to claim a tax write-off.

When you purchase or lease new equipment, don't automatically jump at the extended service contracts. If they didn't make money on them, dealers wouldn't offer them.

A small, local dealer may not have had a competitive price for the purchase of your new equipment, but they may be cheaper for servicing it than an out-of-town dealer.

Many common office machines aren't difficult to perform regular or preventative maintenance on. Assign someone handy at your company to be the resident maintenance personnel.

PRINTERS

Purchase remanufactured, cleaned, and refilled ink cartridges for your desktop printers, if available, or purchase the ink and refill your existing cartridges yourself. Assign one employee to test this method and track the number of pages printed with a brand new cartridge and a refilled one if you're concerned about the output.

If you are printing a document and then revise just a word here and there, only reprint the pages you changed, so long as your changes didn't renumber the pages or shift information downward or upward.

Check your printer's options to see if you can set a default for two-sided printing. The printer will alert you when you need to turn your pile of papers over. Eliminate mailing labels by printing addresses directly onto envelopes from your contact manager program.

PHOTOCOPIERS

Here's one way your photocopier can save you money. The use of carbon paper has gone by the wayside, but "carbonless" forms are still popular in some industries. They are not without their problems, however. The quality of print on consecutive sheets decreases and there may be more copies than truly needed. Considering the cost of carbonless forms, it might be cheaper to have a one-part form and photocopy it after it's signed or filled out.

Save money by not causing paper jams in your photocopier. Check the owner's manual for the right way to load paper into the paper trays. Or if you're opening a new ream of paper, check for an arrow printed on one end. That will tell you which side goes up. It does make a difference.

When you're in the market for a new photocopier, consider the investment in an automatic duplexing unit. If it's easy for people to duplex, then you'll be more comfortable in demanding employees do so for the sake of saving paper.

Another nice feature that some newer copiers have is the ability to print more than one page onto the same sheet of paper. For instance, two sheets of information on 8.5x11 sheets can be printed (shrunk first of course) onto one side of 11x8.5 paper. In some circumstances, this can be a great feature to have.

Of course, make sure any copier you purchase, or any office machine for that matter, is certified Energy Star efficient.

FAXES

Fax machines have hidden costs that are easy to forget about. Labor, the paper used, the toner, maintenance, long distance charges, time lost for busy numbers, time lost due to malfunction, time lost due to misplaced faxes on the other end, electricity, and wear and tear on the machine. That's a lot of money for a one-page fax! Add it up and try to find alternatives to faxing.

To begin with, some things that get faxed may be cheaper to mail. A five-page document going long distance may cost more just in the phone charges than a first-class stamp and envelope would have. If time isn't of the essence, mail it.

Lease rather than purchase a newer fax machine with better features, such as faster sending times to reduce phone charges or more efficient electrical and toner usage.

Send faxes during off-peak times, such as overnight, to avoid having the message not go through due to a busy number at the other end.

Learn to use the reports feature on your fax machine, as it will notify you of incomplete faxes, both sending and receiving, and track the numbers faxes were sent to. If employees are using the fax machine for personal uses, the report will tell.

Keep it simple. Plain faxes without graphics or bold type will send quicker. If you're receiving a fax, you'll use less toner if the fax doesn't have unnecessary graphics or type.

Fax cover sheets aren't always necessary. There are a couple of different products you can get to replace them, such as a rubber stamp that imprints the first page with a small form to fill in critical information. And there are times when a brief message could be written or printed onto a fax cover sheet, eliminating the second sheet altogether.

Have an in-house fax tracker. Make whoever sits closest to the fax machine responsible for studying the fax usage of the company. They probably already have a good idea about this and make suggestions about reductions.

Overseas faxes can be very costly to send. Sending overnight mail might actually be cheaper and more reliable.

Turn your computer into a fax machine. Learn to use your computer's faxing software to send and receive correspondence. Fax-to-e-mail services will route all faxes to your e-mail account where you can delete them. This will save money from printing marketing faxes that are sent to your machine.

COMPUTERS

Computer monitors have become increasingly energy efficient over the years. Liquid crystal display (LCD) monitors are smaller and lightweight. While more expensive than the traditional cathode-ray tube (CRT), monitors, they are worth the money. They are easy to move to another part of the desk, have nicer swivel and tilt features for better ergonomic use and they are easy on the eyes, causing less fatigue than traditional monitors.

PAGERS AND CELL PHONES

Employees who spend the majority of their time in the office can be reached on the office phones and probably don't justify a company-paid cell phone or pager. While the fees for these items may seem minor, if you have a dozen people using them who don't really need them, you're paying for their personal convenience more than for a work-related convenience.

CHAPTER

25

Theft...
All Around You

D ishonesty is a reality for all companies. Every day there is a news story about an accounting fraud, a CEO who lined his own pockets, employees who steal and embezzle funds, shoplifters from all walks of life, and cheating by the very people who sell you the merchandise in your own stores. Review the 2004 National Retail Security Survey in Chapter 18 for startling statistics on shrinkage.

THEFT BY EMPLOYEES

Starting with the largest revenue-gobbling portion of losses, let's look at employee theft.

Why would an employee with a $1 million salary, a $3 million bonus and over $20 million in the company's stock illegally forge expense account reports to pay for things like kennel fees for his dogs, snakeskin boots, or Bloody Mary mix? It's so shockingly stupid that the discount chain store itself found it shocking and embarrassing. But it's true. Even at the highest echelons of Wal*Mart there is employee theft. The case that exploded in the headlines early in 2006 shows that even employers with high ethical standards can let theft slip through the cracks for years before it is noticed. In the case of this former Wal*Mart executive, it wasn't noticed until after he retired.

Theft by employees is not something that people like to talk about. After all, you've worked hard to earn your employees' loyalty, and the last thing you want to think about is them *stealing* from you!

John Case, CPP, is President of John Case and Associates, a security management firm and leading authority on employee and retail theft, believes that up to 95 percent of employers experience employee theft in some form. Few of them are even aware of it, and have no idea how prevalent it is.[29] According to Case, "employees questioned as to why they stole often rationalized their action and said the opportunity of theft presented itself through lax policies, controls, and management indifference."

Seven Common Sources of Employee Theft

1. **Cyber-loafing.** It would be almost impossible to find an employee who has not engaged in cyber-loafing. Everything from receiving personal e-mails at work to forwarding jokes and non-business related e-mails, there is almost universal guilt of this one. Cyber-loafing costs the employees' time, and it can reduce the company's bandwidth and create traffic jams for those who are using the Internet for company business. Additionally, if one employee downloads or forwards something offensive to another employee, the company could be held liable in a harassment lawsuit! Tracking software can be installed to deter this.

2. **Computer-loafing.** Nearly everybody has been guilty of this one as well. Sneaking in a quick game of solitaire or using company software to create personal items for their own use are all misuse of company time and resources.

---

[29] John Case, CPP, "Employee Theft: The Profit Killer," 2000, http://retailindustry.about. com/library/uc/uc_case1.htm, accessed on May 1, 2006.

3. **Copy-theft.** Personal use of the copy machines is rampant at some locations. If you allow employees to use the photocopier, then charge them a small fee to cover your costs.

4. **Fax-theft.** Personal use of fax machines is also a problem in some offices. Employees should be charged a small fee for fax use. Be sure to include long distance charges in the fee, unless it's a local call.

5. **Office supplies theft.** Note pads, pens, Post-it pads. They cost you money and are intended to be used in the office for company business. Make sure your employees understand the effect that even small items have on the budget.

6. **Postage theft.** Ahh, the innocuous little postage stamp. What's thirty-nine cents, after all? Well, added up by the number of stamps that may slip away over an entire year, and it could be quite a tidy sum. Limit access to stamps, or better yet, use a postage meter and limit access to it.

   Some companies allow employees to mail personal items and pay the company back right on the spot. If you have such a system, make sure all transactions are logged and that the person who's running the system is trustworthy.

7. **Components, tools, inventory, parts theft.** Some of this isn't intentional. I recently rounded up about two dozen specialty markers used at my husband's workplace. They were tossed in a junk drawer after being plucked from pockets when he came home from work. Knowing they rightly belonged to the company, I put them all in a zippered bag and put them in his lunch box the next day. They stayed at work, and since then, he's been better about taking things out of his pockets before punching out.

But what about the employee who doesn't return small items?

Are they really guilty of theft? By definition, yes, because they have reduced the supply of those items available to forward the business's interests. Sometimes a notice posted by the time clock or reminders at departmental meetings will be sufficient to deter these types of theft.

Those who steal intentionally are more difficult to apprehend and almost impossible to reform. These employees have many misconceptions, giving them a way to rationalize their theft. They may believe that they are underpaid while the company is rich so the company won't suffer. They may believe that everybody does it, so they can too.

In a retail setting, employees have different opportunities for theft. A brief list of these opportunities includes:

- Cashiers intentionally ringing up merchandise incorrectly (for less than the actual price) for friends or family.

- Cashiers putting an item in the bag (pretending to have rung it up) for friends or family.

- Customer service personnel performing fraudulent returns.

- Employees in charge of marking down merchandise who do so in their own favor either by marking an item down further and then taking it to purchase or preventing the public from obtaining marked-down merchandise until they have a chance to obtain it themselves.

Retail employees aren't the only ones who steal money or goods from their employer. Workers in accounting departments or management with some knowledge of and access to the company's accounting system can easily perpetuate a number of frauds.

One of the most common of these is fake-vendor fraud. This theft involves a fictitious vendor who's in the accounting system. The company occasionally, or regularly, receives invoices from this vendor. Those who are perpetuating this fraud know when to submit invoices, such as a certain time of month when there are numerous invoices coming in and the checks are flying out the door.

There are numerous other commonalities of the fake-vendor fraud. If you suspect something like this is possible at your company, do an audit of all the vendor data in your accounting program.

10 Telltale Signs of a Fake Vendor

1. It's probably a vendor that has regular activity. If the person who's perpetuating this falsehood gets away with it once or twice, soon the temptation will grow to commit fraud on a regular basis.

2. The transactions are likely for amounts that the suspected person(s) has the authority to approve; otherwise, they'd have to risk a superior questioning the invoice if it's submitted for higher approval.

3. If you can pull up a report that targets just credit memos from your vendors, your suspect vendor very likely will be one of them that you've never received a credit for.

4. Where are the "goods" that your fake vendor supplied? If you have an inventory system that tracks all goods, then you can probably eliminate all vendors who provide physical goods as suspect. Also look at vendors who provide only services as those are easier to overlook as to whether they were truly received or not.

5. Look for vendors who are associated only with one cost center. This may point to the person in charge of that cost center—or not. Perhaps the sneaky employee merely knows that one cost center isn't well monitored.

6. Use your software to crossmatch the invoice dates with the date on the check that paid the bill. Put vendors

whose dates are very close on the suspect list and check them out further. Why? Because the fake invoices from the fake vendor don't come via mail; they're usually slipped in a pile of other invoices on a date that checks are going to be written.

7. A clue in your software may be invoice numbers from various vendors. Odds are your fake vendor has only one client: you. Invoices may be sequential in number, repeating, or so far apart from one another that they're obviously fishy.

8. Another major piece of evidence to consider is the information in your own software about the vendor. All the information you normally put in about each new vendor is not there: no credit checks or history, no names of salespeople.

9. When you nail down a short list of suspect vendors, pull some invoices. Is there a phone number? Try it. An address? Use an online mapping program to locate it. Check the phone book. Fake vendors often have company names that don't really tell what they sell or do. They often have post office boxes for an address as well. These should help you narrow your list down even further.

10. If you feel you've found your fake vendor, pull up purchase orders or requisitions related to the invoices you pulled, if there are any. Unless multiple people are in on a fake-vendor scheme, the requisitions or purchase orders for the suspect vendors will often point to just one person in the end.

*Adapted from the University of Waterloo Centre for Accounting Ethics in Waterloo, Ontario Canada (Web site: **www.accounting.uwaterloo. ca/ethics/multimedia/module2.htm**).*

Biz Wiz Says ... "Don't give all the powers to one person."

—Patrick Walden

Vendor fraud is easy to perpetuate in small businesses with two or more partners where the duties are divvied up by talents. For instance, if one partner said "Oh, I'll take care of sales because that's what I'm good at" and another said "Okay, I'll pay the bills and balance the books," there's a good chance that vendor fraud will someday exist.

In one instance, Walden recalls, a business with two partners failed because the partner in charge of the money had power to approve purchase orders and invoices and also paid the bills. The other partner, trusting the first, never checked up on him. Over time, as the business became profitable, the first partner began to enter his credit card companies and other personal debtors into the computer as vendors. *After all*, he concluded, *I'm half owner in this company; I'm spending my own money!* He rationalized that this was his due because they didn't give themselves raises very often. Over time, the business simply could not sustain paying all its own costs plus that partner's personal expenses as well.

All members of a business partnership should regularly review their financial reports and statements. Even if no fraud is suspected, look for these things:

- Subscriptions and other things you agreed to, or thought you did, are cancelled but you are still being billed for them.

- Negotiated rates that you were promised from vendors but they didn't deliver.

- Mistakes that nobody noticed, such as a huge increase in your phone bill. Since the phone company is paid regularly, the bills may not be scrutinized as closely as they should be. A report over time will show a spike in the bill.

Why don't all partners review their reports and statements? Walden thinks these are most suspect:

- They don't understand the big financial picture and the effect that small things have on it.

- Lack of basic knowledge about financials can be overwhelming or boring.

- They are not interested in anything but sales or inventory, so they leave that unpleasant task to others, trusting they'll be honest.

How do you discover other types of employee theft? It's not always easy, especially when you feel that you do trust your employees.

Four Clues that Point to Employee Theft

1. Reduced profits with no obvious reason.
2. Shortages in inventory that aren't explainable.
3. Merchandise moved out of place in the warehouse.
4. New boxes of merchandise that aren't completely full.

Four Ways to Prevent Employee Theft

1. Document all deliveries. Have the delivery person sign off on what's being taken and to whom and have another employee verify this information.
2. Listen to office gossip closely; rarely does theft go undetected by everybody at the workplace, but employees don't like to tattle on each other.

3. Check files for photocopies where there should be originals such as invoices or purchase orders. Finding them could indicate forgery or tampering.

4. Take a close look at the faithful employee who refuses to leave his job for a vacation or any other reason (including turning down a promotion). He may have access to information that would incriminate him so that leaving the job, even temporarily, might expose him.

If you are paying a company for services and your contract states a specific number of employees to do the job, take a head count and make sure you're receiving the right number of employees every day.

Often the department that secures a contract with a company to outsource a function isn't the same department paying the invoice. Set up a system for invoices to be verified against the contract before being paid.

THEFT BY CUSTOMERS

Deterring your customers from pilfering merchandise from your retail store is known as *loss prevention*. What it boils down to is this: making customers pay for items they take or consume.

There are a number of ways that retailers across the country have tried to reduce theft, and they're coming up with new ideas all the time.

The 10 Most Commonly Used Deterrents to Customer Theft

1. **Greeters.** Wal*Mart was the first retailer to place greeters right at the door. Not only do they greet customers but they also look for items being brought into or taken out of the store. The idea is that your average good citizen will be less likely to turn to theft if he's locked eyes

with the owner of the company. Okay, so greeters aren't necessarily the *owners* of the store, but they do represent the owners.

2. **Electronic Tags.** You never know what's going to be tagged at some stores. Known as electronic article surveillance (EAS), the small tag could be imbedded inside the packaging for a compact disk. It could be in a pair of shoes. Whatever the loss prevention team has identified as a target for theft can be tagged: cosmetics, which are easy to tuck into a purse, or baseball cards, for example. Electronic tagging has become sophisticated — no more obvious and bulky ink-filled tags are required. A small piece of metal covered by tape is all that's required for many systems.

3. **Plain-clothes security officers.** Patrolling the store posed as a customer, a security officer could be checking you out at any time. Don't think they're easy to spot either. You'd be surprised.

4. **Uniformed security officers.** Seeing a uniformed security officer may deter the less-than hardened thief and even make the pros think twice.

5. **Observant employees.** Train your employees to spot the characteristics of a would-be thief. Many retailers have phones located throughout the store for employees to contact the security department in the case of a suspicious shopper.

6. **Friendly employees.** Don't expect your employees and sales clerks to hound the customer, but like the greeter, some people are less likely to shoplift if they've had friendly contact with sales personnel or a manager.

7. **Signage.** Everybody has seen signs in dressing rooms and rest rooms at retailers. They warn about the high price of shoplifting.

8. **Cameras.** Whether hidden or in plain view, being caught on tape is a definite deterrent for shoplifters. The thing is, do stores do enough reviewing of the tapes to catch everybody?

9. **Check-out cameras.** Cameras in the ceiling above checkouts keep customers and cashiers honest. There are actually thieves who wouldn't consider shoplifting but rather their target is the cash register. Asking an employee for change for a large bill and causing a ruckus is a common tactic of these thieves. Train all employees on techniques for handling these situations.

10. In addition to thieves who try to fool cashiers, there is a growing nationwide problem with **organized shoplifting gangs** who steal large quantities of in-demand goods such as over-the-counter drugs and infant formula. These professional shoplifting groups can be dangerous, so be sure to train your employees on the proper procedures for handling them properly.

11. **Parking lot cameras.** Cameras in the parking lot aren't just for safety reasons. They can catch thieves who are snitching items from outdoor displays.

However many of these measures you take, a retail environment is always going to be prone to theft. Merchandise on shelves is simply too irresistible for the kleptomaniac.

One company in Boston has come up with a creative solution to this problem by transplanting their online shopping experience into their retail store.

Imagine going into a retail store that offers more than 8,400 music titles on CDs, records, and even DVDs. That would require a fairly substantial amount of floor space to display all that merchandise. But if you walk into UndergroundHipHop's retail store in downtown Boston, you'll be amazed at their creative use of space. In an area totaling roughly 800 square feet, this store also boasts a lounge where customers can sit and relax, chatting about their passion for underground hip hop music.

Where is all the merchandise? Just like on their Web site, customers shop at a computer in the retail store. The merchandise is all there, mind you, and you'll get your items — at the checkout once you've paid. But to save all the time in stocking the retail store, ensuring that the customers don't pilfer the goods and avoiding broken merchandise, UndergroundHipHop has merely eliminated all these possibilities by not putting the merchandise within reach.

Customers can browse titles and listen to samples (from one minute long to even an entire song) and place their order right at a computerized kiosk in the store.

This is not to say that there isn't any physical merchandise on display. Special displays are set up with new releases or other promotional music and a clothing section is also out front for customers to browse through, but the vast majority of merchandise is kept in the back room which also serves as stock for the company's Web site purchases.

This entire concept, while new to a music store, isn't entirely original. Think of the fine jewelry departments at any department store. The merchandise is in locked cases, and you often have to pay for the item before walking away with it. This is simply an extension of that philosophy, providing a seamless integration of UndergroundHipHop's web store with retail space as well.

THEFT BY VENDORS AND SUPPLIERS

Even vendors and suppliers can become jaded about their business relationship with large corporations and, over time, knowingly fleece their own customers. Employees, customers, and vendors who steal or cheat think that large corporations have bottomless coffers.

Sometimes it isn't the vendor as a company that's trying to cheat but delivery persons.

Seven Ways to Protect Your Company from Unscrupulous Delivery Persons:

1. Ideally, check every box delivered and count to see that the required number of items stated on the invoice and on the box match what's inside the box. A delivery person can easily skim items from certain boxes and hope not to be caught.

2. Make sure all boxes you receive are still factory-sealed. If not, be sure to count those first.

3. When checking boxes for missing or incorrect merchandise, if you can't check every box in full immediately, randomly check them. Open some up by the bottom or side of the box and check for anything suspicious as well.

4. Check every invoice or purchase order when delivery takes place. It's easy just to assume it's all there but if you've got 150 boxes of merchandise, one or two not delivered might take days to notice. By then, it's your word against the driver's.

5. Make sure that the delivery person doesn't load a few boxes back onto the dolly and slip them back onto the truck after you've signed for a complete delivery.

6. If a delivery driver is supposed to remove outdated merchandise, have your employees separate the outdated items and set them aside, away from new merchandise.

7. Don't allow delivery drivers inside the store or stockroom. People become so accustomed to seeing them walking around carrying boxes that, after a while, nobody thinks to question whether the driver is coming

or going with that box.

And sometimes it truly is the vendor company attempting to pull a fast one.

Nine Ways to Avoid Being Defrauded by Vendors

1. Items that don't match the items ordered. You might unknowingly receive a slightly different (or inferior quality) product if you don't compare purchase orders and invoices carefully.

2. Pay for all invoices by check, never by cash.

3. If you receive the invoice from the delivery person, question any charge that is added to the invoice after it was printed at the vendor's location. Call and ask the vendor, if need be.

4. Demand that vendors provide credits and invoices on separate sheets of paper to avoid confusion.

5. Demand that a packing slip accompany every delivery, if an invoice doesn't come with it.

6. Have the delivery person sign the packing slip if any discrepancies are found.

7. Have strict policies regarding when vendors can deliver goods, specifically when you have reliable shipping department employees on hand to verify the delivery.

8. Everything in the shipment, even free samples, should be listed on the packing slip. If it's not on the packing slip, don't accept it.

9. Perform routine audits of your vendor contracts, the terms, and all related invoices, even if the item was checked as accurate when received and/or paid. Make sure your vendors know you do these audits; they may help keep them honest.

CHAPTER

26 Lawyers and Litigation

YOUR COMPANY'S OFF-SITE ATTORNEY

10 Ways to Save Money on Everyday Legal Needs

1. **Squeeze it all in.** Unless items are of urgent nature, wait to schedule a meeting until you have several small items to go over in one sitting.

2. **Write it yourself.** If you're familiar with what goes into a standard business contract, write yours yourself and merely ask your attorney to review it for accuracy. Odds are it will take him less time to review it than to draft it.

3. **Come prepared.** When you have an issue that needs review or advice, attend the meeting with all the paperwork, documentation, or information you'll need to settle the matter. Otherwise, you'll have to schedule follow-up visits or route the needed materials and have an additional time charge for reviewing them.

4. **Bring duplicates.** Make extra copies of all documentation you bring, one for the attorney to file and one to make notes on if he desires.

5. **Shed some light.** Don't mislead your attorney or neglect

certain information that you feel is derogatory or is not in your favor. Your attorney needs a full and completely accurate picture of the entire situation. However, don't waste time with needless information or unimportant details.

6. **Send a memo.** Some things are easier discussed in writing via a brief memo. The attorney can then memo or call back with the answer at his convenience. This may result in a smaller charge than a telephone call because your attorney won't have to make notes of what you asked — you've already written them for him!

7. **Be in-the-know.** Read anything newsworthy that relates to your industry or business type, especially changes in laws or requirements. Print or clip the information and file it for future reference; it may save you some money by answering a question yourself rather than calling your attorney.

8. **Be good to your attorney.** You never know when you will need your attorney for a make-or-break deal or an urgent litigation issue. Don't incite his ill-will by being slow to pay your invoices. Bring goodwill from the law firm by recommending them to others and letting them know that you do so.

9. **For advanced assistance.** If your attorney suggests you consult with an attorney who specializes in some manner, ask for a referral and ask your attorney to negotiate a reasonable rate for you.

10. **Take a deduction.** Some attorney fees may be tax-deductions as well. Discover what they are and use them.

ARBITRATION AND MEDIATION

Nobody plans to get sued by their former employees, their

competitors, or their customers. In fact, most companies desperately hope not to be sued, but it does happen, and the costs of litigation can wreak havoc on a company's budget in a big hurry. Of course, any wise business owner should be insured against product liability and certain other issues. But those policies often insure you for the damages awarded the plaintiff. Do your policies cover you against the actual litigation costs, win or lose? If not, here are some tips to consider when dealing with litigation costs.

The first thing you should always try when faced with litigation is arbitration or mediation. "The parties agree to mandatory arbitration in the case of a dispute." This type of phrase is used in many business contracts and it is proving helpful for a number of reasons.

Arbitration is not a trial; it is a decision made by the arbitrator, often a professional or expert in the industry surrounding the lawsuit. Decisions of arbitrators are final and even though both parties usually end up both *giving* and *getting*, even the *giving* ends up costing less than a trial likely would have.

One reason the cost is lower is because juries often need long, detailed explanations of all the intricacies of the lawsuit, including the ramifications of all possible outcomes, lengthening the hours your lawyers are charging you for.

An arbitrator can be a single person or a panel of persons. Either way, since they are knowledgeable about your industry or business type, they don't need the minor educating of the jury. You can get straight away to the facts and the conclusions of the case. Remember, arbitration is binding. Once the decision is made, all parties are bound by it and cannot later bring the same issue up again in a trial.

Another way to settle disputes is through mediation. Mediation differs from arbitration in that the parties do the talking and agreeing with each other, rather than having the decisions made by an arbitrator. Mediation is also voluntary and not binding; if one of the parties fails to follow through, the other party may return the matter to the courts.

Controlling Litigation Costs

Experience counts. How often has this phrase been used as an ad slogan for a law firm? You see it on their TV ads and in their yellow pages ads. But is it really true? Yes. Consider this: what might take an attorney with a $100 per hour fee three hours to do could take a more experienced and seasoned attorney with a $300 per hour fee only thirty minutes to accomplish. So let's see: pay $300 from the inexperienced guy, or just $150 from the guy who's been around the block a few times.

The point is that merely comparing hourly rates among attorneys is like comparing the price of eggs to the price of chicken breasts. They might be in the same basic category, but they're not the same product.

Determining who's experienced and worth their money isn't as easy, hence the reason many people fall into the trap of comparing by hourly rate. The best way to find an attorney who's worth every penny is by getting referrals from other business owners and friends.

Keep it in check. Lawyer fees can add up quickly. And even though a great lawyer is worth every penny, your pennies may be in short supply. At the start of any litigation, sit down with your company's attorney and outline a time frame and a budget for every aspect of the case.

If your attorneys know that they must stay within a certain budget but still provide a satisfactory outcome to the case, your costs won't spiral later in the process when you may be desperate to win at all costs.

If you feel that your legal bills are suspiciously high, hire a legal auditor to check for duplication or other tactics of sneaky or sloppy law firms.

Seven Other Ways to Control Legal Costs

1. Insist that your minimum billing unit be the smallest time frame possible. For instance, if you are billed at a minimum rate of a quarter hour, then every 3-minute phone call you make to your attorney (or he makes on your behalf) will be billed for one full quarter-hour.

2. Insist on frequent bills if there is an active case currently being worked on.

3. Control your costs by not paying if a junior partner or intern is "helping" on your case for his own experience. Unless he actually contributed, don't pay for his education.

4. Keep a log of all contact you have with the attorney's office, and compare it with your bills.

5. Bills should detail specifics of each duty being billed so you can check for double-billing, even if accidental on the firm's part. Don't be afraid to ask for more details about something.

6. Be sure to ask about and compare all your options. Flat fees, contingencies, retainers, and value billing are terms you should have your attorney explain in detail before agreeing on your costs and how you will pay.

7. Suggest (or demand) that your law firm hire an outside company to do their legal research at a rate much lower than it can be done in-house.

Litigation with former employees can be avoided by having a strict policy against supervisors and managers not discussing issues or problems with employees via e-mail. If the e-mail got into the wrong hands, it could be construed as a wrongful-termination issue.

Additionally, your company's e-mail policy should forbid using e-mail to spread any defamatory information (whether true or false) about anybody, whether it be an employee, a public figure or a customer. Libel suits are all too common these days.

If you are considering the position of plaintiff in a case, consider also the potential for the defendant to countersue you. You might end up paying more than it's worth if this happens. Determine the worst-case-scenario costs before deciding to pursue litigation.

Although you hate to get bills from your attorney, don't hesitate to get him or her involved very early when you have a situation. The benefits of attorney-assisted damage control is well worth the bill.

CHAPTER

27

Outsourcing

Outsourcing is one of those buzzwords that can mean everything from hiring an outside janitorial firm to hiring textile workers overseas. Every company should take a look at where they can put outsourcing — or the act of hiring someone else to do something cheaper than you can do it yourself — to work for them.

OUTSOURCING IN THE USA

The most important aspect of outsourcing, the savings, must be verified and continuously verifiable. And you must also be wary of outsourcing to companies that will bid the cheapest price but may cost more in the long run by working slower or with less competence. Take quality and productivity into account when considering a company to outsource to, just as you would when reviewing your own company's departments for those features.

Another aspect of successful outsourcing is to send out jobs that are minor in terms of your big picture but to the subcontractor is a major job in their area of specialty.

If you have current contracts for services that are outsourced, such as maintenance, janitorial services, and service contracts, regularly review the contracts and make sure that all the work you've contracted for is actually being done to quality standards. You may even find that some contracts are not necessary and can end them. Perhaps things have changed and what once was a small item that could be cheaper done outside the company has become a large expense that would be cheaper to do in-house. Don't just keep paying the bills—ask yourself if you got your money's worth every time you pay a bill.

You should also regularly visit the locations where outsourced work is being done or send a team of your employees over to study their processes and make suggestions on how to improve it. If they can do the work even better, you'll save more money.

Specialized tasks often are those that are most targeted for outsourcing. One example is the laundry department of hotels or hospitals. There are companies that will haul the laundry away and return it all clean and folded. But there are also companies that will send in their workers to do the jobs with either their own equipment or yours. Find the right combination that will give you the greatest savings.

International transactions requiring foreign exchange monies can be complicated and time consuming. Companies that specialize in foreign exchange money wires can do the job faster and more efficiently and often can do it cheaper than your own employees because their size allows them to gain better exchange rates than if you did the transaction at your own bank.

Read your invoices carefully—companies that send employees to your location might charge you for travel time as well as the time they are working.

Many companies outsource their payroll to take advantage of the expertise these payroll processors have with changing tax laws. Legal tasks can be outsourced to specialty companies for things like research or depositions.

A large, specialty project such as a mailing can be done more quickly by a specialty company than asking your employees to drop what they're doing and help out for a day or two, especially when you factor in the costs of lost productivity in your employees' other projects and duties.

Having a company produce a specialty part or provide a specialty service right inside your plant might be a smart move. Printing companies often have an ink manager who is not their own employee but is employed by the company with an exclusive contract to provide ink to the printer. This gives the printing company an experienced employee whom they don't have to pay.

Outsourcing can also be done through an independent contractor. You can hire people for certain functions and pay them as an independent contractor. Provide them with the proper tax forms at the end of the year and report what you paid to them. Since they are not employees as defined by federal law, you aren't required to provide them with benefits.

Universities have moved in the direction of outsourcing their food service in dormitories to companies that specialize in this area. These companies, such as Aramark and Sodexho, can often do the job cheaper and more efficiently and leave the university to concentrate on education. Other businesses that use these services include the United States Marine Corps, stadiums, and large corporations with in-house cafeterias.

You may be able to have your choice of outsourced company take on your current employees whose jobs will be lost. This can increase goodwill and loyalty among employees who might otherwise have been unemployed.

You may be able to continue your company's growth without expanding your physical location by outsourcing just one of your manufacturing processes or products.

If you have a product return department, look into companies that will handle your product returns for you. Outsourcing this often frustrating task can save time and money.

Consider outsourcing a new portion of your business while you test the waters. Rather than build a new location for a new product line, outsource the production to someone else who's already set up for that type of product. If the product is successful, you can take over production yourself if it would be cheaper than continuing the outsourcing relationship.

Outsourcing Overseas

More and more people are thinking of overseas workers when they hear of jobs being outsourced. News reports of the comparatively cheap labor to be had in foreign countries don't really show the big picture about the profits to be had, or not had, by the company that uses foreign labor to make its products.

There are a number of other considerations that may actually make outsourcing overseas less profitable than one might think.

Eight Potential Roadblocks to Profits When You Outsource

1. **Foreign laws.** Even though you may pay less for labor once you've got things up and running, just getting to the up-and-running phase may cost you a bundle. Getting government red tape out of the way can be time consuming and unless you have the language and cultural skills to deal with the foreign regulations, you'll also have to pay attorneys who do have those skills to do a lot of this work.

2. **Foreign vendors.** You'll spend a small chunk of change on travel expenses to evaluate possible locations and vendors to do the work. Sure, they'll likely send representatives to you for initial evaluations, but once you get your short list narrowed down, you'd be wise to go check each one out on-location.

Vendors also might have set up fees and other requirements you need to pay for before they can begin to work on your items. Be sure to get the skinny on all of those extras above and beyond the per-item piece they'll be charging to make your most informed decision.

3. **Start up.** It's not just as simple as lining up a place to do the work and a company to supply the help. The months and months it could take to have a consistent quantity of product being shipped out will cost more than it brings in.

4. If you're making a product that requires skills to produce, the **workers in the new location will need training** just like any other worker on the planet. You may have to have some of the lead workers come to the United States to be trained by your current staff first. This will cost you their travel and housing requirements during the training period and possible fees for working visas.

5. **An entire infrastructure may need to be built** at the vendor's location to obtain raw materials, hardware, networks, and other items needed before start up. These are just a few of the many money-gobbling things that can take place in this time frame between signing the vendor contract and receiving finished product.

6. And once your product does begin rolling off the lines at the offshore location, **what do you do with the American workers** who used to create this product? Chances are you'll need to be laying them off. That option may sound good in one way, but there are costs associated with layoffs too, such as unemployment compensation and severance packages. Did your cost-benefit analysis factor in these costs or the possible costs of productivity lost by employees who did not get laid off?

7. Some companies that have moved production offshore have noted things that took them by surprise. **Employee turnover can be much higher** than in the United States, thus adding to your employee training cost. Employees in foreign countries may not be as proactive as American employees. If they see something that could be changed, they often won't speak up. They'd rather please their bosses, even if they're being told to do something the wrong way. All these unforeseen items reduce productivity and add to the costs.

8. **Shipping the product** to you is something that is hard to envision if you're accustomed to having product roll off your assembly line and be ready to ship to customers the same day. Getting your product overseas, literally, and into port, through inspections and customs and onto ground transportation to your warehouse or customer is far more complicated and adds to the bottom line in costs.

Biz Wiz Says . . . "It doesn't make sense to offshore if you're in a low-cost market."

—Patrick Walden

Offshoring, while popular, said Walden, often costs the same in the long run but reaps less productivity. For many small companies, outsourcing or offshoring could be completely eliminated if an untapped source of less expensive labor were used, said Patrick Walden. This great untapped resource: college students as interns.

10 Reasons to Use an Intern:

1. Arranged interns are not employees, therefore they can be used for a semester or several semesters.

2. You don't pay benefits of any sort to interns.

3. Their wages are less than regular employees.

4. They are eager to please because they are gaining real-world experience for their future and college credits now (in most cases).

5. The colleges often have internal means of posting jobs, professors announce them—no ad budget needed to find these workers!

6. With training they can be come just as productive and knowledgeable as many regular employees.

7. They bring with them the latest knowledge from their own professors.

8. They often work part-time in the school year and full-time in the summers, which often coincides with peak production seasons.

9. They are often able to cover flex hours, after classes and into the evenings, which can be hard positions to fill for something like phone support for west-coast customers.

10. If you have a slowdown and need to end their internship early, you don't have to pay unemployment.

NEW TWISTS ON OUTSOURCING

Don't assume that outsourcing is always the answer. It may be wiser to have one person in-house who specializes in a task rather than hiring it out to a company who may have several different employees working on it. Consistency could suffer.

If your company has a need for a small-scale outsourcing of your customer-service phone calls, a new trend is popping up that's being called "home-sourcing." ·Current estimates place the number of home-based call center employees at 112,000 in the

United States. This number is expected to grow to over 300,000 in the next five years.[30] Companies of all sizes and types are getting involved in this opportunity to cut their own costs yet keep jobs in the United States. While there are obstacles to overcome, such as the hardware and peripherals needed by the person who's working from home, there are great benefits as well.

Here is a scenario that happens time and again: many people simply do not have the patience in dealing with customer service reps in foreign countries whose heavy accents make it virtually impossible to have a conversation. A customer in need of a direct answer may be frustrated by the lack of communication. Speaking to a supervisor often doesn't provide a different experience unless the supervisor's linguistic skills differ drastically.

In desperation, the customer hangs up and tries again, hoping to get someone who speaks better English. If they are not successful, they may go to the company's Web site or find a stateside representative of the company to vent their anger to. It may take several calls to resolve what could have been an easy fix.

To remedy this situation, the in-home customer service rep or call center can be a handy answer. Companies have sprung up to screen potential representatives and handle the invoicing and other middle-man aspects of the industry.

A FINAL WORD

A pitfall to avoid is this: don't forget to actually eliminate the jobs in your company that were outsourced. That may mean laying off workers, reassigning them or giving them jobs that would normally have been filled by a new hire.

---

[30] IDC Press Release, "IDC Finds the Number of U.S. Home-Based Agents Will Nearly Triple as Economic Forces Drive Expansion of Homeshoring," January 4, 2006, www.idc. com/getdoc.jsp?containerId=prUS20036206, accessed on May 1, 2006.

CHAPTER

28

Getting Help From Unexpected Places

PENNY-PINCHING EMPLOYEES

Why should your employees look for ways to pinch pennies and boost your bottom line? In some companies, employees would rather have a root canal without novocaine than actively participate in improving their employer. If this is the atmosphere at your company, you may have a serious problem with your corporate culture. Review the information about corporate culture in Chapter 4 to learn ways you can combat this fast-spreading disease.

If employees don't feel that the very security of their job, benefits, or raise is dependent on their thriftiness, or if they feel that the only ones who will benefit are shareholders and upper management, they won't have any motivation to contribute. This is not to say you should threaten your employees to come up with ways to save money or be out of a job. That wouldn't be too savvy, but employees who are aware of the cost of things and the financial health of the company are more in tuned with the need to be thrifty.

There are two ways that employees can contribute to penny-pinching efforts, informally or formally.

Informal contributions are those small, every day things that conserve energy, supplies or increase the employees' own productivity. These are not the types of suggestions that need to be studied for cost-effectiveness and have a formal implementation plan drawn up. They're just situations where you say, "Let's do this" and it's done. While getting all employees to participate in these informal cost-savings measures isn't always easy — after all, you can't follow every employee to the restroom to make sure they aren't using too many paper towels when they wash their hands, you'll find that if managers and supervisors model these thrifty behaviors, they become part of your corporate culture in time.

Here are just a few examples of simple thrifty behaviors that just make sense:

- If you ask, you'll likely find employees who will donate recent magazines from their own personal subscriptions so you can cancel the subscriptions used in the reception area.

- Encourage your employees to curb their own personal work-related expenses, such as transportation costs. When employees carpool and save money, it's "found" money in their personal budgets. Give a token of appreciation for long-term carpooling, such as a gift certificate for treats at a nearby ice cream parlor.

- Ask each employee to forgo Styrofoam cups and bring in a coffee mug from home. If your break room could use an additional microwave oven or coffee maker, ask employees to donate their old ones when they "upgrade."

- Use the recycling containers avidly and even take paper with one blank side out of the recycle bin to use for scratch paper, to post unofficial notices on bulletin boards or other nonbusiness-crucial uses. If employees see that you're re-using, they will be more likely to do so as well.

- Are your employee restrooms or the break room needing a new look? Sponsor a contest to have teams of employees draw up their best design for a set amount of money in supplies. Employees who are fans of the home-makeover-on-a-budget shows that are all the rage will jump at the chance to show off their do-it-yourself skills.

- If you have a large enough company for a democracy, you can have all employees vote on the proposed designs. The teams with the best designs get to decorate the rooms according to their winning design and budget! Have someone on hand to video or take pictures of the before and after, and put the pictures on a bulletin board.

- Set a time limit just as they do on the shows, such as one weekend: all work must be completed by 6 p.m. Sunday. Come Monday morning, the work will be all done and your employees will be proud of their accomplishments. Beware, though, it may be contagious—they may want to do the boss's office next!

Formal cost-cutting measures are culled from employees through a suggestion program and become permanent changes that are not optional by individual employees. Employees will have to modify their working patterns of whatever is suggested to be able to achieve the cost savings targeted by the suggestion. Employee suggestion programs are the best way to harness the power of your workforce. They drive your company's production and profits, and they have a vested interest in making the company more profitable. Suggestion programs must have several key elements to be successful. Make sure your program uses all these factors:

- **Keep it simple.** Traditionally a box is used to collect suggestions, but it must be monitored. With e-mail being the prevalent way to communicate, how about setting up an account such as suggestions@yourcompany.com? This way employees could even offer suggestions from home.

- **Get the scoop.** Ask employees to do some work on their suggestion. If they currently use a part costing $3.00 but want to suggest an alternative, have them determine (or guesstimate) what the alternative will cost. Let them know that the more research and details they provide, the faster an accepted suggestion can be implemented.

- **Make it worthwhile.** Sharing in the savings is an oft-used technique to encourage suggestions, but make sure it's worthwhile. A suggestion that has immediate and measurable savings of $1 million shouldn't earn the employee a mere $500 bonus.

- **Share the love.** Encourage managers to keep the program active. Give them an extra yearly bonus tied to the number of accepted suggestions from those under their supervision.

- **Include everyone.** All employees, at any level, should be allowed to contribute suggestions for their own jobs and the jobs of others. Sometimes the people doing the job are too close to it to see solutions that are obvious to others.

- **Have two programs.** Consider taking suggestions from your customers and your suppliers and vendors as well. If you have a formal program in place, people will be more likely to participate because they know someone will read their suggestion other than a customer service representative who may not care.

- **Be timely.** Review all suggestions in a stated time frame and respond to all of them, giving the employee (customer/vendor) an initial review and decision on whether the suggestion will be looked into further.

- **Be diverse.** The team who reviews suggestions should include members from all levels of employment. Rotate members quarterly so that everybody has a chance to be on a team at some point.

Just like the informal thriftiness, employees will be less than excited about a formal suggestion program if your corporate culture doesn't encourage it.

YOUR STATE LABOR DEPARTMENT

While there is some congruity among states in their labor laws, there are just enough differences to make this worth checking into. Call your state's labor department or check their Web site for any information that would help you understand your state's laws.

THE FEDERAL GOVERNMENT

A whole chapter could easily be devoted just to all the resources and information available from the United States government for businesses. However, the quickest and best way to learn about all these resources is to go to what's called the Gateway of information on their Web site. It can be found at **www.firstgov. gov/Business/Business_Gateway.shtml**.

Information and links are grouped by topic, by company type or size and includes a list of other related links that are commonly used by businesses.

Make the government your friend, by allowing it to point you to resources and information that will help you be more competitive, more efficient, and more profitable.

The U.S. Department of Energy publishes many pamphlets about energy efficiency. Order online at **www.energy.gov**.

The Small Business Administration can be found at **www. sbaonline.sba.gov**.

COST-CUTTING SPECIALISTS

If you've looked in every nook and cranny of your organization but still can't locate enough places to cut costs, consider hiring a consultant who specializes in finding those elusive places to trim the fat. For the most effective results, negotiate payment based on a percentage of the savings that the consultant successfully locates and implements.

YOUR LOCAL COMMUNITY

Contact business professors and see if they have a class who would benefit from doing a study of your organization as a class project. When energetic youth get involved, you might find a fresh approach that will change the way you are looking at things.

PART V:

Assessing Your Efforts

"Nearly all men can stand adversity, but if you want to test a man's character, give him power."

— ABRAHAM LINCOLN,
16TH PRESIDENT OF THE UNITED STATES

While highly tongue-in-cheek, this fake "memo" demonstrates the zeal of cost cutting gone awry:

MEMO

TO: All Hospital Staff
FROM: Administration / Grounds Keeper
SUBJECT: New Cost-Cutting Measures

Effective January 1, we will no longer have a security force. Each Charge Nurse will be issued a .38 caliber revolver and 12 rounds of ammunition. An additional 12 rounds will be stored in the Pharmacy.

In addition to routine nursing duties, the Charge Nurses will patrol the hospital grounds. A bicycle and helmet have been purchased for this purpose.

Due to the similarity of monitoring equipment, the ICU will assume all security-related surveillance. The unit secretary will be responsible for watching cardiac and security monitors as well as performing secretarial duties.

The Food Services department has been eliminated. Patients wishing to be fed will need to let their families know to bring them meals, or they may make arrangements with establishments like Subway or Domino's. Many local establishments offer free delivery and will give discounts to patients. Coin-operated telephones are being installed in all patient rooms for this purpose, as well as for other calls the patient may wish to make.

The Housekeeping and Physical Therapy departments are being combined. Mops will be issued to all ambulatory patients, providing much-needed range-of-motion exercise as well as a clean environment. Ambulatory patients may sign up to clean the rooms of non-ambulatory patients to receive a special discount on their final bill. Time clocks and time cards will be available on all hospital floors.

As noted above, the Administration is now also assuming Grounds-Keeping duties. If you cannot locate an administrator at his/her office, we suggest you walk outside and listen to the sound of a lawn mower, weed whacker, or snow shovel.

The Engineering and Maintenance departments no longer exist. The hospital has subscribed to the TIME-LIFE "How-To" Maintenance Series of hardcover books which will be arriving bi-monthly for the next three years. Volume 1 "Basic Wiring" has already been received. If a nonelectrical problem occurs, please handle it as best you can until the appropriate volume arrives. An arrival schedule can be viewed at the Administrator/Grounds-Keeper's office. For repairs, a toolbox will be supplied to each nursing station for use within their area.

Cutbacks in the Phlebotomy staff will be offset by performing all blood-related lab tests on patients who are already bleeding.

Physicians will be limited to two (2) x-rays per patient per stay. This is due to the turnaround time required by the local drug store's photo lab. Two prints will be provided for the price of one, so physicians be advised: clip coupons from the Sunday paper if you want extra sets. The drug store will honor competitors' coupons for one-hour processing in emergency situations. All employees are asked to clip coupons for photo processing and forward them to the ER.

To cut our utility costs and monitor usage, we have asked our electricity and gas providers to install meters in every room so that the appropriate costs may be billed to patients, departments, or offices. Fans and portable electric heaters will be available for sale or lease in the hospital gift shop.

The hospital Pharmacy has taken up a bold new experiment. The unwanted fruit, candy and flowers received by patients will be collected and the resulting moldy compost will be used for the production of antibiotics. These antibiotics will then be available for purchase through the hospital Pharmacy and will, coincidentally, soon be the only antibiotics listed on our HMO's formulary.

We appreciate your cooperation in our efforts to reduce our operational expenses. Be advised, further measures may prove necessary if these cost-cutting efforts fail to produce the intended results. Please refer all questions to the Director of Human Resources. You may locate her in parking lots A through D this week, where she is currently installing the new parking meters.

While this obviously is a humorous joke, on a deeper level it does point to the truly illogical and downright stupid things that have been done in the name of cost cutting by businesses of every type and size.

How many cost-cutting blunders can you spot? Eliminating something needed and replacing it with something inferior? Doubling up on work duties by people who aren't qualified to take on the additional jobs? Spending money foolishly in a misguided effort to save it? Those are all easy to see. But did the most important one occur to you: not providing quality products and services to your customer. Obviously no matter what else takes place in relation to cutting costs, you have to make certain that your customer is always served and always happy.

CHAPTER

29

Health Hits and Health Checks

Every time our country enters a time of economic slowdown, the public closely scrutinizes every new forecast, every interest rate increase or decrease, every report about the health of our economy. Companies, uncertain of how long the current slowdown will last, sometimes make hasty and regrettable decisions.

Obviously, there cannot be universally applicable rules in cost cutting. The simple truth is that what works for one company or in one situation or for one generation will not always work for another.

HEALTH HITS

Just because you embark on the cost-cutting journey to better business health doesn't mean it will always lead to that end. Here are some ways that common cost cutting can go awry and place a direct hit to the health of your company when you're working hard to improve it.

Failure to Plan

Jan B. King, author of *Business Plans to Game Plans: A Practical System for Turning Strategies into Action*, doles out some wise advice about planning, or the lack thereof. In her article "The Game Plan— The Difference Between Small Business Success and Failure," **http://ezinearticles.com/?The-Game-Plan—-The-Difference-Between-Small-Business-Success-And-Failure&id=13895,** King notes that mere planning isn't always the ticket.

You can have a business plan, but unless you have what King also calls a "game plan," you're shortchanging your business. While a business plan "gets you in the game," notes King, "a game plan keeps you in the game." She likens it to planning how your team will play the game in the locker room—the business plan—and then how the actual game is played on the court—your game plan.

For those who aren't sports-analogy minded, here's another one. "A business plan is a sales brochure and a game plan is an instruction manual," wrote King.

Having a plan will help you avoid the pitfalls common when one fails to plan properly. An example King points out is that a company's CEO could make a plan to reduce inventory by a certain percentage and by a certain date. But if that's as far as the plan goes, those who are implementing it may take the wrong approach. The sales personnel are going to sell, sell, sell, but what will they be selling? Most likely they'll focus on the items that sell well.

That leaves the company's inventory heavily stocked with the items that don't sell well. Those items should have been focused on in the game plan. The company is then left and short-handed on those best-sellers. So not only did failure to plan not solve the problem of excess inventory, it has created a new problem of not enough inventory.

Developing a game plan involves several steps as outlined by King:

- Get in touch with your desires for your business.

- Delve into what's real for your business today in terms of your business model.

- Be sure about what's happening in your market.

- Honestly assess your company's corporate culture (see Chapter 4).

- Consider your resources: don't try making plans you don't have the resources to implement.

Use these tasks to prepare your "List of Objectives in your Game Plan," then move on:

- **Turn your objectives into actions.** "Create a set of action items for each employee that support the department and then company objectives," instructs King. Be sure to include appropriate measurements to employees can see how they stack up at any time during the game.

- **Keep the lines open.** "The game plan is not only communicated initially, it must be kept alive throughout the year with meetings focused on measuring progress toward the goals. Successes should be celebrated frequently," she said.

Game plans are for short-term achievements, such as winning the current quarter's profit goals. But you should always juxtapose your current game plan against the backdrop of your company's future goals and objectives. You'll find you can use the game plan philosophy to help you achieve goals more quickly than by wending your way through time and making poor planning choices.

When you see that you've suffered from a failure to plan, don't despair; go back and start over, this time using King's game plan philosophy. To learn more about her books and services, check out her Web site at **www.janbking.com**.

Taking the Wrong Approach or Only One Approach

Even if you carefully plan out your approach to cost cutting, you might have unwittingly made the wrong choice. Recall the two approaches: the itch and the rash. If your company was having an urgent crisis and you failed to look at the itch-items, meaning you failed to spot and eliminate all the single items you could have cut from your budget, your processes, or your purchasing, then you may have missed some of the biggest savings.

Whenever possible, the full-body rash approach will provide the best results, but you should always be on the lookout for those zingers: the itches, the mosquito bites.

On the flip side, perhaps you only took the quick-hit savings you found with the itch-approach. And for the moment, it seemed as if doing those things would solve your dilemma. Even if taking an itch approach for quick savings on the balance sheet, make a point of using the rash approach as well so that the very essence of cost cutting becomes infused with your corporate culture.

Review the discussion of the two approaches in the Introduction so that you can properly focus on each when necessary and on both in the long run.

Destruction of Value

Cost cutting efforts are intended to make a company stronger, more flexible, and less debt-ridden. But often what occurs is a loss of the company's intrinsic value. Some loss of value can't be avoided: you lose the knowledge your workers carry with them when you have to lay them off. You lose the investment in a new product line that didn't pan out when you ignore the sunk costs and eliminate it from your lineup.

Keep value-losses in mind when you consider cutting and try to become more efficient so that you minimize your losses of value.

Another way you can de-value your business is by making stupid judgment errors. For example, when you start a new product line and create prototypes, be sure that the finished product uses the same (or better) quality ingredients or materials as the prototype and production runs.

If after this phase you locate a cheaper material to cut costs but it affects the quality of your product, your buyers will be expecting one level of quality and receive a lower level. Not only will you have refused shipments and excess inventory (that you may or not be able to sell in the long run), you will have lessened the value of your company in the eyes of your customers.

Voluntary Buyouts

When a company offers a voluntary buyout, such as Proctor & Gamble did between 2001 and 2003, it can quickly slice its payroll obligations. No one doubts that. However, take a close look at who's leaving. Are the productive employees, who can take advantage of the buyout and still get a good job elsewhere, leaving at your behest? Are you left with the flotsam and jetsam of employees, those who don't really contribute that much and would just as soon keep those paychecks coming, thank you very much anyway. Losing valued, highly productive workers is a value loss, buying out those who weren't productive will produce better long-term effects.

While Proctor & Gamble didn't seem to suffer from that problem with their buyout program, others have. General Motors offered buyouts in the form of early retirement to employees in the early 1990s that left a couple of plants so short-handed that the company then had to offer incentives to get the retirees to come back to work! The lesson here: don't get so zealous about reducing payroll that you leave the company unable to perform basic functions.

Involuntary Layoffs

If they can't afford to be warm and fuzzy and offer buyouts, companies may turn to outright layoffs. However, here are ways that layoffs can backfire:

- Morale and productivity can go downhill if employees come to work every day not knowing if they'll have a job by the end of their shift.

- Morale is weakened by layoffs that target certain classes of workers, such as the blue-collar segments of your workforce.

- However, even-steven isn't always a good choice either, as you may have more expendable employees in one area than another and must lay off unevenly.

- Laying off employees too quickly can backfire if an economic downturn turns out to be much shorter than predicted.

Just as General Motors found itself shorthanded after their voluntary payoff programs, several large investment firms were forced to rehire terminated employees in the 1990s after a brief slowdown that didn't last long. Not only did this cost the companies all the money, time, and effort to rehire, but the morale of the employees had suffered. Not knowing if you'll have a job again as soon as the radar screen shows the next blip doesn't exactly endear employees who have already been laid off once.

Poor Implementation of Planning

A big mistake that's also easy to make is in setting in place a cost-reduction program without consulting with those who are most affected by it: your workers. When employees hear cost reduction, they often begin to worry about job security, loss of benefits, being pushed into early retirement, or going without a wage increase.

Beginning with the management team and working down, be honest and have clear-cut numbers and examples to work from. Management often will have to sell these ideas to employees, so if you can't convince managers of the necessity of cost cutting, you'll likely find even less success in pitching your plans to employees.

However, if you do your P.R. correctly, your managers will buy into your plan. If the management buys in, odds are that at some of your employees will also support your plans. They will cooperate and actually work toward your goals at reducing costs. However, there's a trade-off: they need to know that your intent is to reduce waste and conserve resources. They need to know the reason you're looking to do this now, as opposed to last year. And they need to know what you'll be doing with the savings.

Keeping your employees in the dark can be a big mistake. An even bigger mistake is in giving them false security. If pink slips may factor into the reductions, tell them that up front. Whatever else may be coming that directly affects your employees should be laid out on the table.

An informed and motivated work force might actually surprise you and find a better way to cut costs. Many examples in the previous chapters came from the hard work and suggestions of the employees themselves who, after all, do have a vested interest in keeping your company as healthy as you do.

HEALTH CHECKS

Whether new to business or not, everybody can agree on one thing and that's the certainty of change. How exactly the world economy will fluctuate, grow, shrink, or change in the coming decades and what exactly technology and the Internet will do to change the face of business simply can't be known for certain. Good guesses can be made, but Derek Martin, a management consultant, summed it up well by saying, "If a company is not continuously reducing costs to reinvest in people, process, and technology, it will soon be at a disadvantage to its more fleet-footed competitors."[31]

With that in mind, let's take a look at some indicators of your company's fitness *after* cutting costs. These indicators aren't a guarantee that you will have created a better balance sheet and aren't meant to assure you that your company is now sitting on easy street. These criteria are merely representative of the places you might want to check your company's pulse, so to speak, after some vigorous exercising of judgment in relation to your costs.

Health Check: Exodus

If you've had an economic downturn in your business that has forced you into some serious cost-cutting considerations, you may have suffered from a common side effect: an exodus of employees who don't feel secure enough to wait out the storm and hope for the best.

If you've lost skittish employees, perhaps some of the blame could be laid on the level of honesty you put forth. Did you hold regular meetings with employees at all levels to let them know the state of affairs (and ask for their suggestions and help in the process)? If you didn't, your employees may have tuned into any of a variety of rumors and other nonsense that often crops up in such situations.

Perhaps you lost some employees to a competitor or another strong company in your area. If one company senses the possibility of trouble at your door, they may have aggressively sought to woo away some of your best employees. Here again, this is something that may have been avoided with the proper communication.

---

[31] Derek F. Martin, "Cutting Costs Without Losing Your Shirt: A Strategic Approach to Cost Reduction," 2001, www.refresher.com/!cuttingcosts.html, accessed on May 1, 2006.

If you've lost some good employees, don't despair. Set about rebuilding your workforce or redistribute the duties to your current employees—without overloading them, of course—and move ahead.

Staying positive in the face of an exodus of employees is crucial. If the remaining employees see you sink into despair, however briefly, you'll have a serious problem with the second health check: morale.

Health Check: Morale

After a series of successful cost-saving moves, morale should be higher than before, or at the very least, equal to before any such changes. Here's how one company retained employees and kept their morale high even when it seemed things were at their lowest.

The knowledge that a company is laying workers off to ship production to China can have an averse effect on the morale of employees left behind. The leaders at Marlowe Industries, Inc., in Dallas, Texas, knew in 2001 they had a potential public-relations nightmare on their hands when their workforce plunged from 800 to 200.

The company's cost cutting wasn't funded entirely through sending production overseas, as an entire layer of management was also eliminated. Across-the-board pay cuts were instituted for the remaining employees, with management taking a larger percentage cut than lower-paid workers.

However, Marlowe remained in business due to the extraordinary efforts of the management to communicate with every remaining employee. Monthly meetings with honest financial projections kept everybody on the same page as far as the company's stability. Every step of the restructuring plan was presented to employees and followed up on. Promises about returning wages to their previous level were kept—on time. But what was perhaps the most important item for the employees was that the highest profit production was kept in the USA, true to Marlowe's word.

Rather than see their remaining employees run to other employers or become poor performers, Marlowe found that just the opposite happened. People stayed and remained loyal, perhaps even more so than before the downturn.

Marlowe Industries managed to weather their storm without losing a large group of valued employees after the necessary layoffs. Given the nature of the situation, that alone was impressive. But to come out with a positive morale and the loyalty of the employees was truly amazing.

But having employees who show up to work and have a good attitude will only get you so far. You must have something to show for all your hard work at reducing your expenses. Productivity is the measure of work well done.

Health Check: Productivity

If you were to sum up all functions of a business in one word, it might well have to be *productivity*. Therefore, measuring your company's productivity after some cost cutting is vital.

There are a number of ways that you can measure productivity, including your sales figures, your production numbers, or your report of defects and errors in your product. Whatever measurement you choose to use, make sure you have an accurate "pre-cost cutting" number for comparison.

Numbers don't always tell the complete story, however. People tell stories. Survey your workers. Do they feel that they are making contributions to the company's financial health? Do managers and supervisors feel that their employees' production is at least as high as before, or better?

Health Check: Growth

A company that is overburdened with more employees than it can effectively keep busy is hampered in growing. However, by growing, you often need what? More employees. It's a Catch-22 that can be dizzying to the business owner who is merely trying to keep the proper balance in all things while growing.

Even though it may not be obvious at first, like a tulip bulb planted in the fall and lying dormant throughout the long winter, when spring hits you'll soon see little shoots of life and growth springing out of the dirt surrounding it.

Look for little shoots of new growth in your company. Tiny increases in sales or production. Tiny decreases in lead times or in the number of customer complaints. Find every little measurement you can and track it. Nurture your continued growth by rewarding those who are effecting it. Celebrate it as a sign of new life and the beginnings of a season of growth.

Health Check: Profit

High morale, increasing productivity, and even company growth do not always lead to a healthy profit. In fact, there's no guarantee you'll even be in the black at all. Sometimes there are long catch-up periods after cost cutting where the measures taken cost more money than they are recouping.

When you're back in the black and rising, then you can rest assured that you have done the right thing. And next time you face a situation where you need to look at cutting costs again, you'll do so with more self-confidence and the experience to know what not to do, or how much to do.

Every time you work your way through a cost cutting cycle, you become more proficient and selective. Over time you develop a keen eye and sense of what needs to be done when the numbers are down and things are starting to look a little out of shape again.

As with the old dieting adage "Don't wait until you've gained 20 pounds to get back on your diet;" you shouldn't wait until your company is bloated with extra costs and pointless procedures to start your trimming and exercising corporate leanness. Make it a daily habit and it will pay off over the long haul.

Index

W

This book is dedicated to Fred, Elly & Eva

ABOUT THE AUTHOR

Cheryl L. Russell holds Bachelor of Arts and Bachelor of Science degrees from Winona State University in Minnesota. In addition to freelance writing, she enjoys reading, designing custom dresses for her daughters and other creative pursuits. Cheryl and husband Fred Miller live in southwest Wisconsin with their three daughters, six pet birds and a pair of chinchillas.